FROM CHERNOBYL WITH LOVE

FROM CHERNOBYL WITH LOVE

Reporting from the Ruins of the Soviet Union

KATYA CENGEL

POTOMAC BOOKS | *An imprint of the University of Nebraska Press*

An earlier version of chapter 1 was
published as "A Chernobyl Love Story"
in *Caveat Lector* 24, no. 1 (Spring 2013).

An earlier version of chapter 32 was
published as "Staying Straight in Ukraine"
in *Points of Entry*, no. 3 (2005).

Library of Congress Cataloging-in-Publication Data
Names: Cengel, Katya, author.
Title: From Chernobyl with love: reporting from
the ruins of the Soviet Union / Katya Cengel.
Description: Lincoln: Potomac Books, an
imprint of the University of Nebraska Press,
2019. | Includes bibliographical references.
Identifiers: LCCN 2019007495
ISBN 9781640122048 (cloth: alk. paper)
ISBN 9781640122390 (epub)
ISBN 9781640122406 (mobi)
ISBN 9781640122413 (pdf)
Subjects: LCSH: Cengel, Katya. | Journalists—
United States—Biography. | Foreign
correspondents—United States—Biography. | Russia
(Federation)—Press coverage—United States. |
Russia (Federation)—Description and travel.
Classification: LCC PN4874.C345 A3
2019 | DDC 070.92 [B]—dc23
LC record available at
https://lccn.loc.gov/2019007495

Set in Lyon by Mikala R. Kolander.
Designed by N. Putens.

*To Sveta, Yulia, Nastya, and
all the other Slavic women
who looked out for me*

Contents

List of Illustrations   ix

Preface   xi

PART 1. LATVIA

1. Journalists Invade Former
   Soviet Union   3

2. A Festive Welcome   10

3. The Elusive Dane, Friendly
   Canadian, and Other Post-
   Soviet Workers   18

4. Happy Girl and the
   Flasher   27

5. Big Bad Accidents   37

6. Exile   41

7. The Nice Nazi and the
   Mean Jew   47

8. A God Other Than
   Lenin   55

9. Everything Is *Normali*   60

10. Pagans, Communists, and
    a Hill of Crosses   64

PART 2. CALIFORNIA/ENGLAND

11. Back in the USSR   75

PART 3. UKRAINE

12. A Wife Named Katya 81

13. Downing Vodka Shots
    at Chernobyl 90

14. Pirates, Mobsters, and Other
    Eligible Bachelors 99

15. The Enemy Outside 107

16. Heroes and a Woman
    Named Hope 114

17. Darkness at Dawn 121

18. Radioactive Romance 129

19. Children of Tomorrow 134

20. Wet Dreams 141

21. Home Remedies 148

22. Paddington Bear Gets
    in a Brawl 157

23. Atonement 164

24. Justice 170

25. London Calling 179

26. A Western Town in
    Ukraine 186

27. An Internal Attack 191

28. A Chance
    Engagement 198

29. Ukraine Accidentally Enters
    the War on Terror 207

30. Shallow Graves 213

31. Homeland 217

32. Disappearing Acts 223

33. Taken 228

34. The Missing 238

35. Shot in the Butt 243

PART 4. KENTUCKY

36. A Revolution 255

37. Repeat Performance 258

Afterword 263

Acknowledgments 265

Bibliography 267

Illustrations

Following page 120

1. Eastern Europe and Russia

2. Vladimir Lenin in a dumpster

3. The author at a
   Halloween party

4. A chimney sweep in Riga

5. The author and Jenia
   at a hotel in Yalta

6. Orphans and their
   grandfather in Ukraine

7. A babushka in Ukraine

8. A factory in Ukraine

9. Ukrainian coal miners

10. The author with
    Viktor and Jenia

11. The author with the
    Ukrainian military

12. The author with
    Ukrainian protesters

13. A copy of the *Kyiv Post*

14. The author in Kyiv
    in a U.S. article

15. Press passes

16. The author and Dima

17. Riot police in Kyiv

Preface

Two decades before the 2018 TED (Technology, Entertainment and Design) conference in Vancouver opened with a talk by a Ukrainian journalist about fake news, I was a reporter in Ukraine.

I set off for the former Soviet Union during a sliver of time when the world was relatively peaceful following the fall of communism and the Balkan wars and prior to the fall of the World Trade Center. Peace Corps volunteers, backpackers, and intrepid journalists were among those who found their way to places like Lithuania, Poland, and the Czech Republic and decided to stick around. They congregated in the capitals, turning cities like Prague into trendy hubs. Most of them were male.

I was not. I was also not a drinker, smoker, or fan of the more depressive of the Russian authors, and, let's face it, that's about all of them. But I was named Katya. So in true California fashion I blamed my mother for my Slavic name and headed for a part of the world where breakaway republics still used the hammer and sickle as a government emblem. I crawled around Ukrainian mines, parachuted out of Soviet-era airplanes, and drank home brew vodka in the Chernobyl Nuclear Power Plant exclusion zone, site of the world's worst nuclear plant disaster. It was a great adventure—until it suddenly wasn't.

Georgiy Gongadze lost his head setting in motion the Orange Revolution. Planes toppled the World Trade Center, sparking several American invasions, and I ended up in a Ukrainian hospital indefinitely. That's when I got engaged. We met at Chernobyl. A cousin joked that our children would be radioactive.

I would say he was my first love, but that wouldn't be true. I liked him all right, but what I really liked was the adventure of living in the former Soviet Union and falling for a guy who turned my name into a sweet diminutive.

Men speaking French have always seemed rather dandified to me. But Russian, with its hint of tenderness, melancholy, and strength was another story. Of course I didn't know much about men—or a word of Russian—when I took a job in the former Soviet republic of Latvia in 1998 at the age of twenty-two. I knew a lot more Russian and a little more about men, but not enough about my Ukrainian fiancé, when I left Ukraine in 2002.

This is partly the story of my first romance and my first marriage, neither of which has much to do with the man I married and everything to do with the almost half decade I spent digging up stories in the former Soviet Union in the window of time between propaganda and fake news.

FROM CHERNOBYL WITH LOVE

PART 1 Latvia

1 Journalists Invade Former Soviet Union

Three things you shouldn't do in Chernobyl are visit, drink home brew vodka, and fall in love. I did them all. Not exactly in that order, and not in a single trip, which leads me to a fourth thing you shouldn't do: go back. But then I didn't know any of these things before I spent several weeks in a Ukrainian hospital, where even toilet paper was a luxury. Before I met the Bulgarian doctor who insisted I needed a shot in the *butt*; that's how he said it, not me. And before the Orange Revolution, which really began after Georgiy Gongadze lost his head.

First I need to explain how I ended up in Chernobyl. The best place to start is Oakland, where I was born in the mid-1970s. Then fast forward through an overanalyzed California childhood, skip through an extremely awkward adolescence, continue beyond a sober and far too productive college career, and stop at a water fountain in the *San Diego Union-Tribune* building. The year is 1998, and newspapers are still being read. I was a college senior without a car, majoring in literature writing with a minor in history. I had stretched an internship at the paper into freelance work and wasn't really looking for anything more than a ride home when I spotted the flyer:

REPORTERS NEEDED IN FORMER USSR

Even without the all-capital heading it would have caught my eye. You don't grow up during the tail end of the Cold War in a place like Berkeley with a name like Katya and not wonder about the Soviet Union. (I think one of my aunts gave my sister, Anikke, a Vladimir Lenin ABC book. It was red.) The jobs were not in Moscow but in the capitals of Latvia and Estonia, two countries I could safely say I knew nothing about. But the rhetoric was enticing.

"If you like the idea of covering infant democracy and whirlwind business but cringe at the idea of living in a Brezhnev-era apartment building, don't apply."

I took that as a challenge. I was tough enough, as the posting put it, to be among the "first significant wave of ambitious English-language journalists to invade Europe's wild northeastern corner." Brezhnev-era apartment buildings be damned. Little did I know that those words, written with such authority, had been crafted by a guy not much older than me. Later I would meet the author, Eric, a Wisconsinite who had a talent for rhetoric matched by no one I have ever known. He would later become a lawyer. He could go on and on in several languages on topics as undecipherable to me in English as they were in German or Russian. So of course I slept with him. When the only other option was a bed in a room lacking several walls during a Russian winter, you would share a bed with a verbose intellectual and several plastic coke bottles filled with warm water as well. Nothing happened aside from sleep. I am still waiting for him to run for office.

Back up a bit to a time of dial-up internet. A time before there were programs that brought laptops to children in third world countries. A time when I was trying to figure out where and what Latvia was on a library computer. The first website I checked was the one listed on the job posting, the one for the newspaper doing the hiring, the English language *Baltic Times*, which covers the tiny Baltic countries of Latvia, Estonia, and Lithuania. Like so many websites back then, theirs was "under construction." Luckily for me my British stepfather—who had left his island homeland long before I entered the picture but had yet to become an American citizen—also remained loyal to the most British of publications, the *Economist*. It was within the pages of that hallowed magazine that he found articles on the Baltics and faxed them to me via a perpetual student friend who was crashing at the home of an old man down the street who owned a fax machine. Looking back, I think the man was probably in his early fifties, but I was twenty-one, and he limped, had white hair, and no longer worked.

The descriptions I read of the Baltics were slightly intimidating. A restless and, in some cases, rootless Russian population, leaders who tended toward nationalism, and a business model that seemed to include mafia involvement were just a few of the red flags being raised. But the job posting had hooked me, and the idea of working in a former Soviet outpost was only slightly more daunting than my other plan, which involved trying to get a writing job in the movie industry.

Today it may be hard to understand quite how rare a move this was. With email and the internet still in their infancy, knowledge of and communication with far-off countries was less common than it is now. It hadn't even been a decade since the fall of the Berlin Wall. And despite my name, I was not Russian. I was a California native who had spent the last four years in sunny, self-absorbed Southern California. I was tall and athletic with a perpetual smile. I rode my bike or rollerblades everywhere, worked as a waitress at a bakery restaurant, and went for runs on the beach. I lived on a street with a Spanish name that translated to "quiet road" and survived on frozen yogurt and bagels. The former USSR was about as far from Camino Tranquillo as it gets.

Latvia was not a place anyone I knew had ever heard of, let alone lived in or visited. Lithuania was vaguely familiar due to the bronze medals won by their tie-dye outfitted men's basketball team at the 1992 Barcelona Olympics. But the jobs were in Latvia and Estonia, another complete unknown. Applicants were supposed to state where they would prefer to work. I chose Latvia based on its geographical position between the other two countries, the paper's main office being there and a rumor that Estonians were standoffish.

My mother tried to prepare me for the eventual rejection by explaining that this was the first, and so far only, professional job I had applied for, and it usually takes several applications before an offer is extended. I knew this. But for some reason I felt I had a good chance of landing this job. I have no idea now what made me so sure of myself other than a few good clips from a decent-sized daily newspaper and extreme youth. But when the email arrived asking for a phone interview, the only one taken by surprise was my mother. I prepared with a little more *Economist* reading and as much surfing of the internet for Baltic stories as my patience would allow—the age of dial-up and "website under construction" notices meant you could spend ten minutes waiting for a single page to open.

The phone interview went as well as can be expected when two strangers separated by various time zones and bodies of water attempt to converse. The editor of the paper was not a Boris or a Vladimir but a Steve from New Jersey. He didn't sound much older than me and in fact wasn't.

A few days later he emailed with a job offer. I didn't pay much attention to the details. All that mattered was that I was going to the Baltics. At the time plenty of my fellow college students thought they had heard of the Baltics.

Didn't we bomb them?

Why do you want to go there?

Um, be careful.

But they were thinking of the Balkans, an area plagued by various wars since Yugoslavia began to break apart in the early 1990s; it was an area of the world Americans recognized. Now we also recognize not just Afghanistan but Iraq as well. Of course the Baltics are still a mystery to most. They probably would have remained so for me if I had not ended up living there.

It was Latvia that would later draw me to Ukraine. Or, more precisely, my experience in Latvia led me to Ukraine. As a young reporter, my job options after returning to the United States were likely to include covering school board meetings and neighborhood zoning issues, neither of which held much appeal after I had interviewed diplomats, dignitaries, and former SS members for the *Baltic Times*. Ukraine, with its crumbling coal mines, organized corruption—and of course Chernobyl—had a strange appeal. My peers were chasing the riches of the original dot-com bubble. I was hungering to return to Soviet-era apartment buildings and borscht, neither of which I had ever experienced prior to Latvia.

I had been abroad before moving to Latvia. My family lived in England for a while when I was a teenager. I enjoyed the experience of baselessly being taunted as an American slut and getting shingles so much that, once back in California, I vowed never to leave my country or home state again. So I moved to Latvia. The decision may have had something to do with not knowing what else to do. My sister was in medical school, and my parents had made it clear when I graduated from high school that "home" was no longer with them. If the suitcase they gave me for graduation wasn't enough of a hint, their relocation to England and then a hippy ranch reachable only by dirt road did the trick. Communication was strained; my mom was never at the ranch, and their answering machine worked on solar power and tended to get fried. Eventually they settled in a small Northern California town reachable by both paved roads and societal norms. But by then I no longer connected them with "home."

My sister found security with her boyfriends' families. I didn't have a boyfriend. My best friend had recently married. I had felt comfortable in San Diego, but I had never fit in. I moved off campus the second week of my freshman year because I missed seeing old people. I didn't drink. I looked like your typical California golden child, but I had a tendency toward severe depression. Latvia offered a job and possibly an escape from the weighty emptiness that had returned in college after an almost decade-long absence. At the paper I would be with writers, a breed that I knew had its share of loners and lost souls. In my inexperience I took that as a good sign.

My unfamiliarity with cold climates, the former USSR, and professional jobs made packing rather challenging. I relied on the L. L. Bean catalogue for my coat, hat, gloves, and scarf. I figured a Maine company probably knew something about winter. The boots I special-ordered weighed about twenty pounds and cost almost a hundred dollars. I was figuring out fast that the whole season thing made life more expensive when it came to apparel. Wags was a more reasonable, but just as necessary, purchase. A stuffed toy dog, Wags, I decided would be perfect to crush in my arms when I was scared and lonely and far from everyone and everything I knew. He cost twenty dollars, name included.

Fitting my new purchases in the two bags the airline allowed was not easy. Warm clothes take up far more space than summer shifts. And my list of necessities included rollerblades. I also packed a small pile of books, including a Baltic guidebook, and an even smaller pile of magazines. Laptops and cell phones were not common then, so the only electronics I took were a walkman and a travel alarm. I planned to rent a furnished apartment, so

I didn't pack sheets or towels or other household items. But I did add some decorations, including a small dragon figurine and a cloth moon and star that would hang from a door knob. There were also photos of family and friends and a package of single-use medical needles and syringes. The needles were difficult to obtain but not nearly as difficult as the next item on my packing list: police clearance.

The difficulty did not arise from my having grown up in Berkeley, where just about everyone I knew had been weaned on marijuana. The problem was that there isn't really such a thing as police clearance in the United States, at least there wasn't pre-9/11. My new employer required that I prove I had a clean criminal record in the United States and wanted me to have a police officer state as much.

"You want what?" the cop on the other end of the phone line asked.

I repeated my request for the third time: "I'm moving to the Baltics, and I need a paper that says I have no criminal record in the United States."

"You're going to the Balkans and you're worried about criminal records?"

"No, the Baltics, in the former Soviet Union."

"Oh Russia; I get it."

I decided not to correct him. "So can you write me a paper that says I don't have a criminal record?"

"That's not something we can do. But good luck in Russia."

I opted for an in-person request my second time round and after talking to several people finally was told to send them something in writing. A week or so later I received a letter back saying in effect that I had no record in their town but that I might be a mass murderer in Alabama. I got it notarized to make it look more official.

A slightly larger problem was the request that I bring my college transcript. I had not officially graduated when I accepted the job. In fact I was scheduled to graduate from the University of California at San Diego in fall 1998, three months after I moved to Riga, Latvia. I convinced two of my favorite professors to let me do independent study and brought an unofficial transcript with me. No one has ever questioned how I managed to graduate from college in San Diego while working in Riga. Before I left that summer, a friend bought me fleece pants, and my mom and stepdad held a surprise going-away party. The guests were as surprised as I was.

It was a warm day when I left, made even warmer by the fact that I was outfitted in full winter gear too bulky to pack. Wags went under my arm and a copy of Gogol's *Dead Souls* in my jacket pocket. My new editor spotted the book when we met and was instantly impressed. I didn't have the heart to tell Steve I had barely gotten through the first twenty pages. But I didn't know him yet and didn't know how important he would consider an appreciation of Gogol to be. I also figured I couldn't afford to dismiss any serious impression I had made since I was carrying a toddler-sized stuffed toy under my arm and a pair of rollerblades over my shoulder.

Actually the fact that I didn't know Steve—or anyone else in Latvia for that matter— didn't really cross my mind until I was somewhere in Europe waiting for a connecting flight. I got to talking with a group of American teenagers traveling to Poland on some sort of mission and realized that maybe I should have thought about more than winter boots and police clearance before moving to an unknown land. I would have been even more worried had I known what a departure from protocol it was for missionaries to be quizzing me on my language skills instead of my belief system. But this was before I spent almost a decade in Kentucky and became familiar with the ways of hard-core Christians.

Did I know Latvian?

Did I know anyone in the country?

Had I ever seen a hard copy of the *Baltic Times*?

Did I know if the company had money to pay me?

Did I have a phone number for Steve or an address for the newspaper?

Did I know if anyone would meet me at the airport?

My answer to pretty much all of their questions was the same: no. Except the last one. Steve knew my flight details, so I figured someone from the paper would be at the airport. But I wasn't sure. The missionaries seemed concerned. I figured it was too late for that.

2   A Festive Welcome

The missionaries had been right to worry.

As I scanned the crowds at the Riga airport for a "Welcome Katya" or "*Baltic Times* Reporter" sign, I wondered if I had been too quick to abandon my Catholic upbringing. Maybe if I had paid a little more attention at church, I would be in Warsaw now with a bunch of chipper Americans instead of alone in Riga surrounded by a crowd of dour Latvians.

I had noted the dark mood the minute I approached the gate for my Riga flight, and I would notice it whenever I returned to the region after spending time away. It was as if no one had told the people in the waiting area that the Soviet Union had collapsed and they were no longer prisoners of their government. I have since traveled to countries on four different continents, and at no airport gate have I encountered a darker mood than at those where the destination is a former Soviet bloc country. The usual airport types—crying babies, misty-eyed couples, and impatient professionals—are replaced at these gates by a uniformly subdued group of zombie-like creatures who appear to neither smile nor talk nor move. That the men favor short hair and black clothing and the women high heels and short skirts only exaggerates the general feeling of degradation.

Later my Latvian friends would say my smile gave me away as an American. Even with no one to greet me and a baggage cart weighed down with a year's worth of clothes, I smiled. That is probably how Steve spotted me. I was both relieved and disappointed to see him. I had been hoping for a welcome sign. No one had ever held one for me, and I figured landing alone in Riga, Latvia, was probably my best chance of anyone ever doing so. I was just out of college and still thought the whole sign idea rather romantic. I blamed Steve for ditching it and turning the thing into a game to see if he could spot his new employees. About five of us—three Americans, one Canadian, and a British girl named Denise—were hired around the same time and arrived within a few weeks of each other. Steve picked out all his staff members except one. Denise was barely five feet tall and literally slipped past the six-foot-plus Steve. Only after the crowd had thinned and they were the only two left did they locate each other. When I voiced my disappointment at the missing sign, Steve explained his game of guess-the-new-employee. If I had ever held a job other than waitressing and youth sports instructor, I might have been a little nervous on learning that basically half the writing staff had recently abandoned ship. But right then I was just happy that the man who had promised me a job had actually shown up.

Steve was as easy to identify as an American as I was. Unlike Latvian men, who wore their hair brutally short and moved with a stiff rigidity, Steve's reddish blond hair reached his ears, and he carried his tall, slightly pudgy frame in a relaxed, laid-back manner. At his side was a woman who resembled Snow White. Her skin was a creamy pale, her hair a dark black, and her smile as friendly and sweet as the storybook character's. Yulia was the paper's entertainment editor and, as I would soon discover, its social core. She bridged the gap between each group that separated us—Russians and Latvians, foreigners and locals, advertisers and journalists—belonging to all and fully to none. It is a role I later learned to play and only recently have tried to avoid. One who understands so many is understood by few.

Yulia and Steve ushered me to a boxy, nondescript car driven by an equally nondescript driver. Steve insisted I sit in the front seat, which seemed generous until I realized there were no seatbelts. If we crashed without seatbelts, I believed the backseats probably offered a better chance of survival. And once we got started, a crash did not seem entirely out of the question. The car moved fast, weaving around other vehicles that appeared to follow no particular order on bumpy roads that lacked clear lanes and traffic signage. We kept to a wide street with lots of ugly apartment buildings and quite a few trees. I don't remember much else because once I was seated in the car, exhaustion took over. I had been in transit for more than sixteen hours, and it took all my concentration to keep up with Yulia and Steve's conversation. At some point Steve asked the question I had been dreading: "Do you want to go by the office?"

Having never held a professional job before, I figured it was a trick question. I assumed that after paying to fly me across an ocean, my employers would be eager to start collecting on their investment and I would be expected to begin work that afternoon. Age and corporate America have taught me to be less accommodating, but back then I didn't think "no" was an acceptable answer. I said yes, adding in a hesitant voice, "Can I drop my stuff off before I start work?"

Yulia giggled. Steve assured me that they didn't expect me to work that day. They just wanted to show me the office. I wasn't totally convinced. But I was feeling a little better about the situation and listened closely as they began to list the merits of my apartment. After I accepted the job, Steve informed me via email that a nice apartment was available in the suburbs of Riga and asked whether I wanted them to secure it for me. Having no idea what a "nice Latvian apartment" looked like and no clue how I would go about finding one on my own, I said yes. Now I learned that Eric had been the apartment's former occupant. The same Eric who had written the job posting that caught my attention. Apparently shortly after trying to entice writers to join the paper, Eric had taken a job with a German wire service and moved closer to town.

My apartment definitely seemed far away from things. We passed apartment complex after apartment complex interspersed with forest, and still we kept traveling deeper into the bowels of Soviet-era suburbia. It wasn't a scenic drive. Yulia tried to distract me by talking about what she considered my apartment's best feature, a piano. Eric was a bit of a musician and had entertained guests with his playing. I could neither play the piano nor read music. It might have been a good time to learn music, but I decided learning Latvian would be more useful. Some of the apartment's other highlights included its first floor location and proximity to a market and an English-speaking landlady. The closeness to the market and first-floor location in a building that lacked elevators were the first features I learned to appreciate.

It only took me one trip hauling several gallons of drinking water. My landlady's language skills came in handy when I had to explain to her that the apartment above had flooded and water was seeping from my ceiling.

But on that first day I didn't have the context to appreciate any of the apartment's merits and struggled to hide my disappointment. My building looked exactly like every other apartment building plopped down in a small settlement of Soviet-era apartments in the outskirts of Riga. People talk about Stalin-, Khrushchev-, and Brezhnev-era buildings, but to me they were all the same—tall, badly built, and drab. Mine happened to be a five-story box of bland gray. Inside the furniture dated from an era I have not come across outside of the former Soviet Union. There was the obligatory plastic-topped table, bed made of large foam pillows, and doily-like cloth decorations. I did note that it was sunny and spacious. I also noticed that the toilet flushed with a pull chain and had long since ceased to be white in color.

It was the first apartment I would not be sharing with roommates, unless you count Jeremy. A little white mouse, Jeremy didn't move in until later. Or it was several months before I first saw him sprint across the living room floor. I named him after a guy I had had a crush on at the YMCA where I had worked during college. Then I tried to kill him. Or at least capture him. I bought the Latvian equivalent of a humane mouse trap: sticky paper that Jeremy was supposed to get stuck on. I planned to take him outside and cut him free once caught. How I would cut around a wild mouse's little paws without getting bitten was not something I had spent a lot of time contemplating. In the end it didn't really matter because Jeremy never stuck to the paper. I came to consider freeloading roommates another advantage of living on the first floor.

The babushka that entered my one-bedroom apartment so she could lean out my window and cut roses from the sole plant in a half-mile radius was more of an uninvited guest than a resident. All the same, I tried to disturb her as little as I disturbed Jeremy. She had knocked on my door one weekend early into my stay. When I opened it, she let out a quick burst of Russian and barreled in. I made it clear I didn't understand and figured she would go away. Instead she took my hand and walked me into my own kitchen. She opened the window above my sink, pointed to herself and then to the red roses outside the window. Then she started opening my kitchen drawers. Although I like to be respectful of my elders, I was starting to feel annoyed by the intrusion. But not knowing how to protest, all I could do was shrug my shoulders and watch as she leaned out my window and used my scissors to cut what may well have been my roses. She thanked me and left. I never opened the door to a neighbor again.

After I unloaded my luggage and had a look around, Steve and Yulia enquired whether I was up for taking the tram to the office. I hadn't slept in about twenty-four hours and was feeling a bit shaky on my feet, but Steve seemed to think a tram ride was a good idea. I agreed. I tried to pay attention as Yulia picked her way between the apartment complexes, following worn footpaths to a cement slab where there were some shops and a tram stop. It was the middle of the day, so the tram was empty and we were able to sit down. I didn't realize what a luxury this was until the following week, when I had to take the tram during commuting hours and struggled to find space to breathe. Back then the tram seemed exotic to me, with its trolley pole and tracks and old-school conductors who walked up and down its length punching tickets.

As we crossed the clear blue waters of the Daugava River, I caught my first glimpse of the German Art Nouveau and nineteenth-century wooden architecture for which Riga is famous. We got off in the Old Town and walked down a curvy stone street that echoed with every step. Downtown Riga was a world apart from the Soviet monstrosities of its suburbs. Here the city was full of character, color, and life. The streets wound and curved, revealing new wonders at every turn: stone arched walkways, colorfully painted buildings with large wooden doors, decorative carvings atop equally decorative structures. I didn't see any Soviet-looking babushkas here, just young professionals lounging in outdoor beer gardens, strolling on the cobblestones, and congregating in the square.

The *Baltic Times* occupied the second floor of a large old house. There were two doors located on either end of a long wrap-around enclosure that split into two main areas, advertising and editorial. Tall windows looked out onto a cobblestone square. It was late afternoon when we arrived, and a dozen or so people were gathered around a long table eating cake and drinking in celebration of someone's name day. I don't remember whose name day they were celebrating, but the office was in a state of excitement, and the only work being done was that of eating, drinking, and generally being merry. The local staff seemed a little embarrassed by our interruption—not by Steve being the boss so much as by him being an American. I was rather shocked by the lack of productivity, but Steve had lived in the country long enough to tolerate the regular name day celebrations. These were not the quick, ten-minute sheet cake breaks we have in America, where everyone scurries back to their cubicle with their piece of cake, but the prolonged celebrations of a very different culture. In Latvia the most common excuse for these interruptions was a name day, literally a day on which one's name was celebrated. Because of the many different names in Latvia, there are many name days. In summer there also tended to be any number of other excuses not to work. The sun shone for almost eighteen hours, and people spent just about as much time in the outdoor beer gardens. We had a perfect view of them from our office windows.

I don't remember how I got back to my apartment that first day, but I am pretty sure it involved Yulia's finding someone to drive me home because there is no way I could have found my place on my own. Even if I had been able to locate building numbers and street signs, which I wasn't, I would have still been lost.

At the time in Latvia, mattresses and bottom sheets were as common as seatbelts, which means if you are an active sleeper like me, you usually ended up tangled in a mass of sheets and cushions. Jet lag and the almost constant Latvian summer light made it hard for my body to distinguish day from night. I awoke late the next day, untangled myself from my sheets, and set about unpacking. I took a shower but was a little unsure whether the rust-tinged water that came out of the tap was getting me clean. It was definitely not warm, a common but bearable occurrence in summer and a slightly less common but unbearable occurrence in winter.

It was a Saturday so I didn't have to go to work, but I was meeting Steve and Eric downtown in the afternoon for food and a song festival. I was almost as excited to meet the legendary Eric as to attend the equally legendary festival, a week-long celebration of singing and dancing that occurs only twice each decade. Having read about the Baltic singing revolution and its role in bringing down the Iron Curtain, I was thrilled that I was going to be able to hear a part of history. Latvia's recent history was like that of many small countries surrounded by larger powers. During World War I Latvia's Russian rulers were replaced by Germans. After the war Latvia had its first taste of independence and experienced rapid economic growth, a high standard of living, increased literacy, and authoritarian nationalism. The country's new tagline was "Latvia for the Latvians." The Molotov-Ribbentrop Pact between the Soviet Union and Nazi Germany was the beginning of the end of independence for the Baltic states, and by 1940 the states were Soviet republics. In the first year of Soviet occupation 35,000 "anti-Soviet" residents were deported from Latvia out of an estimated total population of 2 million. A brief interlude of Nazi occupation saw 120,000 deported or killed, half of them Jews. Then the Soviets returned and deported, executed, or killed 150,000 Latvians. The missing Latvians were replaced with workers from other Soviet republics, and the ethnic Latvian population shrank from 77 percent prewar to 52 percent by 1989. Now on its second independence, Latvia was trying to create a new identity for itself and its people. That night we saw only the beauty of national pride. Soon I would see its other side.

The evening began with what I would come to consider a traditional Latvian meal: lots of meat and not much else. Eric was the biggest surprise; he was smaller and slighter than I expected. He wore his shirts tucked in and his pants fitted and had the floppy brown mop favored by the Beatles. He had the formal mannerisms and speech pattern of what I took to be an earlier generation; in fact he was just more eastern prep school than western public school. It was comforting to be with Americans, even when Steve and Eric attempted to speak like street thugs. Having attended high school with the real thing, I wasn't impressed. When they switched to the subject of Latvian culture and literature, I knew their high school education had surpassed mine and listened attentively. With Eric one did a lot of listening. I decided then and there he would never be more than a friend.

Having never really experienced an adult relationship, I was not consumed by wanting to be in one. I had dated in college and liked the excitement of a crush, but I did not want to get attached. In high school my role model was Estella from *Great Expectations*, the girl raised to break men's hearts. I feared losing control and being dependent on someone else, not monetarily so much as emotionally. I had watched both my sister and mother cry over men and had promised myself I would never to do the same. It was a good plan—until I fell in love.

There was no danger of that happening with Eric. He fascinated me as a friend, but I was already tired of his talking and was relieved when other voices took over at the festival. Our seats were toward the front and to the right of the outdoor stage. It was warm and still light even though it was already late in the evening. The female performers and some of the audience members were dressed in traditional long, full, colorful skirts with aprons and puffy blouses. Their hair was done in braids and decorated with fresh flowers. The male performers also wore traditional clothing, but like most outfits worn by men, theirs were unremarkable. A number of different groups performed songs and dances, all of which involved much audience participation. I had no idea what the words meant, but the music and what it stood for was beautiful. I tried to imagine what it had been like a decade before, when the Latvians had protested Soviet oppression by breaking out in traditional song. While it took more than the defiant singing of banned cultural songs to bring down the Soviet system, the singing marked the start of Baltic independence. And most of the adults and older children attending only their second festival post-independence had fresh memories of what it had cost them to bring back the song festival. I shut my eyes and listened, longing to have belonged to something so exciting and half wishing for another occupying force just so I could see it overthrown with music.

Everyone stood for the last song, swaying and singing as I imagined people had during the 1960s. The closest thing I could recall was when a bunch of famous artists crooned "We Are the World" back in the '80s. This was a hundred times better. And I was a part of it. Surrounded by so many energized people, it is hard to feel alone even when the language is not your own. When the performances were over, Eric and Steve shoved me onto a tram, immersing me safely in a mass of humanity destined for home. On the tram the singing continued as we traveled through time from the historic Old Town to the last stop in Soviet suburbia.

3

The Elusive Dane, Friendly Canadian, and Other Post-Soviet Workers

My stepfather is as close to a survivalist as you can get without actually wanting to blow anything or anyone up, aside from a gopher. And I don't really count that because the propane explosion hurt my stepfather more than the little guy in his burrow.

It was my stepfather who taught me the importance of stockpiling water, among other things. So there was no way I was buying anything less than two five-liter bottles of water at a time, even if it meant my fingers almost fell off from lugging the bottles by their thin plastic handles back to my apartment. That is what I spent that first Sunday doing. By the following Sunday I had stopped using the clean water for brushing my teeth and instead braved what came out of the faucets. At times this was a clear liquid resembling water, at times it was a rust-colored fluid, and at times it was nothing.

I had to stop several times on that first trip home to relieve my crushed fingers. No one noticed, and no one came to my aid. I congratulated myself for being tough and independent. I had quickly decided that I wasn't going to be defeatist. I couldn't be. If I left Latvia, I would be seen as a failure in California and as a spoiled American in Latvia. I have always been driven and can usually push myself in order to accomplish something. It is afterward that I fall apart. So while there were moments of melancholy, I kept them in check. This task was made easier in the weeks and months to come by the presence of our tight-knit group of young, unsettled expats. Unfortunately none of them lived near me, so I was on my own shopping that first weekend.

I bought some frozen dumplings called *pelmeni*, which were filled with a pureed mixture of meat whose origins I did not care to know, some cabbage *pirozhoki*, and some carrots, all items I found old women selling near the tram stop or in my little market. None of the salespeople spoke English, but they all understood when I pointed to the items I wanted. I was slightly embarrassed by the stares I received for my pointing, but hunger triumphed over any serious social scarring. Shopping never really got easier. Daniel, one of the paper's other new Riga additions, called our method of selecting our purchases "point and shoot." You pointed at the item you wanted behind the counter and hoped the woman serving you would hand you milk and not tampons. Many things were still operating under the extremely trusting and efficient Soviet style. In its simplest form this meant you told someone behind the counter what you wanted and they handed it to you. In its more complex incarnation you told one person what you wanted, paid a second person, and then returned to the first person to retrieve your purchase, waiting in line each step of the way. In some ways it made sense. There was no danger of becoming a consumer-driven Western-style society—it would have simply taken too long. By requiring customers to spend so much time in line, you prolong what would otherwise be an extremely short shopping experience because of the lack of actual items. Of course to us Westerners it was beyond perplexing.

The solution seemed to be to study Latvian. An understanding of the language might have lent itself to an understanding of the culture, or at least saved us from having to endure yet another line after having pointed at the wrong item. It is hard to distinguish crackers from cookies when they are stacked on a distant shelf and encased in unfamiliar packaging. The lessons lasted several weeks. Neither fully Slavic nor Scandinavian, Latvian as a language made no sense, and learning it made even less. We started studying Russian.

Eating out was straightforward thanks to the sample plates restaurants tended to display. After identifying the items, you simply pointed at a plate and a similarly decorated one was produced from behind the counter. Then there was Lido, the Latvian version of fast food. There were about four choices, all some sort of meat and carbohydrate combination, and all you had to do was memorize the number of the dish you wanted or point to its picture. I liked number three, a mushy beige mushroom, meat, and rice concoction. Unfortunately it left me a bit sick and seriously craving some greenery. I'm not a vegetarian, but I am from California and rather fond of fruits and vegetables. I do not count peas in mayonnaise as a member of either category. In Latvia, at the time, the idea of not eating meat was not something you mentioned in polite society. Daniel and I found our fix of vegetables and spices at a purple and pink house on the outskirts of town. Almost like an Indian buffet, the canteen served a number of vegetarian dishes for a single price, plus it offered musical accompaniment to the tune of repetitive Hare Krishna chants. The food was meant to entice Latvian converts, but the only people it ever brought in were hungry Westerners immune to the chants of bald monks.

At the time most Westerners living in Riga lived downtown, not in what I liked to call the Soviet ghetto. You didn't see many young, unaccompanied females from the West; men, yes; married couples, yes; but women on their own, not often. If I kept my mouth shut and pretended to know where I was going and what I was doing, I could almost pass for a local. On the tram to work Monday morning I pushed and shoved as well as the regulars and practiced the Latvian word for excuse me—*Atvainojiet*—over and over in my head. But never out loud; I was too scared I would say it wrong and nobody would understand me.

On my first day I arrived at the office at eight thirty and was surprised to find it already unlocked. Daniel was as anxious to please as I was. We eyed each other warily, unsure if we were competitors or collaborators. Journalism is a strange business. As new hires, we both felt a need to prove ourselves. I sat in front of the computer Steve had pointed out to me during our brief visit the Friday before and listened to Daniel type. I had arrived early, but I now had absolutely no idea what to do. I settled on emailing my mother that I had arrived safely. Email was my main mode of communicating with people back home, and the only place I had access to email was at the office. Before long, a fair part of every day was spent sending desperate messages home about important stuff like the lack of peanut butter or some other emergency. Because of the time difference the reply seldom arrived before the following day, by which time I had usually come up with some sort of solution.

The rest of the staff started showing up around nine. There was a steady stream of greetings for the next hour as they passed through the newsroom on their way to the advertising room. The majority of the staff sold ads; half a dozen of us wrote for the paper; a few organized the rest of us; and several did various odd jobs I never could adequately define. The atmosphere was set by the advertising department, all women, most of them young. That first day the boldest of them smiled shyly at me and tentatively approached, as curious as a child. As a young woman from America I was an oddity, a rare treat for them to fuss over and befriend.

After studying the daily routines of my new colleagues, I started sifting through the archived papers, seeing what had already been covered and what might still need to be written. I scanned the wires for stories from the region and formulated some ideas of my own. My early stories were as ambitious as they were bleak: Latvians held hostage in Chechnya, Soviet-era crimes, and asylum seekers.

My interest in Soviet-era crimes coincided with a Baltic-led diplomatic mission to confront Soviet and Nazi crimes, although Soviet crimes were really the focus. In Latvia there was actually a head prosecutor for the "investigation of totalitarian crimes." His name was Uldis, and he was a cheerful and friendly man of sixty who possessed an almost bottomless anger. His office was filled with files and yellowed documents of the horrors done to Latvians by the Soviets and Nazis. He was so pleased that a Western journalist was interested in his life's work that he recounted, with an almost morbid glee, the day when fourteen thousand Latvians were sent to Siberia. He pushed in front of me photos of grotesquely misshapen bodies, faces with tongues swollen out of their mouths. He pointed at photos of half-buried dwellings and explained that was how Latvians lived in Siberia, underground, "like moles." "Like moles," he repeated, shaking his head.

He displayed a photo of a torture room, placing a pudgy finger by a bucket-sized hole in the floor. "That is for the blood."

His English was limited and he often slipped into German by accident, but his simmering anger and collection of documents said all that he couldn't.

Uldis was eleven when he was put on a cattle car bound for Siberia. The year was 1949. Passengers had to relieve themselves in front of armed KGB guards. "We covered our eyes," he said.

Many died on the journey. Uldis survived and spent five years on a collective farm in Siberia before escaping and making his way back to Latvia. When he returned, the world he had known was gone, everything taken from him and his family. He was a pariah to be avoided, a ghost returned from the dead. In time he scratched his way out of the shadows, digging like a mole for the surface. But what had been done to him was still hidden, and he would keep digging until he felt the international community adequately acknowledged the injustice suffered by his countrymen. "What was done to me means nothing compared to what was done to Latvia," he said.

But he was wrong. It was what was done to him, the country and life that was taken from him as a child and never fully returned, that captivated me. I knew the saga of Siberia, but Uldis was the first real person I knew who had been a part of the saga's making. He said he wasn't after revenge, just truth. But he knew the truth would offer its own revenge. Years have passed, but if Uldis is still alive, I believe he is still waiting. No matter how much is written on the subject, how much is discussed, it will never be enough. What Uldis couldn't understand was that when the acknowledgement comes, it will be too late. The time for that was more than seventy years ago, when he was on a cattle car bound for Siberia.

With my lurid fascination for such stories it made sense that I would be named features editor. I was both honored and overwhelmed by the promotion that came within months of my hiring. Steve still edited my stories, but he was a light editor and I feared my writing would suffer without more extensive editing. Now I was an editor, responsible for editing other people's writing. My promotion came with no pay increase, although it did come with added hours, mainly the one night a week I stayed late to lay out the two or three features pages. I also pretended to assign stories to a limited staff that tended to do what they wanted regardless of my instructions. The layout process was an interesting one that involved picking up a packet of pictures from the bus station. For some strange reason I didn't fully comprehend, photos for the Lithuanian stories arrived not via email but via bus, an actual bus. A staff member would pick up the pictures at the bus station and run them back to the office, where a designer would scan them in while I watched.

My role in this process seemed to be to keep the designer company and occasionally type in short explanations of the photos that accompanied feature stories. Two designers alternated working with me, and neither seemed interested in my suggestions as to the placement of the photos or the articles. Imants was plenty interested in me (and pretty much any other girl he came across) and tended to make the night go much slower than necessary. A skinny blond with a small, fine-boned face and a little too much confidence, Imants was about as close to romance as I would get in Latvia. He was enough of a jerk that my plan to not get attached was easy to implement. Whenever I would start to feel close to him, he would do something that would remind me how childish he really was, something that usually involved criticizing me. The other designer was more efficient, less interesting, and married.

In addition to laying out the feature pages, I was responsible for filling them with my own stories and those that came from our Lithuanian and Estonian bureaus. Denise and Rebecca headed up the Estonian bureau; they were both rather busy with news and business stories, so I seldom bothered them for features. Denise was the little Brit, and Rebecca was an almost as petite American. Paul and Rokas in Lithuania usually kept me well stocked. I never really assigned the Lithuanian staff stories; they just sent me what they felt like writing. I could count on Paul, a former Peace Corps volunteer, to send an interesting human interest story, and on Rokas, a nationalist, to send something that involved at least a dozen references to the great Lithuanian people and nation. I tried to tone Rokas's rhetoric down a bit, but if I cut too much, I wouldn't be able to fill the pages. I would also have to deal with the wrath of Rokas, no small thing even administered over a phone line.

The rest of the small cast of characters who filled the office and my very limited social life in Latvia included the gorgeous blonde Elena, who worked in advertising but was more focused on finding a foreign husband who could save her from ever having to return to her native Belarus. (She is now married to an Italian and the mother of twins.) Elena always had a sense of mystery about her that made you want to whisper when talking to her. That may have had something to do with the fact that she came from a country run by a dictator and that her status in Latvia was tenuous. She sported stunning inexpensive outfits purchased on trips back to Belarus. She assured me affordable cute clothing was the only thing worth taking from her country.

Yulia was in charge of arts and entertainment and making sure that just about everybody was happy. Officially she was the chairman's secretary, but Rud probably made a total of three appearances while I was at the paper, so there wasn't a lot she could do for him. We figured the elusive Dane had some secret, nefarious business going on outside of the paper. We of course had nothing on which to base this theory other than overactive imaginations and the fact that Rud seemed to show little interest in the paper.

Raisa was the real boss. A tiny blonde spitfire of a Russian, Raisa once tried to sweeten a business deal by offering me as an English teacher. Her own English was limited and relied heavily on a single phrase: "Friends, you are somehow welcome." Timor was a young Russian with a shaved head who dressed all in black and answered every question with a shoulder shrug and "I don't know." I liked Timor but not enough to pawn him off on an American friend several years later, when he had come to the United States and was in need of a wife in order to stay. The last I heard he was touring the United States with a circus. Timor's job was one of the undefinable ones you found in many post-Soviet businesses. But he always had a smile for me, even when he didn't understand a word I was saying.

Timor was stateless, born in Latvia but not Latvian. He was one of the many who did not qualify for Latvian citizenship, mainly because of a lack of language skills. At independence Russians accounted for about 30 percent of Latvia's population. To qualify for citizenship they had to pass a Latvian-language test, something many of them were unable to do because under Soviet rule Russian was the main language. Unless your family was Latvian, you didn't learn to speak much Latvian. While I was there, a referendum that would allow the easing of citizenship restrictions for noncitizen children born post-independence barely passed. Timor couldn't vote for it. Yulia was also unable to vote. She was from Daugavpils, a mainly Russian city where

Latvian is barely heard. Yulia was self-conscious about her Latvian skills and did not have the resources to apply for citizenship at the time. Nastya was Russian as well, but she had been taught Latvian and thus was eventually able to obtain Latvian citizenship. Nastya was almost the exact same age as me but infinitely wiser and more practical, which is why she was named business editor while I was put in charge of features. She also happened to be dating Steve, which immediately shrunk the already slim dating pool for us Western women, something Rebecca seemed to lament most.

It would turn out Rebecca was right to be concerned. Latvians and Russians embraced the Soviet ideal of equality when it came to women. They were happy to let them work, clean, cook, and take care of the children. All they asked in return was that they look beautiful and not have any fun playing sports like soccer and basketball. In the dating game this meant we were left to choose between American men, who were looking for leggy Russian model types happy to answer to their every whim so long as there was a chance of a U.S. visa, and local men, who expected everything but personality from their partners.

Friendships were easier. I managed to make a halfway decent impression on my new cohort by showing up without light bulbs. Apparently the last young American reporter had thought she would not be able to find light bulbs in Riga and had packed quite a few of her own. I had many questions about this, not least of which was: if she didn't think the country had light bulbs, how did she know it had lamps? I was careful not to mention my needles and syringes.

I was not the only American female addition to the Latvian office. Sandra came from Alaska. She was a middle-aged divorcee who paired an ill-fitting lavender suit with panty hose and Birkenstocks every day. She could often be found in the morning asleep at the same computer she had been sitting at the night before. In Ukraine I would meet others like her. They tended to leave chaos in their wake and view expat life as an escape more than an exploration. I believed the line separating the explorers and escapees was determined by attitude and age, and I was safely on the exploratory side in both cases. In reality it wasn't so well defined, which may be why I disliked Sandra so much. It may also have been because she seemed to hate me.

She forged my signature on at least one occasion and had a special bitchy tone she used to mock me. When Daniel and I were talking she was at her worst. "Daniel," she would say. "We need to talk."

It was a hissed command, and it would be repeated until Daniel went over to listen to her conspiracy theories, many of them based on my evilness. Sandra and I were not close. Daniel and I were. Our friendship was one more thing Sandra held against me. Daniel was the only one nice enough to associate with Sandra, and she guarded their one-sided friendship jealously. Daniel was the Canadian. He was a bit older than me and for some reason intimidated by my daily newspaper clips, even though he had been editor of a college newspaper. Once he got over that, we became close and spent our weekends wandering the countryside together, doing laundry and going to theaters to watch movies that probably went straight to video in the United States. I would ask his advice about the break-dancer I had a crush on, and he would talk vaguely about relationships. When he was too nice to turn a girl down, I played the role of his girlfriend. We all knew it was pretend.

Phil wasn't exactly an employee of the paper. When I arrived, I believe he had officially already been fired from the *Baltic Times*; he was fired and rehired rather regularly. Or maybe he was just away on a legendary drinking and streaking binge. I'm not sure if those two went together but both were what Phil was known for, and that Halloween he dressed as a leering flasher. Phil was a Latvian American who wasn't very fond of Russians but did share their love of alcohol. When he worked at the paper, he would usually wander in some time in the afternoon, spend a few hours hunched over his desk, and produce an incredibly well-written story before disappearing again for several days. There were rumors he had locked himself in his apartment and done nothing but sleep and drink for several months. There was also a plausible rumor that he had pushed a colleague down stairs or out a window while drunk. I would run into both his temper and his nudity later.

4 Happy Girl and the Flasher

Our Halloween party attracted national attention. I went as a Spice Girl, and a picture of me with my midriff exposed made the country's daily newspaper.

Summer came to a close quickly, the endless days of sunshine transforming into long days of darkness well before the end of October. Before fall fully set in, there was a work outing to a beach followed by a forest picnic. We roasted hot dogs on sticks and ate tomatoes sprinkled with salt. The Eastern European cookout is not unlike an American barbecue, only it is done in real nature instead of in backyards. This idyllic country scene is tarnished only slightly by the fact that bottles and wrappers are usually left behind and most women dress as if they were headed for a nightclub, not a forest. Our Latvian office excursion was no different, which probably explains why I was the only girl to race down the sand dunes with Steve and Timor. Nastya and Yulia were exceptions; having spent time in the United States during high school, both acted and dressed more like I did. But they were local and had family and friends nearby, so it was Daniel with whom I ended up spending most of my time in Latvia.

"Where are we going this weekend," I asked Daniel one Friday afternoon. He hadn't exactly invited me, but as soon as I discovered he spent his weekends exploring the country, I signed on to become his companion. He would choose a spot in his guidebook and map out a route, and we would do our best to follow it. That Saturday it was an ancient castle. We started our day at the bus station and did our best to find a bus that was headed in the general direction, a difficult task with our limited language skills and very basic guidebook. Luckily Latvia is a small country, so even though we always got lost, we never ended up too far off track. This time we ended up walking quite a ways in a little town before we came upon a patch of grass, a bench, and the remains of a very old stone castle. Tired from our hiking, we sat down to admire the site and plan our next move. Although we kept our voices low, our English words quickly attracted attention, and before long a group of young men had taken to staring at us and laughing. I was tired and unamused by the attention and asked Daniel to do something.

"Shall I tell them you're available?" he joked.

"I'm serious."

"So am I."

None of the young men were vaguely attractive, or I might have had a different response. The castle, on the other hand, was extraordinary. I had seen well-maintained and manicured English castles that were as organized and decorated as their modern counterparts, but I had never seen anything this wild and untouched. There were no gates or guardrails, no repairs or attempts at historical decorations; just a crumbling mass of stones on a green knoll overlooking a Latvian village. I circled the structure and spotted a very narrow and small opening that led to a dark and winding staircase.

"Let's go up," I said.

"I don't think we're allowed," said Daniel.

"I don't see any signs saying we can't."

"That's because you can't read Latvian."

"Okay. But if they really didn't want us to go up there, wouldn't there be a barrier or a gate?"

Daniel looked skeptical. He was more physically cautious than I. But I could tell he was equally curious. So I used the one argument that never failed: "When are you ever going to be able to climb a castle like this?"

I looked around. The young men had lost interest and moved on, and there was no one else in sight to sound the alarm. I bent my head and took my first step up. Daniel followed. The steps were small, worn, and wobbly. I placed my hands on the walls to guide me up the dark and twisting stairway. It was longer than it had appeared from outside, and as we continued to climb, I had visions of it all crumbling on top of me in an earthquake.

Finally I saw light and climbed up into a room where sunlight poured in through gaps in the walls. I pranced around, standing on my tiptoes to look out at the town below. There was no one else, just Daniel and me and our imaginations. I tried to picture all the people who had walked on these stones, not tourists but adventurers and, at one point, royalty.

Daniel was the first to mention that we might want to leave before someone discovered us and reported us to the local authorities. He was already writing the headlines: "Western Journalists Jailed for Entering Ancient Castle"; "Canadian Sent Home for Disrespecting Latvian Heritage"; "Westerners Beaten for Trespassing." The bareness inspired our imaginations. Today the spot is probably roped off. But back then there were few English-language signs and even fewer Western tourists outside of Riga. We got stared at, laughed at, and fussed over. We stumbled upon gorgeous ruins and ruined landscapes. By fall we had seen much of the country and took to spending our weekends at movie theaters.

We watched summer fade from our office window, looking down on the square where beer gardens had once blossomed to see children heading back to school with huge bouquets of flowers. It is a Latvian (and Russian) tradition to bring teachers flowers on the first day of school. It also seemed to be a tradition to wrap little ones in layers once the seasons changed, whether or not the weather had actually turned cold. The heating mechanism in homes seemed to be on the same strange system. There was a date when it came on. If it snowed and fell below freezing before that date, you froze. If the date arrived while it was still warm, you simply opened all your windows. It seemed tragically flawed, but nobody seemed bothered enough to change it. Everyone just hoped the snow would wait until the heat arrived.

I was more impatient for the snow to come. I had seen snow before but only on ski trips. I had never been present when a city was blanketed with its first snowfall of the season. I was home when it finally arrived, and I called Daniel in excitement. Although he was quite familiar with snow, Daniel still loved the silence and peace of a fresh snowfall, and we made plans to walk by the river near his apartment. I wrapped myself in my long coat; put on my hat, scarf, and gloves; and boarded a tram that would take me closer to the center of town, where Daniel lived. The whole ride I stared out the window, noting how different the familiar scenes looked now blanketed in white. At Daniel's I waited impatiently as he slowly and methodically prepared for the winter weather. Once outside, I skipped and slid along the streets, laughing at the wonder of it all. My fellow Rigans seemed less enthused, pulling their hoods close around their faces and hurrying back indoors. Only the children appeared excited by the scene, lugging their sleds to the tops of hills and sliding down over and over again.

The streets were enveloped in a quiet more peaceful than any I had ever experienced. Even the Daugava River that crossed Riga was still. Not quite still, I discovered on another walk without Daniel, when I took a few steps too many on its frozen surface. I am not sure what inspired me to try walking on the frozen river. But something about its smooth surface attracted me, and the idea that I could walk on water was hard to resist. I gingerly took a few steps out and then watched as the ice began to crack, one fissure spreading into another. I leapt back onto the snowbank as a hole opened where I had been standing. With Daniel I didn't take such risks, content to walk beside him and share in the beauty and peacefulness of the moment. With Daniel I let myself become attached precisely because he wasn't a boyfriend and would never be one.

Daniel did a lot of walking. I jogged and improvised workout routines in my living room until Nastya invited me to attend her aerobics class. I would have preferred a treadmill, but in its absence I thought aerobics might work. The class was held in an apartment building that happened to have some weights in a room. There was no sign outside the building, just a big Russian guy who offered little greeting. Inside we walked up several flights of stairs, paid a woman sitting at a desk, and squeezed into a closet-like space to change with a cluster of other women. Our class was held in what had probably once been a bedroom. I am always a little flustered the first time I take an aerobics class, struggling to learn the routine and steps, turning the wrong way at the wrong time, and toe-tapping when I should be sliding. Add the fact that the instructions were in Russian and I was confused enough to feel like crying. The instructor wasn't very sympathetic. She wore a lot of makeup and even more jewelry. She counted in sets of ten and shouted but did not actually ever do any of the exercises with us. The floor was concrete and the air circulation poor. I never showered there. It wasn't much of a workout, but I did learn to count to ten in Russian.

Nastya figured our knees would give out from something else before the aerobics floor would do us in. She was realistic, not sentimental. While other Russians shut their ears to the growing unrest in the late 1980s, she hired a Latvian tutor. She studied business because she understood it was another language that would be needed in the new Latvia. I should have understood business would be a big part of Radio Free Europe's coverage of an emerging democracy, but somehow that slipped by me when I signed on to freelance for the organization. I wasn't familiar with its work and had only chosen to freelance because Sandra practically drooled over the head regional honcho when he paid a visit to our office. After the meeting Sandra cornered the regional boss in the hall in her aggressive and inappropriate way. If Sandra was after him, I figured he must be important, so I followed him outside when he left. Unfortunately I spent far more time figuring out how to avoid Sandra and get him alone than figuring out what I would say to him once I did. I started simply.

"I'm Katya," I said.

"Yes, I know," he said. "We met in the office."

He wasn't rude about it, just a little impatient. He smiled and looked like he was about to say goodbye, so I figured I better launch into my sales pitch fast. "I really admire your mission, what you do is so important . . . and as a features reporter I see a lot of what is going on here," I stumbled.

I had no idea what I was saying. I had no experience in radio and wasn't sure whether Radio Free Europe was a government thing or a journalist thing or a combination of both. All I knew was that ambitious Western journalists in the Baltics worked for more than just the *Baltic Times*. Outside of Latvia our little paper didn't have quite the name recognition as Associated Press, Reuters, or Radio Free Europe. If I wanted to advance in the industry, I knew I needed to get another gig. Sandra seemed to hold Radio Free Europe in high esteem. And while I would never defer to Sandra on fashion, philosophy, or just about anything else, I deferred to her on ambition. She had already snagged an opportunity with Voice of America, one she guarded jealously. She trusted no one and had a questionable relationship with the truth, probably aggravated by her lack of regular sleeping, eating, and socializing patterns. But she had somehow landed a freelance gig before me. I was determined not to be upstaged by this semi-deranged older woman who came to work with her hair uncombed and her emotions equally out of check. So I asked this man I barely knew who worked for a radio station I hadn't heard of if he would give me a job. "I would love to freelance for you," I said, pressing my card into his hand.

He smiled and said something on the order of, "I'll see what I can do." He was about to go when I stopped him once again to ask—no, to demand—his business card. I followed up with an email a week or so later. Eventually, probably to get rid of me as much as anything else, he put me in contact with the local office. The editor there had far more experience than I did, but because his boss had put me in touch with him and because I was American, he treated me with more respect than I deserved. My first assignment had something to do with the International Monetary Fund. I was close to tears when Nastya came to my rescue. On that and all my subsequent wire stories Nastya patiently explained the terms I didn't understand, walking me through the ins and outs of international business reporting. My stories ran on the Radio Free Europe website, and Nastya always pointed them out to me. I loved seeing my byline next to such a recognized name as Radio Free Europe, even if I had only recently come to recognize it myself. I knew Nastya's name had about as much right to be there as my own, but she never said anything.

Nastya was endlessly generous, unless you made her full name, Anastasija, sound like a medicine—as most Americans did. She was hard-working but practical, using work time to shop if the right store presented itself on the way back from an interview. She could even handle Sandra, who as a business reporter fell under Nastya's direct supervision and was not above jabbing Nastya for her youth and relationship with Steve. When Sandra raised her voice, Nastya would stay calm and in her slightly New Jersey/Russian accented English explain her reasoning. When Phil raised his voice at me, I ran out of the office in tears. Of course Phil was a little rougher around the edges than Sandra, and due to his maleness, penchant for nudity, and drinking, he was slightly more intimidating. I had also always found tears to be a good avoidance technique. (It had worked at the airport when the agents were trying to charge me extra for my overstuffed baggage.) Nastya, my Soviet twin, born a day apart from me half a world away, was made of tougher stuff. She possessed the Russian talent for keeping disappointment at bay by maintaining low expectations. She had been dating Steve for quite a while, but when we talked in private, she told me she never expected to marry him. He would go back to the States and find an American wife, and she would stay behind in Latvia and be happy.

Most of the other Latvian women I met were less practical. But they were almost all sexy, at least the young ones. In summer they braved the cobblestone streets on four-inch spike heels, albeit sometimes with an ankle wrapped in an ACE bandage. In winter their hair was fluffy and smooth, despite having been smashed under a hat. I don't do heels, and when I removed my winter hat, the only fact evident was static cling. I made a concession on the shoes. When I brought out my big clunky boots, Imants almost died laughing. Then he insisted I glide on the ice patches as he did. He kept laughing when I fell. I ditched the boots but stayed friends with Imants, demonstrating a patience for obnoxious men I no longer possess.

Imants and I had noticed each other right away. He paid attention to all the new women. And in Latvia I paid attention to any man who paid attention to me. Imants would make sexist and ethnocentric comments that he knew would aggravate me. He was unpredictable and uncensored. I came to look forward to the afternoons when he would stomp into the office with his bicycle, interrupting the semi-professional atmosphere with his noise and childish humor. He wanted to be an opera singer and I was told he had a beautiful voice, but he never sang for me. One afternoon not too long after I arrived, he invited me to walk out with him.

"Why do you have a Russian name?" he asked. We were in the square below our office, and he was pushing his bike along beside us. I decided to stick with the short version of the story. "My mom liked it," I said.

He shook his head and let out an exasperated sigh: "Americans." A minute later he was back with another question: "Why do you wear such ugly shoes?"

"I think they look nice," I said. I loved my sand-colored suede Hush

Puppies. I had stopped wearing my boots. But my Hush Puppies were comfortable and practical, and the box they came in had a picture of a dog on it. I wasn't about to give them up.

"A Latvian girl would never wear those," he said. "Latvians have great taste. They are better looking than anyone." And yet it was an American woman he was walking beside. "I'm going to head back to the office now," I said.

I waited a minute to see if he would apologize. He stopped walking and looked at me. Then he leaned in close and kissed me quickly on the mouth before getting on his bike and racing off. I was mad he had thought he could kiss me after insulting me. And even madder that he left before I was able to kiss him back.

It was Imants who introduced me to a group who played basketball on Saturday mornings. I in turn brought along another woman, our Irish copyeditor. Sinead and I were both tall and athletic. We spent most games running up and down the court without the ball because our male teammates did not like to pass to us. The morning game on the Saturday of the Halloween party was the one time Imants gave me the ball: he threw it at my back. After the game he seemed annoyed that I wouldn't be taking the tram back home with him but instead getting a ride with Sinead. The party was downtown. Sinead lived downtown and had invited me to shower at her place before heading to the party.

I had come up with the haunted house idea, but Daniel and Daniel had taken it upon themselves to throw the party. Canadian Daniel shared a downtown apartment with American Daniel. Downtown apartments were usually out of the question on our salaries, but by splitting the rent, Daniel and Daniel could afford a nice place. They shared a bedroom on whose walls American Daniel had hung posters of Buffy the Vampire Slayer. He was from Wisconsin and worked for DSL (Digital Subscriber Line). He was funny and thoughtful and rather short in stature. He invited guests to count the nails in the walls of his former apartment when he had a moving party. There were hundreds of them. It was dark and small and most likely, we determined, a former torture chamber. The place he and Canadian Daniel shared now was airy and inviting, on a top floor with a view of the river and the city. It also had an attic, which I immediately decided would make a great haunted house tour. I wrote a script for it, enlisting American Daniel to provide the props for my scary story.

Nastya provided the finishing touches to my costume. When she arrived, she took one look at my unmade-up face and whisked me off to the Daniels's bedroom. The shared bedroom was fodder for gossips, but I spent a lot of time with both Daniels, and I never got the feeling they were anything more than friends to each other.

"Where's your makeup?"

"I'm wearing some lip gloss," I said.

"Come on, you're a Spice Girl and you're not wearing any makeup?"

She spoke more with surprise than annoyance. I had never worn much makeup and was not skilled in its application, relying on my older sister to fix me up when the occasion required it. At that point I didn't even own any eyeliner or mascara. "We can use mine," Nastya said. "Sit on the bed."

She did my eyes and then covered my pastel lip gloss with a deep purple lipstick. She brushed my hair into two high pigtails. "Now you look like a Spice Girl," she said.

We walked back into the living room together as Posh and Sporty Spice. With my midriff-baring top and makeup I received more male attention than usual. At the time I was most comfortable as the friend, the cute athletic girl who could beat a boy in basketball. That night I was more of a lady than an athlete, and the men around me treated me differently. Instead of the teasing and joking American Daniel and I usually engaged in, he noticed when I got cold and offered me a shirt. I liked wearing what was clearly a man's shirt; it made me feel like I belonged to someone, even though American Daniel was far too short for me and I still bristled a bit at the idea of belonging to someone. It also caused Imants to fix me with icy disapproving glares. He barely moved from the couch, just sat there drinking and fuming in silence, acting too cool and mature to take part in the fun. I was a bit of a late bloomer, so high school–style behaviors weren't out of place for me.

The party was a weird mix of loud music and booze and bobbing for apples, which the Latvians seemed to particularly enjoy. With the DSL office staff, our office staff, and several non-work-related friends there was a good mixture of expats and locals. Pretty much everyone dressed up except Imants and Timor, who came in their uniforms of dark jeans and sweaters and sat on the couch together. Evidently word of our expat Halloween party got out and attracted a newspaper photographer, who posed us for a picture in the haunted house attic. In the photo Daniel is holding a pumpkin, Steve has a candle, and Eric has a coffee cup (most likely not filled with coffee). Cut out of the newspaper shot is Phil, who has a beer in one hand. His other hand is turning down the edge of his Speedo. I am the lone woman in the shot, and the caption in the newspaper refers to me as "Happy Girl." I suppose that was the best cultural translation. And at the time it was pretty accurate.

5   Big Bad Accidents

Arnolds was my introduction to Chernobyl. Not the legends and rumors that swirled around the infamous nuclear power plant but the actual place. You might think "beauty" and "Chernobyl" have no business being mentioned in the same context, but once they did, and Arnolds was not the only one I met who used the phrase "scenic" to describe the site of the world's worst nuclear disaster. He was just the first.

Arnolds was sent to Chernobyl in 1986 to help contain radiation escaping from the fourth reactor at Chernobyl Nuclear Power Plant. He went willingly. Except in those days "willingly" was a euphemism for not wanting to be blacklisted. He didn't in fact know where he was headed until he was already en route.

He was young then. They had all been young: 5,300 Latvian men between the ages of twenty-three and thirty-five armed with cloth respirators sent to "clean up" and contain a radioactive disaster zone. A little over a decade later Arnolds was still relatively young, but he had a hardness about him that obliterated any sense of youth. He spoke slowly and cautiously, as if the socialist machine that had told him there could be no "big bad accidents" in Soviet society were still operating. He had been a Latvian officer in the Soviet Army and was sent to Chernobyl "to see what it looks like."

As radiation seeped from the damaged reactor, Arnolds worked eighteen-hour days to seal it. At first he was not even allowed to leave the contaminated zone at night. A month and a half later he returned to Latvia. The reactor was buried under a three-hundred-thousand-ton metal and concrete sarcophagus. Arnolds and the other workers had been protected by ordinary clothing and, at night, cloth tents.

Some died right away. Others fell sick over time, succumbing to a variety of ailments. By the time I met Arnolds in 1998, he belonged to the 45 percent of Latvian survivors classified as disabled. He wouldn't go into details about his health; he just kept reiterating that he and his comrades were too young for their bodies to be failing them. For me and many Westerners of my generation, Chernobyl represented all that was wrong with the Soviet system. After Chernobyl the Soviet system was unable to deny the lengths to which it would go in order to avoid admitting a mistake. It would sacrifice its own people for its reputation.

The headline of my story was "Big Bad Disasters." Subtle it was not. Most of my stories back then were rather melodramatic. It was hard not to be. When you visit towns that were used as bombing ranges, sometimes with people still in them, understatement is not an option. In California I'd attended what one might call a "diverse" high school, basically an inner city school, so I was familiar with guns. Bomb threats on test days, sure. But real bombs? Not in Berkeley. So when I spotted my first one on assignment in Zvarde, a Latvian village turned into a bombing range, I trudged off toward it excitedly. Valdis yanked me back.

"Not all of them have exploded," he said. He was sixty-nine years old and showing me around his destroyed hometown. I stepped back. Way back.

A younger bearded man accompanying us showed more sense than I, at least on this occasion. His plan to build a home on the crater-pocked and scrub-covered land brought into question his overall judgment. But in this instance he was cautious as he approached what to me looked like a very large and substantial child's toy rocket and pointed out its detonator. There had been no boom—yet.

I wasn't sure how a government could have overlooked clearing bombs from a 214-square-kilometer territory, but then I was even less sure how one could turn a farming village into the biggest bombing range in Europe. But that is what the Soviets had done to Zvarde from 1953 to 1993. Only there was no village any more, its three thousand residents having been forced off their land and its name having been erased from maps. I interviewed a man whose father had returned from World War II to find his hometown vanished and much of his family deceased. The father relocated his remaining family to America.

Those who stayed were allowed back on the land once to harvest hay in 1955. Somehow their presence was not conveyed to forty-five pilots, who dropped bombs on the land anyway. That was the only time the people were invited to see the weaponry up close. But with twelve to one hundred bombs falling in the area daily, it was no surprise when the windows of a nearby school were blasted out; twice fires were ignited, and bomb fragments were found on roofs. The man whose father had left for America came back to Zvarde in the late 1980s and early '90s to protest and was summarily sent packing and banned from ever returning to the Soviet Union. Now he was back trying to claim what his father had lost. His name was Valdis. He had been born here and still remembered the community that had once called it home. As we toured the area, he pointed to new growth where four trees had once stood. "That's where we lived," he said. He clambered over the ruins of a crumbling wall. "My sister was confirmed in this church."

The picture I took shows a white-haired man standing on a sliver of stone in the middle of wilderness. If it was just the ruins of wartime, it would not be so remarkable. But it was the remains of a war conducted in peacetime by a government on its own people. It was like Chernobyl, only few outside Zvarde had ever heard of it because its poison had not spread on the wind like Chernobyl's. Valdis pointed to the place where he used to buy chocolates. It was a heap of stones.

"I pay taxes on this," he said. He laughed with the absurdity of it. Or maybe to keep from crying; it was hard to tell.

"Will you build on it now?" I asked.

"No, I'm not that crazy," he said.

He lived far away, in another country. All that was left for him here was the past. Even the village cemetery had been bombed. Before they left, the Soviets completed the destruction by bulldozing the graves. Then they placed a cross by the wreckage of one of their planes that had crashed during a 1992 bombing. They asked the Latvians to look after it. I am not sure if they saw the irony in this. The Soviets weren't known for their sense of humor.

It was difficult to listen to Arnolds's and Valdis's stories. But for me, retelling them in the newspaper was a way of making amends for the wrong I felt the West had shown the region by refusing to see the horrors hidden there for so long. On paper, communism sounds peachy, and I had met many in America bewitched by its promise of a classless society. I wanted to show them the reality they had long avoided: it was a society built on fear separated into two classes, those in power and those kept from it. The truth had seeped out but only in bits and pieces. In Berkeley I had known people who still believed Lenin was a good man, not a mass murderer. What I saw and heard in Latvia left no doubt about the brutality of the system. And while some might focus on the tragedy of it, I have always found inspiration in what people are able to endure, maybe because it makes my own problems seem small by comparison.

6 Exile

In Latvia the pain of broken families, messed-up marriages, and ruined childhoods was amplified by war, exile, and occupation. In the almost decade after the fall of the Soviet Union, Latvians long exiled from their own land were slowly making their way back. The Soviet legacy was waiting for them. In many cases the older generations, the ones that remembered an independent Latvia before World War II, were slower to return. They wanted to keep Latvia as it was in their memories. It was the younger generations, those in their twenties and thirties who led the homecoming. Latvia had never been their home, so it was easier for them to accept the changes.

Phil, who wrote for our paper, grew up in Australia, attending Latvian camps where he learned the dances and songs of his ancestors. He was stocky, with light hair and olive skin and a sexy Aussie accent. Despite a premature hunch in his spine, Phil could have been considered attractive in a rugged asshole kind of way. He could be sweet and flattering, complimenting me and the other women in the office. He was also intense and argumentative, stepping close and letting his spittle land on your face when he was angry or wanted to get a point across. When he ran out of arguments, he would utter the phrase "Act your age" with all the disgust he could muster. It was as if he had inherited the fight his ancestors had lost and was now trying to revive it. I had grown up fearing my stepfather's rages. I wasn't going to get close to another powder keg. Not all of the younger returnees were so bitter. Those who could see their way past old wrongs were able to integrate into the community and even become leaders. The others, like Phil, remained exiles, just as their parents had been.

It was even harder for the original exiles. They came looking for houses they had once lived in, stories they had once been a part of, and families to which they had once belonged. Unfortunately the country they remembered no longer existed, and thanks to the ever-generous Soviet government, in many cases neither did their property. The houses and apartments were still there; they just belonged to someone else due to the Soviet Union's re-gifting policy. I am a big fan of re-gifting, but only when the gifts actually belong to you. The Soviets took it a step further by re-gifting what belonged to others. This made for rather awkward encounters when the original owners decided to return. In some cases the original owners were told they had forfeited the rights to their homes when they left the country. That many had been exiled or forced to leave did not seem to matter.

Those who were granted their homes back had to continue renting them to the current tenants at the current price for seven years. Paperwork went missing, laws were redefined, and cases dragged on for years. If the original owners did finally find themselves in full possession of their former homes, they were faced with the fact that what had once been a family home was now communal flats. I interviewed an elderly woman who was told she lacked the proper documentation to claim her family home. She was Jewish and had lost her entire family in the Holocaust. There was no documentation.

But that was just the material loss. When you were denied your home, you could hate the laws that kept it from you, but when a family member refused you, the blame was harder to place. There were those who had gone missing during the years of war and occupation who didn't want to be found. I was told that by the Red Cross workers who did the searching. When they didn't think the family could handle the truth, they would tell them the relative could not be located. If they were Jewish, it was never a lie.

At first Voldermars seemed like he was one of the ones who wanted to be found. He wrote to the Red Cross, telling its agents that he wanted to see the church where he was married, the home where he had lived, and the embankment from which he had left Riga in 1943. Under German occupation he had been one of many Latvians sent to Germany to work and fight. He now lived in Scotland and wanted to see his hometown one last time. He didn't mention his Latvian wife and children, but the Red Cross looked for them anyway.

By the time the Red Cross brought him to Riga in 1998, he no longer recognized any of the landmarks he had mentioned in his original letter. When I interviewed him at his daughter's home, he wouldn't talk about the war and couldn't recall what happened to him after it ended and before he settled in Scotland. He was ninety-one years old. His memory might have been fading. Or it might have been too sharp.

Voldermars was elderly and stooped but basically healthy. The years had not treated his Latvian son as kindly; sitting next to each other on a couch, they made a strange couple, the weary looking son and the alert father. Voldermars's daughter, Biruta, stood behind them. She had not seen her father in fifty-five years, and she peppered him with questions in his native Latvian.

"Where did you go after the war?"

"Did you think of us?"

"Did you try to return?"

"Did you marry?"

Sometimes her father would answer—but not the questions she asked. When he did answer, it was through a translator. He was no longer able to speak his own language. When they pressed him on Latvian and Russian words, the best he could do was offer a few broken lines from bawdy wartime songs. He said he tried to find them after the war but was told they had been sent to Russia. Biruta didn't understand. I didn't either. For years the family had waited for Voldermars to return. His wife, Olga, had waited until her death in 1990 without ever remarrying. The children had never known another father. Voldermars never remarried either, but he had a girlfriend back in Scotland. When Biruta asked him to stay a few days, he turned her down. When she insisted, he told her he wanted to be with his girlfriend. The translator tried to soften the blow, but there isn't a polite way to translate the rejection of a father.

The family had no idea where he went after he left Latvia in 1943, no idea what his life was like or who he became. It was clear by the end of the interview they never would. They had been reunited, but the man they met wasn't the same man they remembered. There was a distance between them greater than the language divide.

It wasn't just Latvian families that were destroyed. In the independent Baltic states some of the loneliest places were the Russian military bases. I visited one in Estonia where only women and children remained. For years the mini-village had been closed off from the rest of the country, a secret Russian Army post where Estonians were not allowed. The Russian families had everything the locals did not. They knew nothing of shortages. Some didn't even know they were in Estonia. Then the army left. A few of the soldiers told their mistresses and girlfriends they would come back for them. Others didn't even bother with the pretense of affection and attachment. They simply abandoned them amid a sea of Estonians who despised them. The shops that once sold all the goods you couldn't get in the rest of the country quickly emptied. The schools that once offered instruction in Russian were eaten up by dust and decay.

No soldiers ever came back for the women and children that remained. But a headstrong Estonian woman did. She convinced an organization to fund Estonian lessons for the women and a camp for their children. A tight-knit group of teenage girls attending the camp showed me the half-empty apartment buildings where they lived with half-dead mothers. The girls were beautiful and young and confused. They giggled as they repeated simple English phrases to me in thick Russian accents. They told me about how locals came and stole metal and fixtures from the empty apartments at night. They talked about Russia, a country where they had never been, and Estonia, a country they had never known. They tried to disguise their hurt with pride. But they had been abandoned not just by their fathers but by their fatherland as well. They were citizens of neither Estonia nor Russia, relics of a society that no longer existed.

I couldn't fully understand their isolation, but I understood being left behind. During my parents' divorce and a long childhood hospital stay I had felt abandoned. My parents, distracted by their own problems, had almost lost custody of me. My mother did her best for me and my sister, but she didn't like to be alone. She needed the emotional and financial support of a man. Marriage was a necessity for her. For me it was a risk. It was something altogether different for the women of Latvia who set their sights on marrying American men. When the Soviet system collapsed, it took the jobs and roles of many men with it. Men long dependent on the government for employment found themselves without work and without the skills to find it. Women were faced with the same dilemma but in some ways found it easier to adapt. They had always been respected for being mothers and so had more than one role to fall back on. Men had drink. There was no escape for them. But the women had a way out through marriage. It went against everything I wanted for myself. But when I met Irina, as much as I found her style distasteful, I understood her and her female clients.

At the time, Eastern European mail order brides were just starting to become popular. Irina had been quick to pick up on the business opportunity. In her forties she was too old to try something new abroad but not too old to dress the part of a marriage broker. She wore her long blonde hair in two braids. Any thought of innocence was overshadowed by her black leather jacket and bright red lipstick. She posed for the photo I took while nibbling on the end of a pair of sunglasses. They weren't even hers.

Her office was small and decorated with marriage certificates. She was not ashamed or embarrassed to show me her catalogues of eligible women. She pointed to pictures of women in bikinis and evening dresses. She spoke in a mix of broken English and Russian that her assistant translated. The women, she said, "are cultured and have feminine desires to get married and have a family." I tried not to take offense at the implication, especially when she complained that Western women put their careers before relationships. That was my goal. I had watched my mother tie her future to that of a man, and it wasn't an existence I wanted. But I didn't blame these women for wanting it. I didn't see any better options for them. Some of them weren't citizens. They didn't speak Latvian; they couldn't find work. Their futures in Latvia were limited. They had found a solution. Irina pointed out the hobbies they listed in their profiles. The most common were sewing and cooking. "Feminine," she said. "Like Western men want."

Irina breathlessly listed their other virtues. They were "unspoiled," "loving," and "exotic." I listened, ignoring her broken phrases and simple remarks and instead hearing the underlying drive of an enterprising businesswoman. When she was done she summed up her role as that of a "happy maker."

"You mean matchmaker," her assistant said.

"No, happy maker," she said.

And while I knew happiness was not really her goal, I wanted to believe it just might be the result.

7 The Nice Nazi and the Mean Jew

I saw him one night. Lenin. He was in a dumpster. A paint can had been placed askew on his head and two bottles of vodka lined up in front of his chest. The dumpster was outside the newspaper's office, and I hurried inside to get my camera. When I returned, an empty pack of cigarettes had been placed in front of his chest. It was dark, and the chalky colored Lenin bust was just barely visible in my viewfinder. I wondered where he had been found and who had placed him upright in a full dumpster. I waited in the shadows for a while, listening to the laughter as those who passed pointed him out to their friends.

The post-Soviet years were a utopia on top of a bureaucratic nightmare. The culture was schizophrenic, leaning toward the West while still being pulled eastward by Russia. There was an openness and sense of new beginnings among Latvians and confusion and fear among the Russians who made up a majority in many cities. Latvia was entering the World Trade Organization. Its school system was close to collapse because it planned to lay off all teachers who had not obtained citizenship. There were social orphans whose parents were alive but otherwise incapable of caring for them, often because they were drunk and unemployed. There were poor pensioners. There were huge flower markets.

There were also supermarket bombings. Every few months someone would plant a bomb outside the city's major supermarket and bust a wall and mess up the sidewalk a bit. Luckily for us, the supermarket never felt threatened by these small inconveniences and kept its doors open. There was some talk that it was the mafia trying to get its cut of the business. The supermarket was a new thing and only available downtown, so I would shop there after work and lug the items home. I bought bread, *pirozhoki*, and vegetables near the market in my neighborhood. They were cheaper and fresher. There was a little bar right by my tram stop, and most nights people would down a few shots there before venturing home. I may have been the only sober customer to purchase the *pirozhoki*. They were more grease and dough than anything else, but I was a lazy cook and they counted as food.

Trying to buy hot water bottles was more frustrating. Daniel and I were at a pharmacy using the Latvian words we had been told translated to "hot water bottle," but the woman behind the counter wasn't getting it. We even drew a picture, but still the woman remained impassive. Eventually it became clear she knew what we were asking for but didn't want to give it to us because she didn't think two young people needed hot water bottles. "The customer is always right" was still a foreign concept. When we finally got the woman to sell us water bottles, they were a blessing—until they began to leak. If there is anything worse than a cold bed, it is a cold wet bed. I ventured back to the pharmacy, figuring the second time around things would be easier.

They weren't, not the second time, nor the third. On each occasion I went through the same pantomime, and the woman behind the counter feigned the same ignorance. The comedy became almost tragic when I tried to buy adhesive bandages. The woman wanted to sell them to me individually, something tantamount to a sin for an individual raised on the Costco model of "buy everything you can fit in your car." In Riga it appeared I would have to travel to the store each time before I showered in order to have a bandage for the ankle I would invariably nick shaving.

In this consumer desert there was an oasis of service: McDonald's. It was just a few blocks from our office, and we went there when our water was turned off. Our office was a microcosm of the country and its capital. Like Riga itself, the majority of our people were Russian. We also had our returnee and the adventuresome expats. Then there were the Latvians. Imants was still a student and worked only part time. He was also too childish for anyone to take seriously. There were a few other Latvians, but the only one with a major role was our translator, Lauma. She was the source through which much of our data were filtered. Every morning she would read the papers and let us know what was going on. Because Riga was still dominated by Russians and because Russians tended to be more initially inviting than Latvians, most of us expats hung out with Russians more than Latvians. In some ways this left us doubly isolated; in others it provided us with a clue to a population Lauma didn't always want to include.

Lauma was fluent in Russian, but she wouldn't speak it. She had been forced to speak it for most of her life, and now that she didn't have to, she had no intention of ever speaking it again. She insisted anyone raised in Latvia should speak Latvian. She had a point. The only problem was that under Soviet rule Latvian was not emphasized, so unless you came from a Latvian family, you had no real way of knowing the language. There were a few similar words, but most were drastically different, one language belonging to the Slavic family and the other to the Baltic. In Riga and other big cities you could get by with Russian; it was only in the countryside you needed Latvian. I knew neither. I was studying Russian but only informally. I was totally dependent on Lauma.

One afternoon I decided to interview the young guards who watched over the Freedom Monument. Built during Latvia's first independence and off limits during the Soviet years, the monument featured a huge bronze woman holding up three stars symbolizing the three regions of Latvia. Her name was Milda, and a guard could usually be found keeping her company. I figured the guards would have stories to tell. I chose to talk to them on a day so cold I couldn't even take my fingers out of my gloves to write. Lauma explained my mission to the young guard on duty at the time, and we both waited for his response. When it came, Lauma was silent.

"What did he say?" I asked.

"I don't know," she replied. "He's speaking Russian."

"Lauma, please."

She turned back to the young soldier and spoke to him in Russian. The words she translated back to me were her own: "He was born in this country, and he doesn't speak Latvian. He was raised in Daugavpils." Daugavpils was Latvia's second largest city and almost entirely Russian.

"He probably didn't hear a lot of Latvian there," I said.

"He should speak Latvian."

She tried to continue the interview in Latvian, insisting he must, he should, he had to know the language of the country where he had been born. But he didn't, and I never got the answers to my questions. I heard later that Lauma's ten-year-old son came home in tears from karate one day because he couldn't understand a word the Russian instructor was saying. She had refused to let him learn Russian, putting him at a considerable disadvantage in Riga at the time.

Lauma also didn't like to talk about the past. She was in her early thirties, but her attitude was inflexible and rigid. She wore her hair stylishly short, except her bangs, which were long. Her features and frame were delicate, but her eyes were sparks of defiance. She mentioned once the hard years after independence, when there were long lines and empty shelves. That was when she had married. She didn't talk about her husband. People said he traveled a lot and was paid well. She seldom laughed and was quick to take offense. Like with Phil, there was anger inside her. He expressed his in harsh shouts. She expressed hers in damning silence.

Aside from not wanting to translate Russian, Lauma was generally accommodating of my youthful pursuits, even riding down a luge track with me. We brought her son on that one. Even Lauma had to admit that the 1,420-meter luge and bobsled track the Soviets left behind in Segulda was something special. It had sixteen curves and a maximum speed of 125 kilometers per hour. The manager who showed us around was called "Mad Max." I didn't ask about the name. But I imagine it probably had something to do with the 90-kilometer-per-hour record he held for sliding down the track on a shovel. The story of how an icy rollercoaster ended up in flat Latvia had a lot to do with the fact that the man who introduced the luge and bobsled to the Soviet Union was Latvian. I don't remember much about my ride except being very cold and going very, very fast. I also remember being surprised at how many times I ended up creeping up on the track's curved edges. I am not a screamer, but I am pretty sure a scream escaped my mouth on at least one occasion. I went down on my back, feet first, as Mad Max had advised. Even Lauma's son was silent with fear when I met him at the bottom.

The chimney sweep was more Lauma's style. Latvians love their legends, and he had created his own. His father had been a chimney sweep, and he had been carrying on the tradition for the last forty-two years. He wore the traditional tall black hat and little black jacket fastened with gold-colored buttons featuring chimney sweeps. People regularly stopped him on the street to rub the buttons for happiness. "Do you think that really brings happiness?" I asked. Lauma translated his reply: "Life without believing and hope is not living."

We were seated in the little attic loft where he lived. He was a small, impatient man with a soot-covered face.

"Have you ever fallen?" I asked.

"You can fall only once," he said. "And if it had happened you wouldn't be talking with me here."

I took that as a no and noted so in my notebook. He was more accommodating when it came to legends of wealth and betrayal. He talked about cleaning the chimneys at an old morgue where legend had it a woman's body had been chopped up and put in pies during the war. He cleaned for a couple who he later found out had hidden gold in their basement.

The day we went on a rooftop to watch him work was icy and cold. The roof was slanted and covered with snow. I crawled through an opening rather like a manhole cover in the attic and inched my way toward the flat middle part of the roof. Lauma followed, squatting like I was, close to the roof's surface. I slid a few feet, and Lauma grabbed my hand to steady me. Then we both slid. The edge was near but still a few feet away. We sidestepped back toward the center, shivering from more than just the cold.

The chimney sweep fixed me with a look of annoyance. I had missed the best shot, his initial appearance on the roof. It turned out he had only let us on the roof because he wanted copies of the photos I took. For a lot of assignments I reported, we couldn't get the newspaper's usual photo service to attend. I had a pretty good camera, so I often ended up taking my own pictures. This was one of those occasions. I wasn't a professional photographer, but I also wasn't a complete amateur, and I did not take well to being told what to do by the chimney sweep. I ignored his instructions, which was easy to do because he was speaking Latvian and the translation reached me too late for me to react. I was pretty pleased with the shot I got. He is looking down the chimney, a rope over his shoulder, a cleaning tool in his hands. Above is a blue sky, below the city of Riga, cold and clear. I keep a framed copy of the photo on my wall and one of his buttons in my jewelry box.

Looking back, if not with the wisdom of age at least with a greater understanding of the high cost of health care, I understand Lauma's hesitance to accompany me on some of my more risky adventures. But I was in my early twenties, and having already had several close calls with death, I took life for granted. When an American in our circle ended up in the hospital with unexplainable stomach problems, I was openly sympathetic but secretly suspicious. Wasn't she tough enough to handle a little stomach flu? And if she wasn't, why didn't she just go home? It was only later, when I found myself in a Ukrainian hospital with similar abdominal pains, that I understood not all pain can be ignored. And the solution isn't always to leave the country, although in the end that is what we both had to do.

There were several strains of Latvian nationalism, none of which I can recommend but most of which I came to understand. One of these belongs to the Latvian soldiers who fought with the Germans during World War II. Unfortunately the Baltic Legions happened to be members of the Baltic Waffen ss units. Every year they would march in downtown Riga to commemorate their war dead, and every year news outlets from around the world would carry coverage of the parade. Photos of old men waving the red and white flag of their country would run above the words "Nazis march in Latvian capital." They were condemned outright. I watched the parade with a stringer for a Western wire service. Neither of us could believe it. When I first heard about the march, I imagined it would be a small skittish gathering. In reality it was large and cumbersome and unapologetic. While leery of talking to Americans, the Latvian soldiers were also eager to explain how they ended up on the wrong side of history. The legion was created in 1943 under German occupation. Although termed "voluntary," it was one of those "voluntary" things that was ordered by Hitler and carried out by a draft. While they were never connected with any war crimes, members fought in German uniforms, many of which bore the infamous ss identification. It wasn't really a good look.

The men I talked to explained that they had worn those uniforms not because they supported Nazi ideals but because they had been told they were fighting for a free Latvia, one not occupied by Communists. Now, in the postwar era, Western Europe and America seemed to be okay with this as long as they kept relatively quiet, a sort of "don't ask, don't tell" scenario. Only the guys didn't think they had anything to be ashamed of and wanted their country and the world to recognize their heroism. One of the men I spoke with was still slim and straight-backed, like the soldier he had once been. He was patient with me, explaining what it had been like in Riga during World War II. His voice was so soft I had to lean in close to listen. He told me about the friends who had served with him and died beside him. Then he asked, not so much accusingly as curiously, how my country could criticize his actions when it had left Latvians to fight off the Russians and Germans on their own. As much as I sympathized with him, I knew his argument was a tough sell, especially for a country trying to join the European Union.

The Jewish rabbi I interviewed had a more politically correct and sympathetic story. He had been exiled to Siberia in the immediate postwar years and had experienced near starvation, among other hardships. There were very few Jews in Latvia at the time, and I was never sure why he had decided to return. But there he was. So I wanted to interview him. It had been nearly impossible to get him to meet for an interview, and I had reluctantly agreed that he could see the story before it ran. He was the only rabbi in town, and it was the only way I could convince him to talk to me. So after writing the story, I returned to his office with a hard copy. I didn't want to email him a copy he could hold onto.

He stopped me almost as soon as I started reading.

"Let me hold it," he demanded.

"No."

He sulked. I continued reading.

"That is not the right way to say it."

He snatched the paper from me and started scribbling over my text. I extracted it from his hands, ignoring his written comments. "I am only asking you to comment on the accuracy of the piece, not the style," I said. I kept reading. He continued to interrupt, arguing over trivial details.

"You can't mention the glass of water like that," he said.

"Why not?"

"That is not the way I want it told," he said.

"It is just a glass of water."

"You cannot understand what I went through. What it was like."

He was echoed by his assistants, who reiterated that he had suffered greatly and needed to be treated kindly. I had no problem with treating him kindly. But I was not going to bend the rules of journalism simply because he wanted something phrased differently. I was young and looked even younger and was commonly mistaken for a student or intern. I bristled whenever my experience was questioned. Now I might laugh at the whole situation, but then I was furious.

"I am the journalist, and I decide how to write it."

"It is my story, and I no longer want you telling it."

He tore the paper from my hand. I tore it back. We were both acting like children, but neither of us would give in. I grabbed my bag and fled, a little round rabbi in hot pursuit. And that's how I spent my time with former officers of the Waffen ss and a Jewish rabbi.

8 A God Other Than Lenin

A funny thing about the snow in Latvia: it didn't melt. Days passed and still the white fluffy stuff remained. Only it was no longer fluffy—or white. I had seen snow before but just on short visits to cold places. I guess I never thought about the fact that after I left, the snow stayed. And in Latvia it stayed for a very long time—until May—with more and more continually piling up. It presented tragic ends I had never imagined, including death by falling icicles and ice fishermen falling through the surface of lakes. Every year a few died, no doubt relations of the poor drunk souls who die in the country's lakes every summer. Then there are those who meet their demise while drinking and hunting. There are just some things that don't go well with heavy drinking—mainly Slavic men.

For my own survival I took to looking up when walking alongside buildings on sunny days. Inside my apartment, where a glass of water left out overnight was likely to freeze, the hot water bottle became my constant companion. I taught myself a form of sliding and running that managed to both keep me warm and moving forward and also undoubtedly entertained my more hardy Latvian neighbors. The snow made it difficult to rollerblade in Latvia; it was better in Ukraine, although skiing was a more appropriate pastime. In Kyiv there was even a ski slope—or a hill with a line that pulled you up the slope if you could endure the strain on your biceps and the burn in your hands long enough to reach the top. That is where Dima and I went on our second date. Our first was on New Year's in the new millennium. After meeting at Chernobyl, we had to keep it epic.

Living in Latvia, I spent New Year's Eve in Moscow. I also took a winter trip to Stockholm. I had quickly tired of the winter scene in Riga. By November the icicles that formed on Steve's beard had lost their novelty. The same held for watching children slide down frozen streams. Waiting to see how long Sandra's panty hose and Birkenstock uniform would last proved an all too brief distraction. A pair of boots even clumsier than mine surfaced not long after the first snow fall. She kept the lavender suit and pantyhose, just adding the winter footwear.

I never received a satisfactory answer as to why it happened, but every once in a while, the water simply ceased to come out of the taps. Sometimes it lasted hours, sometimes days. Hot water was more prone to this interruption in service than cold. When that happened, you either smelled or had a convenient excuse to shack up with your boyfriend. When I had neither, I paid a visit to the friendly Irish. If nothing else is imported, every post-Soviet city ought to welcome a few Irish expats. They go a long way toward cheering things up. Riga's Irish included Sinead, whom I had invited to play basketball with me; her husband Dermot; and their toddler daughter, Seresha. Dermot had a real job in finance for some big company and a real apartment in the city center with modern amenities like a washing machine and an individual hot water heater. When the family was out of town, I was given the key to their place, where their Latvian cleaning woman found me semi-dressed and dancing to the Beatles. I don't believe she had ever seen *Risky Business*. Even if she had, I was no Tom Cruise. As soon as my clothes were dry, I packed up and headed back to my Soviet ghetto. My other musical memory is of meeting one of the voices behind Milli Vanilli; he was in town with his band for a charity concert.

At a press conference for the event, a Russian journalist asked the group why Russians were depicted as the enemy in one of its videos. The band members looked at each other, unsure how to answer. Finally one of them said, "It's just a video." Back then Latvia was a place where '80s bands past their prime could pretend they were still stars. There was a rumor of Duran Duran or Depeche Mode coming for a concert, and all the women in our office, and in Riga in general, were ecstatic. I had stopped admitting a fondness for both bands back in high school. But Latvians were so behind on things that they still believed bands like Duran Duran and Depeche

Mode were hip. It was the same for most other 1980s rock and pop groups. Latvians had largely missed out the first time these bands came around and were determined not to do so again.

We spent Christmas in Nastya's apartment eating homemade pizza while wearing reindeer antlers. There isn't exactly a list of what to give your twenty-something daughter living in Latvia, so my mother sent me red felt reindeer antlers and a pair of sparkly red gloves. The gloves were meant to be used like a loofah in the shower, but the tags had been cut off, so lacking an explanation, I assumed she was giving me Michael Jackson attire. I know I wore them at least once. I must have been feeling particularly nostalgic.

Prior to the pizza party we attended Christmas Eve services. Aside from Eric and Daniel, I don't believe any of us were particularly religious, but suddenly we all thought it would be a good idea to go to church. I remember giving Nastya pointers on what to do, her Communist education having completely skipped over worshiping any God other than Lenin.

"Stand now," I said, jabbing her in the side.

A few minutes later I yanked her down: "We kneel now."

The singing was self-explanatory; the sermon less so.

"No clue," I whispered in her ear. "I think they're speaking Latin."

A day or so after Christmas Eric somehow managed to convince a man at the Russian Embassy that I would be writing a story for his German wire service despite the fact that I spoke not a word of German. We were both given visas to Russia. Eric surely was meant to be a politician. And like with any good politician, it was never clear exactly what his politics were. Or maybe that is just because when Daniel and I paid him visits after depositing our laundry at a nearby laundromat, I tended to drift off when he launched into his monologues. Being Canadian, and thus more polite, Daniel did his best to stay awake and most likely neutral.

I was fast asleep when the overnight train to Moscow reached the border, and a rude guard woke me and demanded my passport. Several scowls and harsh words later he returned it. I worried about Eric, who planned to overstay his visa. I pictured him stuck in some tiny room at the border while gruff guards quizzed him on things he would have no way of answering.

In the end it was much simpler. He gave them some money. I think that is how most of us obtained our "invitation letters" to the country. For a Russian visa you needed an invitation, and for that there were businesses that would sell you one. In our case Eric's colleague in Moscow had taken care of the paperwork, making our trip to the Russian Embassy in Riga relatively painless.

In Moscow we toured a famous graveyard; then we sat in a coffee shop drinking tea. We walked around Red Square—and sat in a tea shop sipping more tea. We looked at the Kremlin, then drank tea at another tea shop.

Most of my trips to Moscow went this way, a little sightseeing and a lot of sipping. That's what happens when you visit Moscow in winter. You drink a lot of tea. The Russians drink a lot more than that, but for me it was simply tea. It was Orthodox Christmas time; nobody was doing much of anything besides eating and drinking anyway, so our sipping tours were quite well accepted by the local populace. We spent New Year's Eve in Red Square with a mass of humanity. It was the warmest reception I received in Russia, with plenty of people offering me sips right out of their champagne bottles. There is a rumor that New Year's Eve during Soviet times was celebrated at the same time across the Soviet Union's eleven time zones—very convenient for those in Moscow, very inconvenient for those elsewhere. A bit like everything under communism. The Muscovites I met waxed poetic about those great times. I understood their nostalgia; they were from Moscow, the center of the Soviet empire and a stronghold of tradition. After the celebration they emptied Red Square and pushed their way onto the last metro train. Within an hour Red Square was silent and empty.

We got out of Moscow almost as quickly, spending much of our visit at a friend of a friend's dacha an hour or so outside the city. It was a half-built structure in a neighborhood of half-built houses. It seemed everyone had run out of money midconstruction. Certain rooms, including the bedroom where I slept, lacked walls. It was a strange situation, and after one night of sleeping with plastic Coke bottles filled with warm water to keep away the chill of the outside, which in this case was an entire side of my room, I was the worse for wear.

"You can have my room," Eric offered the next morning.

"That wouldn't be fair," I said. "I'm the extra person; I wouldn't feel right if you slept in the unfinished room."

I also didn't want his family blaming me if he got sick from exposure. He didn't want me to become ill while he was playing host, so we were at an impasse. Ever practical and solution-oriented, I proposed the obvious: "Why don't we both sleep in your room?" Eric looked at me a little funny: "There's only one bed."

I had noted this, but being from Berkeley, I was not worried. I remember waking up one Saturday morning during my sophomore year in high school to find a teenage boy snuggled between two girls on the pullout couch in the living room. They were my sister's friends, and they insisted they were all just friends. I believed them. Eric seemed to need an explanation though. So I offered one: "We can share," I said, "as friends. We can even have separate blankets if you want."

He insisted a few more times that he would simply sleep in the unfinished room. But that night, when the reality of the wind chill dawned on him, he climbed into the bed opposite me in the room with four walls. We were definitely just friends, and the only benefit we got out of sleeping in the same bed was warmth.

My next trip to Moscow was also in winter and involved a lot of walking. I remember dropping my cell phone on the street at one point and my hands being too cold to pick it up. But then I was with the man I would marry. When I got too cold, he would encircle me in his arms. It was a work trip again, only this time I was actually working. So was he. It was the first story we did together outside of Ukraine. We fought a few times, but waiting for our train at the station on the return trip, I ended up sitting on his lap, my head buried in his chest. I was never one much for public shows of affection, but then before I met him I had never really felt the safety of someone else's arms. It was probably an illusion because he was as cold, broke, and tired as I was at the time. But I felt safe.

9 Everything Is *Normali*

The date was an accident. The computer was freezing up, and both of us were a little stir crazy. It was late in the evening, and all I wanted to do was go home. But Imants hadn't even finished laying out the entertainment section. We talked about movies. I told him I would never watch Robert Redford's *The Horse Whisperer* because it was almost three hours long and I didn't watch movies over two hours. He agreed it probably wasn't any good because it was a girl-and-horse story. When he finally got to the features section, I no longer cared what the photo cutlines said. The other designer would take a cigarette break when I wrote cutlines, but Imants liked to stay by me talking nonsense and making it impossible for me to string together a coherent sentence. Tonight I was too tired to tune him out and somehow ended up agreeing on a bet. I don't remember what the bet was about, but we both agreed that whoever won it would get to choose the movie we would see. It was a weird way of asking me out, but I accepted it. I lost and Imants chose *The Horse Whisperer*. I think he did it as much to annoy me as anything else. He talked through most of the movie, mocking the sad scenes and generally ruining the dramatic effect. I ended up liking it.

On the tram ride back he conveniently missed his stop and claimed it was too late to catch another tram to his house. He asked to sleep at my place. I let him follow me home and even made out with him for a while on the couch. Then I headed for my bedroom. He tried to follow.

"You're sleeping on the couch," I said.

"It's so hard," he said. "I won't be able to sleep."

"Hmm, maybe you should have chosen a shorter movie so you could have caught a tram to your place and slept at home."

"Katya."

"Imants."

I shut my door. There was loud grumbling from the other side of the wall. I knew it was just a show. In Latvia the beds aren't really that different from the couches. Imants was just being Imants. We were more competitive with each other than caring. When we went ice skating, he had to go faster and jump higher than I did. He would speed around the rink—actually an outdoor tennis court flooded and frozen over—with a recklessness bordering on dangerous. He was all about upstaging me, and if I was ignoring him, he wouldn't hesitate to flirt with the nearest female. I went out with him because, really, there was no alternative. Maybe it is because they are surrounded by beautiful women, but Latvian men seem immune to feminine charm. You can be wearing a skin-tight leather ensemble, which many women did, and the men won't even notice. The most common Latvian expression is *normali*. No surprises, no emotion—just the flat *normali*. Normal; it didn't even need a translation it was such a dull word. Imants at least noticed. He just noticed everyone. The list of Western women he had flirted with and kissed was long. I was okay being another name on that list as long as he was no more to me than I was to him. His immaturity made that easy for me.

It was harder in Tunisia. I have always been close to my mother. That spring she expressed an interest in visiting me. I told her that would be great so long as we could also escape somewhere warm. We ended up spending a week in Tunisia. The few days we spent in Riga beforehand had been tiring for both of us. She found my apartment depressing and my cleaning skills lacking when it came to the toilet. I tried to explain that the discoloration had more to do with the water than anything else, but she had never lived in a post-Soviet apartment and didn't quite understand the setup. In Tunisia we were immediately reminded why Western women avoid traveling alone in certain sections of the world. If I had been invisible to Latvian men, I was anything but to their Tunisian counterparts. I wore long pants and shirts out of respect for the culture, but still my light hair and eyes attracted attention, and after almost a year of invisibility a part of me was flattered. I knew better than to respond to most of the attention or spend much time alone outside of our gated resort. But my mom didn't run, and I have never been able to resist a jog on the beach. I attracted my first companion within five minutes. He lasted five minutes more. Others followed, all paying more attention to talking than pacing. They fell off almost as quickly as they joined. Except for one; he talked less and ran more. A half hour later he was still running with me.

I don't remember his name, but he was young and smart and eager to show me around his city. When he took me to his home and introduced me to his mother, I decided he must respect me at least a little. He decorated my hands and feet with henna designs whose meanings I decided it might be better not to know. We made out on the beach and then on his roof. I couldn't get enough of his affection, as if storing up his kisses and compliments for the emotional void I would be returning to in Latvia. I was slightly embarrassed remembering the stories I had read about lonely Western women who pay Mediterranean men to be their lovers. But I wasn't paying him and I wasn't enraptured enough to think we had a real connection. I was also smart enough not to sleep with him. I had been raised in the San Francisco Bay Area and had a healthy fear of AIDS and other sexually transmitted diseases. I didn't really think anything would come of it, but when he asked for my phone number, I gave him the *Baltic Times* number.

A few weeks after I got back he called the office. Nastya answered and spoke to him in French. She smiled when she came to get me. It was awkward trying to talk to him in the office. But I didn't give him my home number. I was back in Latvia and focused on work. In reality I didn't even talk to my family much while I was there, which may be one reason my mom wanted to visit. I sent emails and wrote letters to my grandparents, but phone calls were infrequent and uninformative. I couldn't describe what my life was like in Latvia and didn't feel the need to try. I received other kinds of attention.

Swedish Save the Children flew me to Stockholm for a day to advise the organization on the situation of children in the Baltics. It was the first (and aside from one disastrous interview with Reuters) only time in my life I wore the kind of power suit working women like my mother wore back in the 1980s. It was teal, and I felt as awkward and out of place in it as Sandra looked in her lavender attire. But I was only twenty-two and I was advising a large organization about an entire region's needy children. I felt I needed to impress. I prepared a little paper with talking points. No PowerPoint presentation, just a piece of binder paper. We came up with an essay contest with prizes that would encourage writing. I would organize it; the organization would fund it. I was feeling a bit cocky about my "expertise" on the condition of Baltic children. It was easy to get a big head in Latvia.

When I visited cities for the paper, it was not uncommon for my presence to be announced publicly. The first time this happened I was sitting in the back seat of a car. I was gazing out the window at old military fortifications when I heard what sounded like my name on the radio. The woman serving as my guide smiled. "They just announced your visit to our city on the radio," she said.

I wanted to ask how they knew I was there, why they cared, and if they had announced my visit on all the stations or just that one. But I was a professional journalist. I was supposed to be indifferent to fame. So I just smiled and said, "How nice."

10 Pagans, Communists, and a Hill of Crosses

I was seated across from three seasoned Soviet-era prisoners. None of them were cuffed or shackled, so I assumed their infractions, although now more than a decade old, were relatively minor. It was my first visit to a prison. For all I knew, it was normal to meet prisoners in an office with only the prison director offering supervision. Earlier, when I had asked him if I could speak with a few of his charges about the new criminal law, the director seemed bemused. He didn't think I knew what I was getting into. He was right.

I imagined I would question men who had robbed a store to feed their children or something romantic like that. I had yet to meet enough prisoners to be cured of the notion that they are basically good people who made bad decisions. In my naïveté I believed they were all remorseful men looking for redemption. It wasn't that I hadn't seen bad things in my life. I had. I just still wanted to believe in good. I still do. I don't know how else to be.

The three I met were brought up to the room by a guard who, to my dismay, promptly left after delivering them. It was time for me to start the interviews. I stuck with the basics: name, age, occupation, or (in this case) crime.

The first prisoner's response translated to murder. I tried to make my source more sympathetic.

"Just one murder, right?"

No, multiple.

"It was in self-defense though?"

He shook his head. No.

He wasn't helping me with my theory. He offered no excuse, no regret, nothing, no emotion at all. I gave a nervous smile. He didn't smile back.

Still trying to paint a compassionate picture, I asked why he had killed the first time. I think he said he didn't have a reason for strangling his girlfriend to death with his bare hands. In my head I tried to determine the time it would take me to reach the exit. I didn't ask about his subsequent murders. I cut my losses and moved on to the next guy.

The answer was the same. Murder.

And the third. Murder.

I wondered if the prison director had tried to find the least sympathetic prisoners on purpose in order to scare me out of my attempt to humanize them. If so, it had worked. My ambition to see their side of things had largely vanished. They had killed people—many people as far as I could tell—for no good reason. I didn't care what happened to them any more so much as I cared about what happened to me now that I was sitting across from them. Eventually I asked what they thought about the new criminal code. They didn't care much. They had been locked up too long and seen too many new initiatives to believe anything would change for them. They were still behind bars. And I for one was glad of it.

Later, on other assignments, I did meet some more sympathetic cases. Their situations were hopeless. Fleeing fighting or political persecution in their native African or Asian countries, they had gotten caught in Latvia on their way to a better life in Western Europe. It was unsafe for them to return home and impossible for them to move on now that they were behind bars. They never stood a chance sneaking through Latvia. It wasn't as if they could blend in. There wasn't much diversity in the Baltics. The closest you got to seeing anyone of color were the gypsies. And everyone knows how Europeans love gypsies, or Roma. Being American, I was infatuated with them. They offered a bit of color, chaos, and racket among a rather cold and stoic populace.

At a rural Latvian school dedicated to educating Roma children, teenagers studied in the first-grade classroom. While their Latvian counterparts sat quietly at their desks, the Roma children danced in and out of their seats like American youngsters pre-Ritalin. The teacher explained that the Roma students colored with violet and red while the Latvian kids favored calmer tones. If they didn't understand something, they asked questions. They were warm and expressive and energetic. They also tended to marry by thirteen and drop out long before graduation.

The school was a Soviet leftover. Under the Soviet system companies were encouraged to hire Roma, and police tried to make sure the children attended school. Now no one wanted to hire them, and donors found excuses not to provide the school with books. It wasn't anything new. Roma had been in the region for centuries, and their presence was even noted in several Latvian fairy tales. They are said to have come from India, and their language is close to Sanskrit. Most of those I met spoke a mixture of Latvian, Russian, Romani, and English that was hard for anyone but them to understand. The Latvian teacher who showed me around the school pointed out Roma differences not to set them apart, but to try to help me see the world through their eyes. It was a unique perspective. Death, she explained with the help of a translator, is celebrated because Roma are happy when a person leaves this difficult life. In one of the first classrooms we visited, a boy I took to be about eight or nine jumped around me excitedly.

"What's your name?" I asked.

"Dollar," he said.

"Oh, does that mean something in Romani?"

He looked at me like I was a little slow. Then he looked at his teacher.

"It means dollar," he said. "Like your money."

The teacher explained that "Dollar" was a popular name among the Roma. "They think if they name a child Dollar, he will have a lot of money," she said.

Dollar was thirteen and had been in the equivalent of first grade for seven years. He still couldn't read or write. He seemed bright. I wondered why he was still at such a low level, but he didn't have any answers. Later the teacher told me. Dollar's mother regularly had to go to Russia for work and took him with her. In Russia he wasn't accepted in the schools because he was Roma. He didn't want me to know this. He told me he was going to be a doctor. He stayed by my side most of the day. When the teacher tried to shoo him away he remained firm. "Bodyguard," he said pointing to his chest.

He was barely four feet tall and scrawny. When any of the other Roma children got too close to me, he would gently prod them back. They all wanted to ask me the same question: "Are you a friend of the gypsies?"

I said yes and hoped I could stand by my answer once I left the protected safety of the school. I liked the Roma and often joked I was part gypsy. When I was sixteen, I bragged to friends that I had moved more times than years I had been alive. It was true. My mother was a single working woman in the 1980s; moving was just what we did. Our moves were not dramatic—from one rented home to another—but they offered a kind of fresh start. In Latvia all of us expats were outsiders making our homes far from the familiar. We had entry into many groups but belonged to none. We were special and also weird, the new girls or boys who are both admired and feared. We were not unlike the Roma, who called the world their home but claimed no country as their own. Before I left the Roma school, the teacher gave me a Latvian/Romani dictionary. I still keep it in case I should ever need to translate between two languages I don't understand.

Another language I don't speak is German. But the older Latvians did not let this small inconvenience stop them from attempting to converse with me in that language. They seemed to believe anyone who knew English should be able to understand German, and despite my pitiful attempts to speak the language, they continued to hold fast to this belief. One source I regularly met with seemed surprised every time he slipped into German and I fixed him with a blank stare. I had told him each time I saw him that I didn't speak German, but he liked to test me. Like many of his generation, he seemed to think I was refusing to speak German out of modesty or stubbornness and not because I had no idea how to speak it. They were reminders of their country's Germanic past.

The younger generation had different occupiers, and it had different language instructors: the Cartoon Network. It was Tom and Jerry and the Looney Tunes gang who taught them how to speak English, a detail I discovered while researching a radio piece for the BBC World Service. Having grown up with a British stepfather, I was familiar with the BBC World Service and thought it the epitome of great journalism. One of its programs, *Europe Today*, was doing a segment on English in Eastern Europe and called the only English language newspaper in the Baltics to find a reporter to help. Nastya and Steve, being a couple, had decided to take vacation at the same time, leaving me in charge. As acting editor-in-chief, I was able to inform the editor at *Europe Today* in full confidence that I would be the best person for the job. I failed to mention I was also the only person unless she wanted to deal with either a woman who had a questionable relationship with the truth or an unreliable drunk. The editor was happy to have me do the piece. I believe she may have regretted it later, when I showed up in London looking for an internship. When people useful to my career tell me to keep in touch, I take them at their word.

Friends were a little harder to keep close, especially friends made in a country in which neither of you belonged. It was inevitable we would leave. None of us, except maybe Nastya, planned on staying in Latvia forever. But before we all went our separate ways, we had one great day together celebrating Jani, or Midsummer's Eve, the longest day of the year and an official holiday in Latvia. Throughout history Latvians have maintained a close relationship with nature, which is reflected in their language, folklore, and art. On Jani it all comes together when everyone heads to the country to spend the holiday among the forests and strawberry fields. People leap over raging bonfires and weave straw wreaths for their heads and get hit with branches in a homemade sauna. At the office we all decided we could at least manage the going to the country part. A colleague had a country home outside of Riga. On the afternoon of Midsummer's Eve we took a train there.

As the train slowly made its way through the countryside, I looked out the window at people collecting sticks and brush from the fields for bonfires. On the train old men carried buckets for mushroom picking, and women wove wreaths made of branches. I brought a soccer ball. At the house we picked strawberries, wove wreaths, and kicked my ball around. It was the exact picture of country life I had conjured up as a child when I begged my mother to relocate to the country—with the exception of the Euro pop music someone was playing. It was an idyllic pagan festival with warm stew and "his and her" saunas. Inside the wooden lean-to that served as the women's sauna I tried to avoid the branches the other women were hitting each other with. But after watching Nastya undergo the treatment,

I realized it was more of a pleasant tickling sensation, like a back scratch, than the rough and hurtful process I imagined it to be. The harmful part seemed to come when a certain number of leaves stuck to you, thus making it likely you would become a wife. Several of the women were desperate to get the leaves to stick. I was determined that nothing stick to me, especially a Latvian husband. My cowardice continued when it came to the rinsing segment of our experience. The men plunged into a cold lake naked. The women simply poured water over themselves in the sauna, an act of both modesty and cowardice.

Afterward we warmed up with a bottle of sweet wine and a round of singing by the bonfire. I didn't recognize the Latvian classics, but luckily there were a few Beatles hits. I don't believe John Lennon ever pictured a Russian with a shaved head singing "Strawberry Fields Forever," but until you have heard the ESL version of Beatles classics, you haven't really experienced the band.

The point was to stay awake until the sun went down and then remain awake until it rose again a few hours later. I can't remember what the point of jumping over the bonfire was other than to eliminate those who probably should not be reproducing anyway, a Latvian version of the Darwin Awards. Maybe we were fitter to survive than most because although few of our jumpers were sober, none were seriously injured. Still, after seeing several leapers barely make it over the waist-high flames, I opted not to jump despite Imants's goading. It was hard to let him succeed without meeting his challenge, but I was slightly older than he—and more sober.

Sometime after the sun came up, we went to sleep in a barn filled with hay and animals. Sleeping in a hayloft is not as fun as it sounds. Hay itches. It doesn't cover you like a blanket. And farm animals don't sleep in, even on holidays. Imants also seemed uninterested in sleep and got the wrong idea when I huddled next to him under the blanket we had been forced to share. I helped him understand with a few good jabs to the ribs. He got me back the next day by attaching himself to a girl on the train ride back to Riga. I didn't miss him.

Soon people started making their exits from the paper. All of us "new hires" had been in the Baltics more than a year. I guess we figured it was time to move on. I would have stayed. But after Daniel left and it became clear Steve wasn't necessarily going to stick around, I reconsidered. I didn't want to be editor. And I didn't want to be in Riga without Daniel. There were many things he didn't share with me, but there wasn't much I didn't tell Daniel. I even fantasized about living next to him when I was older. In this dream I would have boyfriends that would come and go, but Daniel would always be there. Of course I would let him date as well. It was a nice idea and probably better thought out than my marriage. But then I dreamed this when I wasn't in love. And I never tried to translate it to America.

In a country where men regularly make fools of themselves proving their manliness—ice fishing and bonfire jumping—there was no false bravado with Daniel. He openly avoided large dogs and took tentative steps when the sidewalk was icy. He seemed comfortable sticking out, getting lost, and even traveling alone. Not long out of college, I was still in the phase of wanting to fit in and be accepted, something that had been pretty much impossible in school because I didn't drink. Daniel seemed to have accepted his outcast status in Latvia, and I tried to do the same. I also copied his practice of reading books set in the region in which you are living. I spent many cold, dark Latvian nights with a hot water bottle and a copy of Tolstoy's *Anna Karenina*. It was Daniel I called when Sandra was particularly bitchy or when the snow was just so beautiful I had to go for a walk. I knew it would be hard after he left, so the first weekend he was gone, I planned a trip to the hill of crosses in Lithuania.

I set off Sunday morning on a bus bound for a rural Lithuanian village from which I would catch another bus to the legendary hill. The manmade mound had been constructed during Soviet times, when the people would plant a few crosses there and the Soviets would promptly bulldoze them. The people kept planting crosses and the Soviets kept bulldozing until there now stand several small hills covered in crosses of every kind, size, and make. Daniel had been enthralled by the place and insisted it was easy to locate.

I arrived in the village around midday with a half hour to spare before the next bus took me to the sight of the crosses. An hour later, when the bus had still not materialized, I asked the old woman next to me if she knew where it was. Although I was speaking Russian, she answered in Lithuanian, so all I caught was the gesture she made toward the clock. It was an hour off. At least that is what I thought until I checked a number of other clocks and realized there was a time difference between Riga and the village. The next bus would not arrive for another hour. I sat down on the wood benches and began to cry. I kept on crying, only stopping in time to wipe my eyes and board the next bus headed to the hill of crosses. My fellow passengers must have thought I had some sort of religious experience. But I was just sad. I missed Daniel more than I had ever missed a friend. Although purely platonic, my relationship with him was the closest I had ever been to a man. In a way I think it taught me how to be vulnerable around men and helped me understand the benefits of a relationship, an emotional one if not a physical one.

Of course I wasn't thinking any of this at the time. I was just thinking how much I missed the adventure of my first year in Latvia and the little group of friends I belonged to. I wasn't ready for it to end, but it was ending all the same. Daniel had left, and I knew others would soon follow. I didn't want to be the last one out. I've always found it harder to stay than to leave. The bus dropped us off in an empty field, and I once again was overwhelmed with exhaustion and sadness as I tried to figure out where in the world I was. It was then that I spotted a hill in the distance. When I was several hundred feet away from the small rise, I began to hear the most beautiful and eerie sound—the sound of thousands of crosses jangling in the wind.

I wandered around reading the names and words on the crosses, studying how people had piled them on top of each other, hung them around each other, and transformed a field in the middle of nowhere into several small outcroppings of faith. I bought a small wood cross for my sister from one of the many booths on the side of the road. I planted her cross halfway up the bigger hill in the shade of a larger cross. Then I stood there and listened to the sound of faith, the sound made when the wind moves thousands of crosses.

My religious reverie was interrupted by the sound of American accents. I stopped thinking about eternity and started thinking about tonight and how I was going to get home. I made friends with the midwestern family to whom the accents belonged and got a ride back to the bus station in their rented van. I arrived just in time for the evening bus to take me back to Riga. Only the bus didn't stop. The one that came two hours later stopped, but only to let passengers off. Apparently the buses back to Riga on Sunday night were always full and seldom stopped. It was almost midnight when I finally boarded a bus bound for home and several hours later when I climbed into my bed. Daniel had been right about the crosses. But he had been wrong about how easy it was to find them. It had been damn near impossible without him.

I left Latvia a month later. I headed back to California because I didn't know where else to go. I didn't have a job, but I figured if I could find work in a country where I didn't speak the language, I could find work at home. My replacement at the paper arrived the day before I flew back to the States. With nothing left to do but ship some packages home, I made a point of showing the new guy around Riga. He was a nice kid and a distraction from any thoughts I had about my future. I thought I was a pretty good tour guide, although looking back, I think my penchant for revealing the whole truth may have contributed some to what happened next. He probably didn't need to know about the hot water shortages, freezing winters, and shortcomings of Soviet-era housing on such a beautiful fall day.

I had been back in California a week when Yulia emailed. The new hire had lasted a week. I guess it was a good thing in the end because it was the guy who replaced the guy who replaced me whom Yulia married.

I was in California only six months before I was headed to Ukraine, where I would meet the man I would marry.

PART 2 California/England

From: Timor   1/2/2000 5:26 PM
To: Katya

Hello, Katya!

Merry Christmas and Happy New Year!!!
>   Or
>   Scary Christmas and Merry New Year! (joke) =)
>   How are you? What's new?
>   By the way, where is my ticket? (to USA) I'm waiting. . . .
>   Ok, see you next week!
>   Timor

To: Timor   1/17/2000 8:07 AM
From: Katya

Hey Timor,

Happy New Year, sorry a bit late. Did you do something fun? I was waitressing. How are things in Riga? Last night I listened to a kid count to 100. The parents gave the kid my tip and he walked off with it. Besides not being able to find a job life is good.
>   I'm still working on that ticket. I think I should wear a pin at work that says give me a big tip and help buy Timor a ticket. Just kidding, I think.
>   I think I'm going to go see a movie.
>   Talk to you soon,
>   Katya

11 Back in the USSR

I'm going to fast forward through the brief and demoralizing stint in California that followed my stay in Latvia. Suffice to say most newspaper editors didn't feel my experience interviewing Latvian members of parliament and former Nazis qualified me to cover school board meetings. While I did get a gig cocktail waitressing at a hip sports bar, serving twenty-somethings Sex on the Beach and Fuzzy Navel drinks wasn't exactly the kind of excitement I was after. And the boyfriend who worked as a guard at San Quentin State Prison was not as interesting as he sounds. He might have been—had he ever talked. But he didn't.

Middle of nowhere Georgia seemed far less interesting and exotic than an English-language newspaper in the real Georgia. I can't remember how I set my sites on the country of Georgia, but once I had, I put way more effort into wooing the paper than I had ever put into wooing a man. The editor of Georgia's English-language newspaper was impressed with my work from Latvia. He didn't question my interest in working in Georgia the way American editors questioned my interest in working in Texas. Unfortunately he had more pressing matters on his mind—like finding a regular source of electricity and keeping the government from shutting down his paper. Latvia had been difficult. Georgia seemed to operate under a whole new scale of hardship.

None of this scared me off. Back then I thought the more brutal the conditions, the better. Besides, there was nothing for me in the States: no serious boyfriend, no car, and, most crucially, no career. (I did have a hamster named Mishka. I found him a good replacement home.) My stepdad and mother were headed to London and invited me to come along. I arrived with bronchitis and everything I thought I would need post-London to start fresh in Georgia or another equally exotic location. Having no clue what one would require in Georgia (or anywhere else I might land), I pretty much repacked what I had taken to Latvia. I knew my lodgings in London—a pullout futon in the hall/kitchen/front room of a one-bedroom flat—were temporary. As soon as my stepdad was done sprucing the flat up, he planned to sell it. I loved London, but the Tbilisi of the world fit my budget better.

While in town, I figured I would take advantage of the opportunity by interning at the BBC. Before leaving California, I had applied to the same radio program that I had worked with in Latvia. My contact had been doing all she could to get me in, but it wasn't working. Once I got to London and could talk for more than a minute without hacking, I started calling the BBC—every hour. When the phone calls didn't work, I went in person. It took several weeks, but finally I was granted my internship. The BBC seemed almost as baffled as I was as to how I had managed to make it in. I don't think the editor I had worked with really expected it to happen. Americans don't work at the British Broadcasting Corporation.

As the situation in Georgia continued to deteriorate, so did my chance of securing paying employment there. The editor I was courting did offer me a job. He just couldn't offer me a salary. I didn't see that working out and began to focus on other countries where the hammer and sickle had wreaked havoc. There were plenty to choose from. But I had my standards. After the isolation of Latvia I wanted a country Americans cared about—or at least recognized. I also wanted a place less intimidating than Russia itself. Ukraine was bigger than Latvia and viewed by the West as a buffer zone with Russia. It was a country that had a lot going for it news-wise. Ukraine had been a part of the former USSR, one of the founding republics when the Soviet Union was established in 1922. It bordered Russia, had once been a part of the Russian empire, and was still home to the Russian Black Sea Fleet. It had recently emerged from an almost decade-long recession that featured five-digit inflation rates. Although it had a new currency, the *hryvnia*, everyone still called the currency rubles. It was the land of oligarchs and mafia. And if that wasn't enough, there was always Chernobyl.

That in fact is how I chose where I would live. I didn't look into health care, living standards, or climate. I considered language but only briefly. I also didn't look into whether Ukraine's English-language newspaper happened to be hiring. I had decided where I wanted to go. Now I just needed to make it happen. I had a plan for my future, and I was going to stick to it whether it made sense or not. No one else had offered anything better.

I sent the *Kyiv Post*'s managing editor an email. Greg was a bit baffled by my fascination with the country. He was familiar with Western men wanting to come to Ukraine for the women. But I was a different breed. I don't think he understood why I was so set on landing in Ukraine. His counterpart, Diana, one of the few Western women at the paper, definitely wasn't crazy about the country. There wasn't much Diana was crazy about back then, including, I would come to find, me. But I think they were both curious about me and vaguely impressed by my Latvian clips. After a few more back and forth emails they sent me an editing test and then a job offer.

I paid a visit to the Ukrainian Department at the BBC to obtain contact information for counterparts in Kyiv. The heavy-set older men who greeted me had thick accents and limited use for pleasantries.

"Why you want to go to Ukraine?"

"There is a job there."

"You speak Ukrainian?"

"No."

"Russian?"

"A little."

"You know nothing about Ukraine?"

It was a statement as much as a question. I felt the need to defend myself.

"I spent fourteen months in Latvia."

They scoffed. "The Baltics don't count."

I knew the Baltics were considered to have had it easier under communism. The Baltic Sea region was where top officials vacationed. But they still had Lenin statues and limited access to Levis under Soviet leadership, so I thought I had experienced the former Soviet Union. But I had had only a taste. I wouldn't understand this until later. Even if I had, I doubt I would have changed my plans.

PART 3 Ukraine

From: Katya   6/19/2000 9:10 AM

To: Anikke

Hi Niks,

Still haven't gotten the package but that is no surprise it takes a really long time because the people in customs like to test everything out first—I think they have probably already read the two books that I ordered months ago.... I wish I could call you right now but I can't. I'm at home and feeling a bit sad for no good reason. I love being by myself but at the same time I am a bit lonely. Too bad the guy selection here is almost nil. Want to watch a movie but the only one in English this month is some shoot em up, all the others are dubbed into Russian. My Swedish music channel has disappeared and I am growing tired of watching Ruski TV. On the up side I started Russian lessons and the intern is really nice and we hang out a lot.... I better go, my bath water is getting cold—I compose email from home and send from work. The church bells just started ringing again. I am close to a church so on Sundays I hear the bells for a long time, it is really pretty.

    Love woofys

12 A Wife Named Katya

If I thought my welcome in Riga was lacking, then my reception in Kyiv was downright dismal. One of the newspaper's drivers picked me up and deposited me at Greg's apartment. On the way there I noted that everything seemed to operate on a larger, louder, and faster scale than in Riga. There were more billboards, more cars, more people, and more noise. One road led away from the airport, and it was wide and straight and lined with horse-chestnut trees. It all seemed rather impressive until we got off the main road. There were no clearly marked lanes of traffic on the side roads, and drivers weaved around like racers jockeying for position as they tried to avoid the more substantial dips and ruts of the side rode we turned on. This time I didn't even inquire about a seat belt.

The driver didn't talk much, and he smiled even less. His skin was rough and greasy and his teeth stained. He was missing a finger or two. We headed first to the Soviet apartment building sprawl of the suburbs. The building we stopped at was slightly nicer than some I'd seen but generally little different from the usual model: big, old, and drab. Inside one of the lower units Greg was busy feeding two large dogs. They belonged to him and his girlfriend. Dog ownership was a domestic feature slightly at odds with my vision of an American living in Kyiv. It implied a rootedness I had not expected to encounter. Greg spoke to the driver in a Russian that sounded as harsh and impatient as any Russian man's. The more ways I noted that Greg belonged, the more I felt out of place. My Russian was rudimentary, and as much as I loved dogs, I couldn't imagine feeling settled enough in this region of the world to own two large ones.

Greg was nice but distracted. His curly dark hair was shoulder length and tucked behind his ears. His blue eyes moved rapidly from one thing to the next, like he did. He looked to be in his midtwenties. He shoveled some chunks of meat into his mouth, and then we headed to the office to meet Diana. (Greg was the main editor, and Diana was right below him. I was a few rungs down the ladder.) The ride was brief and didn't involve any new sights other than the usual Soviet-style office building monstrosities. There were more of them in Kyiv than I had seen previously, but that didn't make them more impressive, just more present.

The *Kyiv Post* was located in a drab office building on an equally drab street. The elevator tended to get stuck, and you risked suffering smoke inhalation if you took the stairs, where all the smokers congregated. Later a ping pong table was set up on the landing outside our office. It was an interesting concept and would have provided fine data on the effect of smoke inhalation on exercise had anyone been interested. Of course it would have been skewed toward the male population because the men seldom allowed their female colleagues to play, which, from a Darwinian perspective, made some sense.

My entrance that Sunday preceded the ping pong table by several months and elicited a more subdued response. Diana was the only person in the office, and she sat in front of a computer at the far end. She didn't bother to get up; she just pushed two unfitted bed sheets my way—fitted bottom sheets being on the list of things that had yet to debut in Kyiv. She placed a set of keys on top of the sheets. "There you go," she said. "Do you need anything else?"

I wasn't sure how to respond. When I didn't say anything, she offered a little more information about the apartment where I would be staying. It belonged to another reporter, Jake, who was out of town. Jake had agreed to let me stay as long as I took care of his new kitten. He didn't have extra sheets, so Diana had arranged to loan me some of hers. Her task complete, Diana turned her attention back to her computer. She was cute, with short wavy dark hair, soft features, and a slight lisp. She looked to be in her thirties, her tall frame a little too filled out to still be considered slim, her attire more fun and practical than sexy. American women were a rarity in the former Soviet Union, and I was curious about her story. I never learned it.

Greg took me to Jake's apartment. He bought me some food, pointed out the route I should walk to the office in the morning, and headed off to meet his girlfriend. The apartment was all I had remembered of Soviet-era housing—and then some. The tiny closet that housed the toilet was so unpleasant and small I left the door ajar when I used it. The carpeting was heavy and dark, and the shelves and table blocked what little light managed to fight its way in through the window. Kyiv was proving to be more complicated and lonelier than Riga. I couldn't imagine my former editor, Steve, leaving me on my own with so little ceremony. But Greg and Diana were more settled and integrated into the community than my *Baltic Times* comrades had been. They were also less invested in my welfare.

I looked at the rotary phone and thought of all the people I couldn't call because of the expense, the unreliable connection, and the time difference in the States. I didn't have internet access, and I wasn't much in the mood for writing a letter that wouldn't be read for weeks. For the first time I truly doubted my decision to return to the region. I was starting to sink into a place I didn't want to go, couldn't go. I needed to get out of my head and out of the apartment. I got out my running shoes and set off.

The neighborhood where I was staying wasn't exactly the kind of place where people went jogging. It was more of an industrial area people walked through to get elsewhere or avoided altogether. I was just about ready to head back to the apartment when I realized I had no idea where I was. There is an urban legend about an expat who gets drunk in some post-Soviet city one night and ends up going home to the wrong apartment because all apartments look the same. You don't have to be drunk to have that problem. At least I never did. By the time I finally made it back to the apartment, I had long since stopped running. I was walking, sniffling, and fixing every person I saw with a glare that warned them not to get too close—not that any of them seemed tempted. Back at the apartment I took a shower with water that came out of the pipes in an orange hue and never got above lukewarm. I caught a glimpse of a skinny kitten, but it didn't seem interested in getting to know me. I forced myself to eat a little bread and cheese, put the sheets Diana had given me on the bed, and retreated under the covers. I cried until I felt the relief of exhaustion and fell asleep.

The kitten attacked at midnight. Over the next few days I discovered it was big on making its presence known at odd hours of the night by pouncing on my head, batting at my hair, or kneading my stomach. I had never owned a cat, so I was unaware that it's normal for kittens to play at night and thought the kitten's sole purpose for launching night attacks was to annoy me. The next day the little devil was nowhere to be found, probably sleeping soundly under the bed and out of reach of my wrath.

I was looking forward to the distraction work would provide and managed to make my way to the office without getting lost. Things improved from there. I found myself sharing a desk with a Scot, the next best thing to an Irishman. Ewan was as friendly as Diana was surly. With his small, slightly doughy build, dark beard, and quirky mannerisms, he reminded me a little of a Hobbit. He loved to read but was too practical and happy to care much about writing. He might have been in his late thirties, but he seemed a little less settled than Diana and Greg and more aware of how difficult relocation can be. Between his accent and his recitation of random facts I sometimes had trouble following him, but I didn't really care. He always had a smile for me. My friendship standards were almost as low as they had been in sixth grade, when I had to buy friends with lunch money.

Ewan, Diana, Greg, and I sat in an editor's section in a far corner of the office. The space was basically one large open room filled with clusters of desks. I was in charge of choosing, arranging, and cutting wire stories for the paper's world page. I also helped edit some of the stories written by the paper's non-native-English-speaking reporters. The latter task ranged in difficulty from frustratingly impossible to barely any work at all. The impossible pieces would later serve as one of my arguments for demoting myself to a reporting position. I told Greg that the stories would be better if I was allowed to use a translator and write my own instead of trying to rework barely understandable texts by inexperienced local reporters. I wasn't a great editor and I had no intention of becoming one.

That first day Greg gave me brief instructions, which Ewan filled out. I didn't think I was qualified to choose the news, but I rather enjoyed the

God-like power it gave me. Part of the elimination process was practical. We were a weekly newspaper read by ambassadors and businessmen, so stories had to have a bit of a shelf life and a business edge.

At lunch time everyone headed to the neighboring restaurant or the corner store, where you could buy yogurt, meat, rolls, and kefir, a sort of liquid yogurt. I stuck with yogurt I could eat with a spoon because it was familiar and because the pictures on the containers made it easy to identify what flavor I was eating. No one invited me to join them for dinner that first night, so I spent my evening alone eating bread and cheese in my dark apartment. There wasn't a TV and I hadn't developed an ear for Russian pop music yet, so I ate in silence.

My second day on the job I inquired about finding an apartment. Although I didn't like Kyiv at that point, I never considered leaving. I had a job and I had a mission, and I wasn't going to let my emotions hold me back. I figured finding my own place, where I could finally unpack and stop living out of a suitcase, would improve my mood. Greg suggested I go through a sort of real estate agent for renters. I had never heard of such a thing and was skeptical about paying someone to find me what I should be able to find on my own. Of course I couldn't find a place in Kyiv on my own. So Greg asked one of the local reporters to help. She called one of the brokers. I gave up and let them drag me to three or four affordable apartments that were pretty much indistinguishable and indescribable. At each place a landlady showed us around, fussing about the space, furniture, and amenities, all of which I found lacking. I'm not very picky, but I have trouble living in dark places that make me want to kill myself.

The apartments we saw the next day were no different. The broker was beginning to tire of me and demanded to know what exactly it was I wanted. I mentioned light and openness. I almost didn't agree to see the next place she wanted to show me because it was $350, well above what I had planned to pay. Most of the places I had looked at had been $200 or under. But the broker said I would love it and not to worry about the price.

The building was in a quiet section of town not far from the botanical garden. It was pre-Soviet, built before taste and beauty were pushed out in favor of conformity. Glass doors separated the bedroom from the main room, and another set of glass doors led onto a small sagging balcony. It had high ceilings and large windows and room in which to imagine more than a drab daily existence. The landlady was pushy but friendly and hugged me to her ample chest. I knew her affection had more to do with the potential money I represented as an American with dollars than my stunning personality, but it was pleasant nonetheless. Her chirps about how she would wash my clothes and feed me stopped when I tried to negotiate the price. A minute before, her eyes had slanted with merriment as her smile pushed her flesh upward. Now they slanted with suspicion. It was amazing how quickly she transformed. It should have been a warning. The broker and my colleague advised me to walk away.

The next day the broker called to tell me the landlady had gone down to $300. It would be extra for laundry. Hugs, I gathered, would be included so long as I kept up my supply of Benjamins. There was only one problem: I had no money. I didn't want to ask Greg for an advance, a wire transfer would take too long, and ATMs were on the same list as Diet Cokes—they didn't exist. In desperation I asked Ewan if he could loan me the money. Not just the $300, but also the money I owed the real estate broker who had showed me the places. Luckily there was no such thing as a deposit, but I did need a little extra for some food, which made the total amount close to $400. That might not sound like a ton of money, but in Kyiv back then, for people like us, it was a fortune. Foreign diplomats, businessmen, and contract workers made American-style salaries and stayed in American-style lodgings. We made enough to live rather comfortably in Kyiv at the time, which was not enough to make it in most cities in America. My salary was around $1,000 a month, and Ewan didn't make much more. We were paid in cash. It was safest to keep it in dollars and only exchange it to *hryvnias* as needed. You could find an exchange kiosk on every corner and count on the rate to change just as frequently.

Ewan gave me the money without asking for a written receipt. He also loaned me a few English-language books. There would come a time when even Diana would help me out. Whether you liked them or not, when only a limited number of your colleagues were born speaking English and accustomed to governments in which elected representatives were not as a rule bribed for favors, you end up sticking together. It's almost like family; you may not be enchanted by the members, but at least they are familiar. Diana could be charming when she wanted and cruel when she didn't. I tried to stay on friendly terms with her, but I never tried to be her friend. I didn't want a close association with a bitter woman. I had understood Sandra's bitterness better; she was old and unattractive and half crazy. Diana was none of the above, but she was mean in the way unhappy people often are. When she encouraged me to do a story on rollerblading, I suspected her of doing so only because she wanted me to admit I didn't have the guts to go out alone in a strange city on my rollerblades.

And at first I didn't, but with enough prodding I finally got up the nerve. I was a little self-conscious riding the metro with my blades slung over my shoulder. But the boardwalk by the Dnieper River, where I had been told people bladed, was only two or three stops from my apartment. I had a little backpack to put my shoes in. It was late spring, and young couples were leaning against a railing kissing, oblivious to the old fishermen next to them sitting on upended buckets. Immediately outside the metro stop a man offered rides on a miniature horse. Closer to the water there were a number of little cafes with cheap plastic seats where you could get a soda. I noticed all of this as I was blading up and down the cement walkway that ran parallel to the river, weaving around women walking in hot pants and high heels and men in dark jeans. It felt nice to go fast and feel the breeze on my skin, and I was tempted to take deep breaths and spread my arms wide, but the road alongside boasted a number of exhaust-spewing vehicles, and I was liable to hit one of the love birds strolling alongside the path if I stretched too far.

Later that summer I would return to the area to try water skiing—pulled by a jet ski. I never managed to get up. I also never managed to get the story behind the water skiing business. The guy who ran it was cagey and crooked and made it sound as if the whole Kyiv water skiing scene was run by the mafia, which it probably was. By the end of the summer I had moved up to sky diving.

At first my impression of the city was limited. Kyiv was larger and more intimidating than Riga, and I had no one to help me explore it. My neighborhood was peaceful and beautiful, and for a while that was enough. A block from my door was a square-shaped park with old men playing chess at tree-shaded tables and an upscale restaurant where the waiters dressed as traditional Ukrainian Cossacks. At the other end of the park was a large statue of the man for whom it was named, Ukrainian poet and artist Taras Shevchenko. Not far behind my building was a wide tree-covered walkway that led directly to a dome-topped Orthodox church from which the most beautiful singing could be heard. A pack of wild puppies hung out in the shrubbery en route to the botanical garden, which occupied part of a nearby hill. The entrance to the garden cost only a few kopeks, but the guards weren't very attentive, and I usually entered without paying. My place was within walking distance of two metro stops and several tram stops, all of which were cheap and semi-dependable.

In time I got to know the rest of the city, which was equally impressive. During Soviet times Kyiv was the third largest city in the Union. When I moved there, it had a population of about 2,600,000. It had domed churches and modern nightclubs, fancy restaurants, and impressive old government buildings. One of Eastern Europe's oldest cities, Kyiv is famous for St. Sophia Cathedral and the Kyiv Pechersk Lavra, both recognized by UNESCO as World Heritage Sites. The locals know Kyiv for Khreshchatyk, a main boulevard along which Maiden Nezalezhnosti, or Freedom Square, is located, as are many government buildings. On weekends and warm summer evenings Khreshchatyk was closed to vehicles and music was blasted through public loud speakers. Like a county fair, Khreshchatyk attracted families, couples, teenagers, and pensioners.

I didn't explore much of this at first. Aside from Ewan, who already had a wife named Katya, my friend pool from which to find fellow explorers was limited. The expats at the paper were older and more settled than the Riga crowd. The local staff was shut off for other reasons. Our office manager, Vika, was friendly but shy and unsure of herself around Americans. The female reporters included Katya, a small serious blonde; Anya, an awkward young woman both physically and socially; and Jenia. There were others, but they tended to come and go, and quite a few were on vacation that summer. Katya didn't seem to need any friends, and Anya was rather annoying. But Jenia had a mixture of sweetness and ambition that about equaled my own, and later we would become friends. When it came to the local male staff, the majority didn't talk much to women. Vitaly did. With his short dark hair, compact muscular build, and unflinching attitude, Vitaly could easily be mistaken for a thug—until he smiled. And Vitaly, unlike the other men in the office, smiled at and laughed with women, treating them as an American man might, like friends and colleagues. A week or two into my stay he stopped me as I walked by his desk. "What do you do outside of work?" he asked.

I wasn't sure how to reply. Reading Ewan's science fiction books even though I was not a science fiction fan seemed almost as pitiful as watching old episodes of *Alf* dubbed into Russian, despite my having an almost physical aversion to the nasal-sounding actor who played the father on the show. I had talked on the phone to my Italian-Austrian friend Sandro once or twice, but the connection was fuzzy, and I was guarded in what I told him. We had met when I was in London. He wanted to visit, but I wasn't sure where he fit in my life and didn't invite him.

Although I was lonely, I had gotten over my initial bout of misery. Greg had recently allowed me to do some of my own reporting. My first story on former collective farms had helped to establish me as a serious writer. In the last issue there had been a letter to the editor complimenting my writing. It was from Daniel, my old Canadian colleague and friend at the *Baltic Times*. He had gone back to Canada but was planning to move to Portugal to work for a wire service. I wasn't sure if all of this is what Vitaly wanted to hear when he asked what I did, so I kept it simple. "I read," I said.

I thought maybe he would invite me to join him and Vika, whom he was dating, for a drink. He didn't. But then neither did any of my countrymen. Of course I didn't drink, at least not then. That didn't happen until Chernobyl.

13 Downing Vodka Shots at Chernobyl

I didn't meet my future husband on my first trip to Chernobyl. That time I was with Viktor, Jenia's boyfriend. Having grown up under a cloud of radioactive fallout, Jenia did not understand my desire to visit the contamination zone that surrounds Chernobyl Nuclear Power Plant. More to the point, she did not appreciate my dragging her boyfriend along with me. But Viktor was the *Kyiv Post*'s photographer, so if there was a story in Chernobyl, then Viktor went to Chernobyl.

We were all reporters. We knew the numbers. The 1986 accident and subsequent fire released about fifty tons of radioactive dust and debris into the air, the worst of this settling in the thirty-km exclusion zone surrounding Chernobyl Nuclear Power Plant. Eighty percent of those who received additional doses of radiation (read conscripted cleanup crew) had become ill. Thyroid cancer rates in Ukraine had increased tenfold.

The thing was, Viktor wanted to go. That was the first time he left Jenia. The second time he left her for a woman. The third time he left her forever. He would be dead within the decade. But it wasn't Chernobyl that killed him, and the wife he left behind wasn't Jenia. Neither was the girlfriend.

I never understood the attraction. Jenia spoke flawless English and had the exotic look of a European with a hint of Asian: blonde hair, pale skin, and slanted eyes. She had the prejudices and insecurities of a Russian, but she also had the ambition and entrepreneurial spirit of a Westerner. Viktor dressed in track suits and didn't speak more than a word or two of English. He was large and gruff and had a tendency to mumble. I had tried to see him differently when Jenia first started dating him. Earlier that summer

I had spent a week in Crimea with Jenia and her family. I didn't have any vacation yet, but Jenia was one of Greg's favorites. I think he was starting to grow fond of having me around as well, so he let us both take a break.

Jenia spent most of the trip talking about Viktor. We shared a couch in her family's living room in Simferopol. Her mother served us fresh fruit, and her father drove us to an underground cave. Crimea was unlike the rest of Ukraine; it was mountainous and had an almost Mediterranean feel. The Russians had gifted it to Ukraine during Soviet times, never expecting to lose it, and they remained fully entrenched. But Crimean Tatars deported under Stalin were returning, and they added a diversity of color and religion you couldn't find anywhere else in the country. There were vineyards and beaches and a climate that reminded me of California.

I ended up getting homesick and taking the train back to Kyiv a week early. I think the way Jenia's mother fussed over her made me more nostalgic than anything else. When I was little, I used to stand on my mother's feet and she would hold my hands and dance me around the room. As I got older, we danced less, but every once in a while we would still pair up, my feet bigger than hers but still always on top.

She never visited Ukraine. She would call, but the connection was scratchy and there was a distinctive click at the start of every conversation. She joked that in Ukraine even the phone tapping was primitive. I was more careful with what I said. Cards and magazines from abroad arrived weeks and even months late. Some never made it. Others looked as if they had already been opened. One of my bags from my London flight ended up in Moscow. I called the airline about it regularly, following its progress on detours through Stockholm and a few other random cities. When I went to retrieve it from the airport weeks later, I was met by a customs agent. I watched as he opened my bag and dug through my clothes. He held up a U2 CD.

"What is this?" he asked.

"A CD," I said.

"How many you have?"

I tried to quickly come up with a low but reasonable number. If something was counted, there was a good chance it was going to be taxed.

"Five or six, I think."

He dug deeper, tossing aside silk long underwear and fuzzy sweaters to reveal Tracy Chapman, Sheryl Crow, and a dozen or so other CDs. He waved several in my face.

"You said five or six."

"Sorry, I couldn't remember."

I probably should have stopped there, but I couldn't help adding a jab about the delay: "It's been a long time since I saw my luggage." He tallied something on his fingers.

"That's $100."

"What! They didn't even cost that much."

A hundred dollars was the normal tax levied on foreigners. In this case it was a dozen CDs, but it might as easily have been six pairs of socks or three wool sweaters.

"I'm not going to pay $100."

"Then you will not have your CDs."

I tried to plead poverty. When that didn't work, I tried tears. I got the price down to fifty dollars. Then I walked away without my bag. Outside I recounted my experience to the office driver. He told me to go back in and pay. Eventually I did, but first I wasted a few more hours of everyone's time arguing the injustice of the situation. I was the only one who didn't understand it was not a question of fairness. The agent had the power to ask for money, and I was in a position to give it. It was a simple transaction officials used daily. Some came to your door asking for your *propiska*, or residence permit. During Soviet times you needed to have the proper papers to live in certain areas. Officially or unofficially this rule was still enforced. I had the right papers, but that didn't guarantee I would be left alone. The first time I opened the door, a man, his face hidden by the brim of his cap, spent five minutes inspecting my passport, visa, and work papers. When he handed them back to me, he didn't smile; he just turned toward the next door. The second time I heard the telltale knocks and ensuing demands before the inspector reached my door. I shut off my lights and kept quiet. Jenia didn't have the right papers, but she knew the price, and when she could pay it, she would open the door. When she couldn't, she would hide.

My door was thick and padded and possessed multiple locks. Inside I made the place as much my own as I could by stashing the knickknacks that decorated the tables and cabinets in drawers. My landlady would come once a month to collect my rent and do my laundry. I would leave the money on the table, and she would leave the knickknacks back on display. In addition to sending out my laundry, I had made other upgrades since Riga. Now that I lived on the sixth floor, I rented a water cooler and had water tanks delivered. I had a mini hot water heater, so when the hot water was turned off, I barely noticed. But when the running water was turned off, I still struggled. My bottled water was too expensive to use for a shower or cooking. My neighbors relied on an ancient-looking truck with a hose that trolled the neighborhood, but I was uncertain how to approach the truck and just went without for a few days. In my neighborhood the shortages never lasted long.

When I was home, I loved to sit on one of the little seats on my balcony and listen to children playing in the courtyard below. Shaded by a tree, I would write in my diary. I tried not to notice the sharp angle at which my cement balcony sloped downward or the heft of the balcony above me. When I was bored with running, I did dance routines to the Russian music channel on my television. I had found a Russian teacher through the classified section of our newspaper, and she came to my home three mornings a week.

Outside the safety of my building, on streets not far from my own, destitute pensioners held out their hands to passersby, and street children with the glassy eyes of glue sniffers stared out from dark corners. Men in uniforms with big guns walked in and out of shops. I was never sure whom they were protecting. Later I would watch rows of police hidden behind shields and helmets strike at protesters. I stood close to report what was happening until Dima shoved me back. Then he went closer to get a better picture. I admired his bravery then. Now I know he was only doing what was expected of him.

I learned how to take the metro to and from work and where to buy carrots and nuts on the way home. I mastered the art of cramming into a mini bus and negotiating with gypsy cab drivers. Then I set about finding a way to visit Chernobyl. I discovered it wasn't that difficult to enter the exclusion zone that surrounded the plant; you just needed to know the right person. In my case that person was Anatoly, a one-time documentary filmmaker who was from the region and thus had a special entrance pass. The zone was once home to two cities, Chernobyl and Prypiat, and seventy-four villages. In addition to receiving large doses of radiation after the disaster, those who lived in the zone were given shoddily constructed homes outside of it and passes that entitled them to special medical care and entrance back into the zone. I suppose accessing the zone had its advantages, especially when it came to bilking foreign journalists. Anatoly offered a number of services: translator, fixer, tour guide—for a price. Later another fee was tacked on: a contamination tax for the value his vehicle would lose by being taken into the exclusion zone. Luckily he did not demand a similar fee for his own exposure. I didn't like the way he did business, but I didn't see another option. (This was before Chernobyl tours became a thing.) I couldn't go to the site of the world's worst nuclear disaster with just anyone, and Anatoly knew what he was doing. At least I thought he did.

On the drive there he told me that the road had been repaved twice since the 1986 disaster in an attempt to reduce radiation. That wasn't because it had seen a huge amount of traffic. Buses stopped going to the area in 1986, and so did pretty much everyone else. There is no welcome sign announcing the entrance, just a military post where you hand over your documents. The soldier who took ours asked if I was scared.

"No," I lied.

"Good luck," he said.

It seemed a strange thing to say, but then I suppose wanting to visit the zone was a strange thing to do. Living in it was even stranger and officially illegal, but that hadn't stopped a hardy troop of babushkas. Former residents of the area, they had hiked for miles with their belongings on their backs and slipped into the zone in the dark of night. Anatoly's late grandmother had been one of them, and he promised to introduce me to several others.

Finding them was a challenge. From the single paved road that crosses the area we saw only trees. An absence of street signs and people meant maps were useless and asking directions impossible. The side roads were unpaved and so overgrown with vegetation it was a rare treat to actually spot a roof, wall, or shop sign. Trees sprouted in what were once entranceways; brambles peeked out from paneless windows, and birds nested in cracked concrete stairwells. A modern community abandoned to time and nature, the place was quiet and creepy in a way an occupied village or empty countryside can never be. When I exited the car, Anatoly warned me to stay on the pavement; the grass and moss had higher levels of radiation, he said.

After the accident Chernobyl was closed off. The phone lines were cut, and no one was allowed to enter or leave. Evacuations began three days after the accident and continued for two weeks. Residents were told they would be able to return in a few days. They were never allowed back. But as time passed, several hundred former residents, mostly elderly, returned. Chernobyl was their home, and outside of it they had never felt comfortable. It probably didn't help that the secrecy surrounding the accident meant outsiders treated them with a mixture of jealousy and fear, envying them their "special status" while at the same time shunning their presence in case "contamination" was contagious.

If you look carefully, you can spot signs of their existence: a shadowy figure or laundry hanging out to dry in a wheat field. Galina's door was open, her garden neat and orderly. She was one of the babushkas Anatoly introduced me to. She returned a year after the accident, when the home where she had been relocated broke in two during the spring thaw. In 1992 a fire almost destroyed her Chernobyl home. There were no fire fighters to help her put it out. One winter she spent a month without electricity. The summer I visited there was no running water, a serious situation for those who are exposed to radiation and are advised to shower daily. At the time a supply bus visited the zone twice a week, but in the beginning residents were completely cut off, and they learned to rely on the land, drinking milk from their cows and eating fish from the lakes and fruits and vegetables from their gardens. They did not seem bothered by the fact that radiation levels in dirt and marine animals were still a hundred times more than normal ten years after the accident.

Like any good Ukrainian hostess, Galina did not wait long to offer me food. I tried the "I'm not hungry tactic," knowing it wouldn't work and I would be obliged to eat the *blintzes*. She was proud that they were stuffed with fruit from her own garden, and I might have shared the sentiment had her garden not been on soil surrounding the world's worst nuclear disaster. Calculating that a babushka's displeasure lasts longer than the effects of radiation, I gingerly sliced into a blueberry *blintze*. As I ate, I tried not to think about the fact that radioactive elements are decreasing faster in undisturbed forested state lands than in private lands that are being farmed. The *blintze* was actually quite tasty.

I can't say the same for the vodka I downed at the next location. This time my hostess was not offering me refreshments out of politeness. She insisted I drink a shot of home-brew vodka before we began the interview. I told her I didn't drink. She shrugged. I started the interview. She greeted my questions with silence. Her husband pushed a shot glass filled with a clear liquid toward me. "Just a sip," he said in Russian.

I shook my head. It was hot, I did not drink, and I knew downing a shot of home-brew vodka from Chernobyl would not be the time to start. This did not seem to bother my hostess. We were at an impasse. The more I refused, the more the couple goaded me. I felt like I was at a fraternity party hosted by a pair of Ukrainian grandparents. Throw in two big Ukrainian men like Viktor and Anatoly, who proved as impatient to see me drink as the couple, and I was right back in college.

I figured it couldn't be that bad. I grimaced and took a tiny sip. Then I gagged. It burned something awful, first my throat and then my stomach. As I motioned desperately for a glass of water, Viktor took a picture. The old man brought me a glass of water procured from I have no idea what source. I didn't care. If nothing else, it was probably safer than the vodka. But just as I reached for the glass, the woman intercepted it. She was a small, bony little thing, but she was fast. She pointed to the still three-quarter full shot glass. There would be no water until I had finished the entire shot. I took a deep breath and tried again. It took me two more attempts before I could get it all down. Viktor captured it in pictures I never saw. Although he had also been "offered" a shot of vodka, Viktor somehow escaped having to actually drink it. This may have had something to do with the fact that Viktor resembled the classic Hollywood version of a Ukrainian, a thug.

I was feeling a bit dizzy as I began the interview. Anatoly was kind enough to point out that my cheeks were flushed. The couple's story was not that different from Galina's. The old man told me about chasing a wild pig out of their wheat field. Galina told me about packs of wolves rumored to prowl the zone. When they first returned, they found their home trashed and their furniture gone.

Anatoly's former family home had also been stripped bare. The bathtub, piano, stove, sink, and even the electrical outlets had been taken. Newspaper cuttings, old school notebooks, and broken toys littered the floor. A calendar was stuck at April 1986, and the walls of his sister's room were covered with pictures of male heartthrobs from decades past. She was probably a mother herself now, but her teenage dreams remained fixed in time.

Anatoly was studying in Kyiv when the accident occurred. His sister and father were living at home. The morning after the accident a family friend had taken the first and last bus out of Chernobyl. He had seen fire on the roof of the plant but was not concerned until he arrived in Kyiv and heard there would be no more bus service to or from Chernobyl. When Anatoly reached his sister by phone, she told him their father was drunk because someone at the plant had told him spirits protected against radiation. She had exercised outside at school the day after the accident. A few days later she escaped in a neighbor's boat. Their father stayed behind to help. He didn't really have a choice.

Sifting through the memories strewn across the living room floor, Anatoly held onto a single photo. When I asked why he didn't take it, he responded, "The dust." If you were to judge by the area's ransacked homes, thieves lack the same scruples. Wiring, plumbing, and furniture from the contaminated zone is probably circulating around the country.

But two fish from a local lake didn't make it out. A cousin had given them to Anatoly, and when we were leaving, Anatoly asked an inspector if he could bring them home. The man laughed. Then he took the fish and tossed them out. We tested our radiation levels by stepping inside a machine and pressing our hands against a panel. With my local treats still cooking in my stomach I was rather apprehensive.

"What happens if your levels are too high?" I asked Anatoly.

"Then you can't leave."

I am not sure if that was his caustic Ukrainian humor or the truth. I did not have to find out. My levels were okay. Back in Kyiv Anatoly warned me to shower and rinse the dust from my nose. Inside my apartment I suddenly flashed back to the shower scene from the 1983 movie *Silkwood*, about a worker at a plutonium processing plant who becomes contaminated. The suspense continued when I washed my nose and grayish dirt emerged. I kept washing and washing and only stopped when my nose became raw. I stuffed the clothes I had worn with my dirty laundry in the back of my bureau. A few minutes later I dug them out and stuffed them in a plastic bag that I then placed back in the dirty laundry pile. I wondered if you could feel radiation. How would you know if you had been harmed? I knew all the science and research, but I also knew there were still unknowns. Just to be safe, I never wore the clothes again.

But I did go back to Chernobyl. It was on the next trip that I met the man I would marry.

I don't know who Viktor married. Jenia married an American. She told me years later in an email that Viktor had died, a victim of another of Ukraine's death traps—the roads. In Ukraine seat belts, traffic signals, speed limits, lanes, and lights are the exception, not the rule. Viktor was driving to an assignment late one night when he got into an accident. He was still working as a photographer in Kyiv. He had a wife and baby. According to Jenia, he survived the initial crash, but his family lacked the money to pay for the medical care that would keep him alive. He died not long after.

14 Pirates, Mobsters, and Other Eligible Bachelors

The ruling oligarchs got to skim millions from business deals and government contracts. The rest of us got bootleg CDs. Paying the equivalent of $1 for a Moby CD was a definite perk of corruption, and I regularly bought albums from private sellers in and around my metro stop. I was haggling over a "greatest hits" album for a '90s group that never had one when Lyosha interrupted. Even then I found him rude.

The CD seller understood my broken Russian; he just didn't like the terms I was offering. Lyosha took it upon himself to "help." Thanks to his kind aid, I ended up paying the equivalent of $2 for my CD instead of the $1.50 I had nearly convinced the seller to accept. Lyosha was to prove equally "helpful" the rest of the summer.

After I bought my CD, he invited me for a drink at a nearby café. I accepted because he spoke English and I felt he owed me at least a soda. I was also curious. His Russian was unaccented, but he was unfamiliar with the going rate for counterfeit CDs in Kyiv. He was twenty-something, with short hair and small eyes hidden behind large glasses. He dressed like an Eastern European man: jeans, dark shirt, and weathered jacket. But the colors of his clothes were more vivid and the material less worn. He sipped his juice through a straw and told me he lived in Australia but had been born in Ukraine. He had the habit of both criticizing and defending his native land in the same breath.

My apartment was nearby, so I invited him over. I had left my passport on a side table, and he picked it up and started paging through it. I pointed out my Ukrainian and Latvian visas and my entrance and exit stamps for Tunisia and Russia.

"You should never leave this out," he said. "Someone like me could steal it."

"Why would you do that? You have Australian citizenship."

He let out a long sigh. When we fought later, Dima would respond with the same exasperation and a variant of the words Lyosha now used.

"You don't understand. You're American."

"And you are Australian."

I took my passport back. I didn't have a better place to put it, so I held onto it until he left. It wasn't that I thought he would steal it. I just didn't want to hear any more of his advice. Lyosha was an expert at finding fault, especially with women. The second time we met he critiqued the outfit of every Ukrainian woman that crossed our path. He thought they dressed like prostitutes. It was true that many found leather pants and transparent lace tops to be appropriate attire for any occasion, but I was growing to appreciate the freedom this granted me. At work I wore sleeveless tops and sundresses without worrying about bringing a sweater to cover my bare upper arms. I wondered what Lyosha thought of the backless sundress I was wearing.

By then we were sort of seeing each other. He was in Ukraine for the summer visiting family and took it upon himself to show me his favorite spots in the city. We were sitting on a hill overlooking Kyiv when he put his arm around me and drew me close. His kisses were both aggressive and gentle and the main reason I kept seeing him. He told me he had recently broken up with his Ukrainian girlfriend because she was too obsessed with money and status. Then he said he liked me because I wasn't like Ukrainian women. It was a backward sort of praise that essentially meant I didn't look like a hooker and I didn't go for men with money, neither of which I felt were such bad options.

Ukraine had lowered my standards in music and men even further than my year in Latvia had. The other CD I was trying to buy the day I met Lyosha was that of British pop king Robbie Williams, a "best of" album for a man who never should have had one and probably didn't outside of bootleg copies. Lyosha was the best of my boyfriend options, my selection limited to drunks, cads, and Western men focused on Ukrainian women. There were also some gay Westerners.

Then there was John. That wasn't his real name, but that is what Sabra called him, and it was Sabra who introduced us. Sabra was the summer intern, and she arrived a week too late to keep me from dating Lyosha but in time to ensure I had other options than being alone. I have always liked spending time alone, but if you spend too much time by yourself in a foreign country, you risk a sort of isolation more extreme than any felt at home. Sometimes walking alone in Kyiv, listening to Russian, and seeing babushkas with kerchiefs on their heads and businessmen in ill-fitting suits, I would wonder what I was doing there so far from everything I knew. It would hit me suddenly, and it was not a pleasant feeling. The best way to avoid it was by spending time with friends who spoke my language and understood my culture.

Sabra was American. She was loud, funny, and large. She spoke Russian imperfectly and unabashedly. She had the kind of short, round body and expressive face associated with a matronly woman and the nurturing personality to match. She had spent two years in the Ukrainian city of Kaniv as a Peace Corps volunteer and had brought two Kaniv friends to live with her in Kyiv during her internship at the paper. John was one of them; Sveta was the other. They were all about the same age, but Sabra was like a mother in the way she looked out for them and me.

Sveta was a timid, out-of-work music teacher with a caustic side. She was a little heavy and tended to wear clothes that made her look even more so and hairstyles that hid her brilliant blue eyes. John was a roaming musician with a slight build and a gentle manner. He was the only Ukrainian man I ever met who wore his hair long. It was blond, and he pulled it into a low ponytail. He wasn't handsome, and he was usually broke, but he was considerate and caring. Sveta and John were always fighting. Sabra was what kept the trio together. John was her boyfriend, Sveta her best friend. I was the tag-along. When I told them about Lyosha, John said he wanted to meet him so he could teach him how to treat a woman. John worried my perception of Ukrainian men would be tainted by Lyosha. In truth I had already developed a rather damning opinion of Slavic men. John was the one who changed it. But I still didn't trust him at first, and it almost cost me our friendship.

Sabra's apartment wasn't far from Khreshchatyk, and on weekends we would head to the street festival scene that was Khreshchatyk. We would line up to buy soft-serve chocolate and lemon ice cream at a kiosk near McDonald's. When he had money, John liked to treat us. When he didn't, Sabra would buy. John carried his guitar with him everywhere and performed impromptu concerts that Sabra, Sveta, and I would attend. It was at one such concert that I met a young woman who introduced herself as John's girlfriend. When Sabra joined me, I told her what I had heard. She confronted John after the concert. The ensuing argument took place in rapid-fire Russian, so I missed much of what was being said. But I understood when John pointed to me and accused me of not understanding his language. I had also understood when the woman told me she was his girlfriend.

The one who didn't understand was the young woman. Unaccustomed to a considerate Ukrainian male, she figured John's attentions meant he was more than a friend. That is what Sabra and I pieced together after John finally calmed down enough to explain himself. Sabra and I had walked the streets around her apartment until late into the night trying to find John, who had stormed off during the fight. It was almost morning when he returned to the apartment. After peace was restored, I made my exit.

My next Russian-language mishap was with Lyosha. When we went out, it was usually just the two of us, but on one occasion he invited me on a cookout with his friends. Outside his friend's apartment complex he pulled out a small video camera and showed me how to work it. As we headed into the woods surrounding the building, he called out instructions: "Film that stump"; "Did you get that joke?"; "Why aren't you filming?"

I had taken a break to concentrate on walking and trying to converse with one of his friends. Lyosha tromped over to my side and yanked the camera from my hands. "I'll do it," he said.

A few minutes later he was back, instructing me to film once again. I took the opportunity to tell him I didn't want to be the videographer anymore. "What else are you going to do?" he asked. "Your Russian isn't good enough to understand us."

He was right; it wasn't, but I had assumed he would help translate. Instead he ignored me, except when he wanted something filmed, and then he would bark out instructions in English. I had always found him rude, but this was a whole new level of inconsideration. When it was just the two of us, he was critical, but he was also tender and protective. Now he was just obnoxious. Even his friends looked at me apologetically. An hour or two in I told him I wasn't feeling well and needed to get back, but he said he was having a good time and wasn't ready to leave. I knew I would never find my way out on my own. Like the Soviet-era housing monstrosities that we had come from, the woods we were in were uniformly bland. The spot ten feet from the apartment where we had set off hours before looked about the same as where we ended up, complete with scraggly trees, a little clearing, and scattered trash. There seems to be an unspoken rule that once you arrive at a cookout spot, no matter how miserable the setting, you are obligated to spend an inordinate amount of time cooking sausages (glorified hot dogs) and various kebabs over a campfire. Or maybe Eastern Europeans actually enjoy it. I had been on several in Latvia, and they were the same as those in Ukraine: substandard food in a substandard countryside setting, "enjoyed" for a substantial period of time. There was also beer and vodka, which I guess, if you are a drinker, makes it all worthwhile.

I sat on a stump with the video camera and watched Lyosha and his friends laugh and joke. When I was close to tears, I picked up the camera and hid behind the lens. On the walk back Lyosha was tipsy and suddenly in the mood to talk. I ignored him, using the camera once again to put distance between us. He didn't seem to notice. Once we were out of the woods, Lyosha told me we would be going to his friend's apartment to continue the gathering inside. He said we would stay only a few minutes. I didn't have much of a choice; he was my ride. When we got inside, he disappeared, and I was left to watch videos in the living room with his friends. The videos were from earlier in Lyosha's summer visit, and everyone was laughing and pointing at them until a blonde woman came on the screen and the Lyosha on the screen kissed her. She appeared to be his girlfriend. The word his friends used was "fiancée." The room went silent as everyone struggled to catch a glimpse of my face without meeting my eyes. I asked who she was, and one of his friends told me Lyosha had proposed to her earlier in the trip, but she had turned him down. Another friend added that Lyosha still planned to marry her. That much I could grasp in Russian. I asked the guy sitting next to me how to get to the metro. His instructions were complicated, but I was too embarrassed to stay. I got up to go. He told me it was dark and unsafe and to wait for Lyosha. I agreed to wait in the hall until he located Lyosha. When Lyosha found me, he was all sweet apologies.

"That video is from before I met you," he said. I was looking down at my feet, avoiding his gaze. "We broke up," he continued. He took my chin in his hand and titled it upward. "Look at me Katiusha. I don't want anything to do with her anymore."

"So you aren't engaged?"

"Of course not. Would I be with you if I was still engaged to her?"

"I don't know."

He laughed and wrapped his arms around me. Then he kissed me hard, and I kissed him back. It was easier than trying to find my way home alone. When he dropped me off at home later that night, we made plans to go out again during the week. When he didn't show, I called his grandmother's house. I asked where he was, and she told me he was out with his girlfriend. Lyosha called later that night. He told me I didn't understand his grandmother's Russian. I hung up. He called several more times. The first two times I hung up after I heard his voice. The third time I listened to him. He never called back a fourth time.

John told me he would take care of Lyosha. I think he just said it to make me smile. The thought of John beating up another guy made us all laugh. When I mentioned a hamster might make up for a missing boyfriend, Sabra figured out how to get me one. Hamsters aren't common pets in Ukraine, and she warned me that the pet shop might not let me spend much time choosing one. I ended up with a cream-colored fur ball I named Malchik Spichka (Little Match Boy). I kept Spichka in a cage on a table in the living room. In the beginning Spichka was a small but pleasant addition. As he grew, though, he developed a huge sack of nuts and began to have a very strong odor and an unpleasant and unfriendly manner. I no longer enjoyed taking Spichka out of his cage, and I started to resent having to clean up after him. Hamster bedding and litter were not easy to find, my landlady hated him, and I was growing to dislike him as well.

When I was a child, I had a pair of pet mice that were both supposed to be female but somehow managed to multiply. We took several to a hill and let them loose. My dad convinced me we were returning them to nature. I decided to do the same for Spichka. Kyiv being a bit wilder than Berkeley, I equipped him with a cage, food, and a little note to prospective owners. Instead of letting him run free, I placed him on a park bench in his cage, hoping someone would decide to adopt him. Then I walked away. When I returned an hour later, he was gone, cage and all. Just like my dad had told me when I was a kid, I told myself he had gone to a better place. I believed it then about as much as I did when I was a kid—not at all.

Sabra took care of Sveta in another way. We had never had a full-time translator at the paper. Before she left, Sabra convinced Greg to hire Sveta as one. Although Sabra spoke Russian, she liked to have a translator on interviews and was impatient with our colleague Anya's less than enthusiastic efforts. Sveta was far more obliging and fun to work with. Her knowledge of Kyiv and her English vocabulary were both lacking, but she was eager to learn and was always using dictionaries and maps. It worked out well; Sveta needed a job and there weren't any of those in Kaniv, and I needed a translator who wanted to help, not hinder, my productivity. Sabra left us together. John went back to doing his own thing, traveling from place to place with his guitar.

I don't think I told Sabra about what I did to Malchik Spichka. We didn't talk much after she left at the end of the summer. She kept in touch with Sveta, though, and of course with John. Sabra knew too much about relationships and American immigration to promise anything, but Sveta and I understood she would probably be making her way back to Ukraine before too long. It wouldn't be to see either of us.

Sveta called me from the funeral. She was in Kaniv.

"John's dead," she said.

"What do you mean dead?"

"I'm at his funeral."

Sabra had been gone several months by then. John was living in Kaniv, and Sveta and I were living and working in Kyiv.

"What should I tell Sabra?" she said.

"You have to call her. You can't put that in an email."

There was silence on the other end.

"Sveta, you okay?"

"Yeah. It's just I think she lives alone. I don't want her to hear that alone."

I remembered Sabra was close with her father. I told Sveta to send him an email telling him what had happened before she told Sabra. I hoped he would be able to comfort her. It was the best we could do.

I don't know if Sveta told Sabra the details. I don't know if she knew them. What she told me over the phone was that John had been found beaten to death in a room tied to a chair. There was something about his performing in a club and the mafia not liking the arrangement. No one really knew. He had no money and no enemies, but he was a performer and popular with women, two things that could put him on the wrong side of the mafia. He was also a joker, and Sveta said he got the last laugh when they were carrying his closed casket to the grave and he fell out. I didn't really see the humor in this, especially when she said he had been beaten so badly she couldn't recognize him. I don't think Sveta found it funny either because she was crying when she told me. I guess she was just trying to find something of the friend she had known in the disfigured corpse that remained.

15 The Enemy Outside

Yulia was silent.

"What did he say?" I asked.

She shrugged her shoulders. "I don't know how to say it in English."

I must have looked concerned because she added: "I'm sure it wasn't important."

That wasn't reassuring. Or true. Yulia—not my Latvian friend but a Yulia I met at the *Kyiv Post*—was translating for me. We were part of a group of about a dozen Kyivites learning to skydive. We were gathered in a basement-like room in the city outskirts listening intently as our instructor explained how to deploy the parachutes we would be using the following day. Yulia had stopped translating the instructions around the time we were being told what to pull to deactivate the emergency chute after the regular chute engaged. I learned this later. All I knew then was that the instructor was forcibly gesturing to a knob on his pack.

"Yulia," I said. My voice was a mixture of whimpering and pleading. "Um, I think I need to know what he said."

The instructor glared at me. He was an old-school Russian military type who had been reluctant to let me in the class. He relented only when I produced the entrance fee and assured him I understood enough Russian to grasp his instructions. There had been three of us at the start. But Olga wasn't eating. Olga was willing to try pretty much anything, from starvation diets to skydiving. In this case the two didn't go well together. Lack of food had made her light-headed and caused her to fail the physical we had to take in order to jump. Olga was a reporter at the *Kyiv Post*, and we probably would have been better friends if she hadn't been Diana's favorite underling. Yulia was also a friend from work, but she worked in IT and was harder to pinpoint than Olga. Yulia had short spiky orange hair and an athletic build. Her husband was British, so she could have lived abroad, but she showed no such inclination. That was strange in itself. What seemed even stranger to me at the time was the way she talked about her husband. It wasn't that she disliked him. It was just that she didn't seem to particularly like him either. The relationship appeared more like a partnership to me than a romance, only it wasn't clear what either partner got out of it. Up until then I believed marriages fell into two categories—miserable and happy. I had yet to learn that there were marriages that existed in between those extremes, marriages that were neither failures nor successes.

I discovered this not long after I married. We were talking about growing old together when Dima informed me that later in life we would both have affairs. At the time I couldn't imagine anything worse. I promised myself to stay in shape, and as attractive as age would allow, as long as I could. I thought that would keep him from wanting anyone else. I didn't understand until much later that that wasn't what it was about.

I may have gone skydiving before I fell in love, but I wasn't a loner with a death wish. I was simply a curious thrill seeker who lived in a country where everyday living was risky. All of us had a different attitude toward safety over there. Some took the issue so seriously that they lived in a sort of constant fear that kept them from truly experiencing the country. Usually they were the ones who had the salaries to afford relative isolation. The rest of us adapted. In the United States I would never ride in a car without a seat belt. In Ukraine I can't remember a single occasion when I wore one. Back home I hitchhiked a total of two times. In Ukraine I flagged down unknown drivers daily. In America I followed the traffic rules. In Ukraine I wasn't really aware there were any. The only rule that all drivers seemed to follow was the flashing of headlights to warn fellow drivers when a police car was in the area.

That is why Jed kicked us out of the car after the accident. He didn't trust the police, especially with a car full of young women. Jed was our publisher, and that was the first and last time I rode in a car with him. We had been coming from a game of ultimate Frisbee, a sport Greg was set on popularizing in Kyiv. I have never been a good Frisbee thrower, but with Sabra gone, Jenia busy with Viktor, and Sveta not much of an athlete, I decided to give it a try. I loved sports, and soccer hadn't gone over too well the few times I had attended games. Greg didn't mind me playing, but the Ukrainian guys he played with did.

Frisbee was a mixture of men and women, locals and expats, plus a few large dogs. We played barefoot on the beach, taking breaks so Greg's Ukrainian girlfriend could smoke. The games ended when the cigarette breaks lasted longer than the playing. Afterward we would all scatter. I was headed to the metro with half a dozen local women one evening when Jed offered us a ride in his car. As the sole American woman, I got the front seat. Another woman sat next to me, and four or five more squeezed in the back. I didn't know Jed well, but I was familiar with the rumors. He had a large personality that almost matched that of the oligarchs. He had a compact and tight build, light hair, and a smile that dared you to challenge him. He was a business mogul, not an idealist. He was young and bold, and I think he liked the image of the playboy as much as he did the actual role.

Leaving the beach, we had to take a half-circle ramp sloping downward. I knew the minute Jed drove onto it that we were going too fast. The momentum of the car took it across three lanes of traffic. We were still moving too fast as we headed toward the far side of the ramp. I saw it clearly as we kept speeding forward and upward. I knew what was going to happen—and that I couldn't do anything about it. I felt a strange calm. I heard a few screams from the back seat. The car went airborne right before the bottom of the ramp. Momentum took it across several lanes of traffic, where it crashed into a median in the middle of the road. Somehow we had not been hit. I had been flung forward but was squeezed in so tight that I had nothing more than a sore spot on my forehead. The women in the backseat had fallen forward as well but had also been grouped in too tight to move very far. Jed was the first to speak. "You guys okay?" he asked.

There was nervous laughter as we twisted and shook ourselves, trying to see if anything was broken. All of us were okay, even Jed. "You better get out before the cops come," he said.

We scrambled out and made our way to the metro overpass. From the bridge above we looked down on the car. Several cop cars were on the scene before our train arrived. We weren't too worried about Jed. He had money.

The crash made the rounds at work the next day, and I made sure to mention the sore spot on my forehead and the bruises on my arms. I figured the experience would serve as good job security. The local women wouldn't sue Jed, but he didn't know I wouldn't.

Public transportation was safer but slower. It took Yulia three days to get to Kyiv by train from Riga. By the time she arrived, we had only two days to spend together before she had to get back on the train and return to Riga. We did the tourist things together, walking down the winding cobblestone street where they sold *matryoshkas* (nesting dolls) and pins and medals decorated with hammers and sickles. I showed her all the views Lyosha had shown me and introduced her to Sveta. Before she left, she made Sveta promise to look out for me. Sveta must have been in Kaniv when I went parachuting with the other Yulia.

It had been an impulsive decision. Someone in the office had mentioned that skydiving was cheap in Kyiv, and when I found it only cost about the equivalent of fifteen dollars, I decided to try it that weekend. Yulia and I were star pupils the first day. After the morning lecture we practiced landing by jumping from small heights in a playground outside, like the instructor advised. Our male counterparts mocked us from the sidelines.

Shortly after our arrival at the airfield the next morning, we spotted the first of them being carried off on a stretcher, a large splint on his leg. "He was too old for this type of parachute," said our instructor.

He looked about forty. Age didn't seem to be a factor for the next man who stumbled toward us on a wobbly ankle; he looked even younger. Yulia and I were starting to get a little apprehensive when we saw our gear. I decided then and there that paying more for equipment you are entrusting your life to might not be such a bad idea. Instead of the high-tech shiny and bright kit I was used to seeing in the United States, we were weighted down with floppy helmets and drab green packs that looked like they had survived several wars, none of them recent.

I heaved the pack on my back and attempted to walk. It was probably good that I would be moving through air and not walking on land because I could barely stand without toppling over. Yulia and I quizzed each other on the crucial step she had struggled to translate—deactivating the emergency chute after the main chute deployed. If you missed that step, you were basically doomed. If you didn't deactivate the second chute, it would deploy, and the two chutes would likely get tangled while you raced toward the ground. Yulia had used a combination of gestures and words to explain this step to me. Then she agreed to go first. Her bravery landed me a slot right behind her in the lineup. We weren't the first ones to jump that day, just the first on our flight. I was starting to think about home and how things would be done differently there, which led me to thinking about how things were done here. That of course was not a good thing to spend too much time contemplating. It was helpful that they loaded us on quickly.

The plane was not of the commercial sort. There were benches instead of seats and an open space where a door should have been. The noise was deafening. I didn't quite understand why we hooked our chutes to a bar above our heads or how we would free ourselves from the plane once we were in the air. But it was too late—and loud—to ask questions. So instead I simply watched the fields and apartments grow small beneath us as we climbed to almost three thousand feet. It looked like we were still flying over houses when the instructor pulled Yulia toward the open door. I followed, bracing myself behind them.

I was still trying to balance myself when I noticed Yulia was gone and the instructor was motioning for me to jump. I had enough time to see the back of Yulia free-falling through white nothingness before I too was floating in thin air. I have no idea how I got there. I remember looking out at my friend and thinking there was no way I would follow her into that void.

And then I was there. I was so scared I couldn't think to scream. There was nothing to hold onto, nothing around me. And for two seconds it seemed like there would be nothing in the future.

Then, just as suddenly, my parachute activated, and I was floating peacefully above the world. After such fear it was utterly calm. I quickly deactivated my spare chute and sank into the silence and stillness. I watched the houses and world below and felt serenely above it all. I was removed from the material world in a way I had never been before and would never be again. Time slowed down, and yet the landing two and a half minutes later came all too soon. I was concentrating on straightening my legs as we had been taught when I hit the ground and a bolt of pain shot through me. I fell hard and lay there a minute or two. I felt my body to make sure nothing was broken. Everything seemed okay, aside from some bruises. I scrambled up and set about rolling up my parachute. It was the first time I had seen the chute in all its glory. As I bundled it up, I decided that seeing it for the first time now, after I had jumped, was a very good thing. The material looked old and rather worn. I wondered how many jumps it had made and how many it was supposed to make before being retired. I had a little too long to contemplate this while waiting for the bus that would take me from the field I had landed in back to the main airstrip.

On board the bus I shared my concern with Yulia. The man behind us chuckled. In broken English he told me the chutes were in great condition compared to the planes. The aircraft were Soviet relics that should have been junked decades ago, he said. We ignored him. Yulia and I were hooked on the rush of skydiving and vowed to go jumping again the next weekend. When that didn't work out, we promised we would go the following weekend. And when that too fell through, the weekend after that. But the weeks turned into months, and we never jumped again. The more time that passed, the less we mentioned the topic until eventually it became a memory of our one jump instead of a memory of the second and third jumps we had promised we would make. We didn't talk about the change, but I think we both knew the more times we leaped, the more chances something could go wrong.

My mother called the next day. She said she had had a strange feeling that something had happened to me and needed to hear my voice. I told her about going skydiving. She took it well. I wondered what our listener thought. The telltale click came a few seconds after I picked up. I learned to expect the click and at times almost waited for it before beginning my conversation, as if the connection was not complete without the mysterious third party. This was more than a decade after the end of the Cold War. But foreigners were still watched, and I was accused of being a spy on more than one occasion. It wasn't a baseless accusation.

I had taken the first steps to becoming a spy. After Latvia and before Ukraine I applied to dozens of newspaper and one government agency, the CIA. Recruiters called my parents' home after I had already moved to Ukraine. Although they did not say who they were, or what it was about, my stepfather figured it out. He tried to convey this to me in coded message over the phone. I had no clue what he was talking about, which was probably the first clue I was ill-suited for the job. The second came when I finally did connect with a man in recruitment while back in California on a visit. The recruiter advised me to read Ronald Kessler's book *Inside the CIA: Revealing the Secrets of the World's Most Powerful Spy Agency*. Kessler made it brutally clear how little control agents had over the use of the information they gathered and the treatment of local sources. There were elements of the work that sounded exciting. But I wasn't sure I could stomach doing something whose end result I might not agree with. I loved my country but not more than I loved individuals. The third reason I wouldn't have made a good spy had yet to come into play, but even then I knew it might be a possibility. Marriage to a local was not allowed.

Peter never married a local. He had a girlfriend, and a child or two, but not a wife. He was a conspiracy theorist and the perfect caricature of a Cold War spy. He chain-smoked, had large plastic-rimmed glasses, and disheveled brown hair. He was of indeterminate middle age, spoke Russian and English, and revealed remarkably little about his past or personal life. He covered politics at the *Kyiv Post* and was always meeting people in bars. He didn't hang out with the other expats on weekends or in the evenings, nor did he hang out with locals. He had countless acquaintances but few friends. When his girlfriend was giving birth, he was at the office. He said the hospital wouldn't have allowed a man to attend, but I still found his nonchalance strange.

When something was going on in politics or someone new was in town, Peter knew before anyone else. He could work the phones and the conspiracy theories better than any of us. I never had a genuine conversation with him. I didn't really know how to talk to him. His language was completely foreign to me. He was elusive and well connected. The rest of us figured he was a spy. He never denied it. Nor did he acknowledge it.

16 Heroes and a Woman Named Hope

That fall Georgiy Gongadze went missing.

I didn't pay much attention at first. Gongadze ran the website Ukrayinska Pravda (Ukrainian Truth). He was a little-known political muckraker, and the rumor was that he hadn't gone home the night he disappeared because he had been with his girlfriend. Government investigators had their own theories. One about the abduction being related to political matters was quickly replaced by one that blamed it on Gongadze's personal life. Another official version had him staging his own abduction. I left it to Peter to figure out what had really happened. I was more into past heroes than present mysteries. I spent the end of summer covering the reburial of a seventeenth-century Cossack hero—or at least his head.

The Cossack reburial was held in the sweltering heat on Khortytsya Island, an isolated sliver of land in eastern Ukraine that attendees reached via non-air-conditioned buses. Cossacks, Slavic tribes known for their autonomy and horsemanship, once accounted for 80 percent of the Ukrainian population. The newly independent country was eager for any excuse to honor its earliest freedom fighters, especially a military leader like Ivan Sirko, who sometimes had sided against the Russians. The outdoor ceremony included prominent Ukrainian Orthodox priests. The attending modern day Cossacks were dressed in bright sharvary pants and fur hats, their hair in scalp locks and swords on their hips. They were quiet and attentive, taking only occasional swigs from the vodka that filled their old-fashioned drinking vessels.

As the ceremony dragged on and the sun grew stronger, the swigs grew more frequent. An hour into the proceedings I struggled to keep my eyes on both the live inebriated Cossacks and their long dead compatriot. It isn't every day you get to attend the burial of a seventeenth-century Cossack, although, the Cossack in question had already had quite a few.

Sirko had first been buried following his death in 1680. His second burial came in 1708, the third in 1967. On the last occasion he was buried without his skull, which was sent to Russia for scientific reasons that seem to have extended into political ones. By the time Sirko was reunited with his skull in the late summer of 2000, all that remained of the romantic warriors who had once roamed the Ukrainian steppes was a bunch of drunk middle-aged men in dress-up.

One begged for a sip from my water bottle. Finding it hard to refuse a man with a sword, I relented. He emptied the entire bottle on his head. I attempted one or two questions. The answers I received were not ones I could print. Sveta and I headed back to the steamy bus. We were convinced we would succumb to heat exhaustion now that we had no water. A kind Cossack offered us a drink, but we knew better than to accept. Vodka wasn't going to make the trip back to Kyiv any better.

The Cossacks had been beastly but beloved. Ukraine's present-day rulers had the brute part down. When our American publisher went astray of the Ukrainian government, they detained him at the border. Tax inspectors were always levying fines, and our working conditions were regularly inspected by government minions for electrical, fire, and other "hazards." Many an opposition paper was shut down for the same. Meanwhile, the people pried metal from still-functioning factories, walking off with manhole covers and street lights to sell on the black market. In one village a local leader told me if the villagers were lucky, their daughters would be pretty and become prostitutes and their sons would be thieves. That was the best future she could imagine.

The situation in Sveta's hometown, Kaniv, was almost as bleak. A former factory town located on the banks of the Dnipro River, Kaniv is best known for being where Ukraine's most famous poet, Taras Shevchenko, is buried. When I visited less than a decade after the Soviet Union fell, the factory that had once employed five thousand kept on only one hundred workers. The apartments were crumbling and empty, the shops bare. It was as if time had stopped in the dusty town. The street lights were infrequent, the manhole covers missing, and the decorative metal railings gone, all victims of enterprising thieves and scavengers. Buses and city workers kept to a schedule all their own, and cars were a rare sight. Most government workers couldn't remember when they had last been paid. Some kept working; others didn't.

Our journey had begun outside a bus station in Kyiv where private drivers waited for passengers. If you were lucky, you would find a vehicle that already had passengers and would take off soon after your arrival. If you weren't, you would wait with the driver until his vehicle filled, a task that could take a few minutes or a few hours. There was no schedule. The only assurance was that it would probably be faster, more comfortable, and more expensive than the bus. Sveta made the trip most weekends. I accompanied her occasionally. The first Saturday I went with her we considered ourselves lucky when a driver agreed to take us and just one other passenger. Sveta and I would pay the normal price. The other passenger had agreed to pay double to make up for the lost income of a fourth passenger. Kaniv is only about a hundred miles from Kyiv. By bus it can take half a day or longer. By car it is about three hours. Sveta and I sat in the back, and moneybags sat in the front. He called us *krasivyye devushki*, beautiful girls. "My beautiful girls, where are you two going all alone?" he asked in Russian.

Sveta did the talking. There were certain times when it was best not to reveal my American status. Judging by moneybags' foul breath, ripe body odor, and leering looks, this was one of them.

"Kaniv," Sveta said.

"Kaniv can be a long ride. Let me take you to lunch. I will treat us all. It has been a long time since I have been in such company."

"We're not hungry."

"Then how about a drink? Beautiful girls must get thirsty?"

He laughed and nudged the driver.

"No."

We continued in silence for a stretch.

"*Stoyte* [Stop]!" he called to the driver. "I need to get a drink."

The driver pulled off the road, and we sat waiting as moneybags went into a shop. He returned several minutes later with a pack of cigarettes. We drove again. Ten minutes later he called for the driver to stop again. This time he was gone longer. "Can't we just leave him?" Sveta asked the driver in Russian. She knew we couldn't.

"I'm sorry girls," he said. "I know he is awful. But he is paying double."

"Why does he have to keep stopping?"

"I think he likes to buy things because he has been without them for so long."

Sveta and I exchanged looks. The whole ride it had seemed as if moneybags was in a rush to consume: beautiful women, food, drink, cigarettes. But we had assumed it was just part of an act. Now it seemed it might be something more.

"What do you mean he has been without things for so long?" Sveta asked.

"He just got out of prison. He's been locked up for ten years."

Moneybags returned before we had time to ask the driver what he had been in for. The rest of the ride was surprisingly uneventful.

In Kaniv I was invited to go swimming in the river by a man with a beach towel. I liked his carefree attitude until I realized he was fall-over drunk. Most of the young people in the city were. There was nothing else to do. The only pressing matter was filling tubs when the water came on. The water worked for a two-hour segment in the middle of the day, during which everyone filled bathtubs and buckets. If you missed the water window, you would have trouble washing, cooking, or using the toilet for the next twenty-four hours. And if it was your weekend to clean the apartment halls, you were in grave danger of being beaten by a babushka. When we arrived, it was Sveta's week, and even though she seldom occupied her apartment, she never missed her cleaning duty. She used a wet rag on a pole to push around the dirt on the stone stairways. I had observed the maneuver many times before, and every time the rag and water seemed dirtier to me than whatever was being cleaned.

The apartment complex was eerily quiet, just as the streets had been. There were hardly any cars outside, either moving or parked. Every once in a while you would see someone sitting at a bus stop. An hour later the same person would still be there. The playgrounds between the complexes were sandy and used only at night, when teenage girls with very short skirts sat on the swings calling out dreams to a city that wasn't listening.

There was no buzz of electricity or hum of technology. There was no hurry or bustle, just static stillness. When Sveta pulled out a pair of walkie-talkies, I thought she was reliving her childhood. It turned out she was calling her parents. The phone wires tended to get stolen. Walkie-talkies were more reliable. When Sveta was in Kyiv, she left her Kaniv apartment empty. There was no one to rent it to and no way to sell it. It was kind of like her teaching job. She was still employed as a piano instructor at one of the schools. She just was no longer paid and so no longer went to work. It was a strange security without security. She was not without skills or possessions; they just no longer held value.

It hadn't always been like that. Her parents had moved to Kaniv to work in the factory. They lived comfortably with their two children, Sveta and her older brother. Then the Soviet Union collapsed, the factory fell apart, their son moved to Russia, and their daughter stopped being paid. The town's dairy farm and bakery closed, and they both lost their jobs. The electronics products the factory had produced had been state secrets in Soviet times, and Sveta's mother still talked about her former job in hushed tones. Most of what she said was in hushed tones. She spoke with a gentleness born out of exhaustion and exasperation. She had short white hair and mischievous eyes. When I came to visit, she would feed me hot dogs and cookies and tell me about her heritage over candlelight, the electricity having gone out.

Her family had been exiled to Kazakhstan under Josef Stalin's rule for the crime of having a cow, ownership of any kind being thought bourgeois. A train dumped them in the wasteland with nothing. Those that survived built simple homes and a community. When she was a teenager, Sveta's mother was sent to work on a collective farm. She escaped for good when she moved to Kaniv and met Sveta's father. She was in her fifties when her world fell apart a second time. She tried working as a middleman, buying goods around the country and bringing them back to Kaniv to sell. But several encounters with highway bandits made her and her husband rethink their options. They opened a small shop that sold everything from bread to secondhand clothing. They tried selling cigarettes and alcohol, but the taxes levied on them were too steep. The taxation system was convoluted and arbitrary. The cost of electricity, rent, and gas more than tripled in three years. Their aluminum door was stolen and their windows broken. They named the shop after Sveta's mother, Nadia, hope. It was one of the many things in short supply in Kaniv.

Both communism and the excuse for capitalism that followed it had failed Sveta and her family. They relied on hope. I was American; I didn't need hope. I had democracy. I thought it shielded me from chaos. But that fall I began to see its holes. For the first time I remember, the international community was questioning the fairness of a Western democracy, my democracy.

I was in California visiting my family when we heard the details about a possible recount of the 2000 U.S. presidential election. We were coming back from the beach, and the political news streaming over the car radio felt far away. I hadn't voted because I was living abroad. But I was American, and I always figured Americans did things the right way. They didn't need recounts. They weren't cheaters. Now I wasn't so sure where I belonged or what was the right way of doing things. The clarity of youth had crumbled, leaving the line between good and bad, right and wrong, as broken as the promises of politicians.

On my way back to Ukraine I stopped off in London for voice lessons at the BBC. My employers wanted me to sound more British, to lose my California accent, to disguise where I was from. My mother was expert at this, and my sister and I hated her for it. When we lived in England as children, her imitation of the British accent felt like a betrayal. She said she couldn't help it, that her voice just changed to match those around her. Like plastic, it bent.

I believed I was made of tougher stuff, but I was bending in other ways. In London I stayed with my Italian-Austrian friend Sandro. He still adored me, and I thought it would be good to like him. But I fumbled with affection for him as badly as I tripped over the tongue twisters the voice instructor at the BBC made me recite. When we were in bed together, I let his hands explore but kept my back to him. I wasn't sure what I wanted, and he could tell. After that trip he didn't call or email much anymore.

My radio stories for the BBC also started to taper off. I had been doing occasional "letters home" for the radio since arriving in Kyiv. I wrote scripts about my trip to Chernobyl and recorded them in the studio. When I got back from London, I did a story for BBC radio on a mysterious skin disease outbreak among children in the countryside. The hospital that was treating the children refused to let me enter, the doctors caring for them wouldn't talk, and the local politicians insisted nothing was going on. But everyone else—the mothers and fathers and aunts and uncles of these children—couldn't say enough. They looked to us for answers. We were as bad as the rest, offering something worse than silence: false hope. Because like them, we didn't know what was happening.

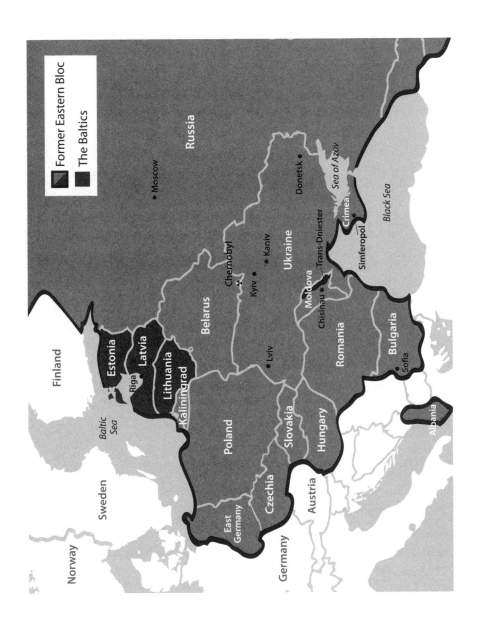

1. Eastern Europe and Russia.

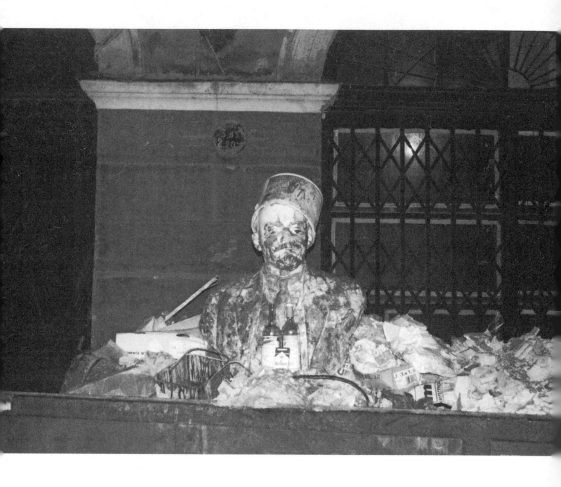

2. Vladimir Lenin in a dumpster in Riga, Latvia. Photo by the author.

3. The author (*center*) at a Halloween party in Riga. Courtesy of the author.

4. A chimney sweep in Riga. Photo by the author.

5. The author (*right*) and her friend Jenia at a hotel in Yalta under the watchful eye of Lenin. Courtesy of the author.

6. Orphans and their grandfather in Ukraine. Photo by the author.

7. A babushka in Ukraine. Photo by the author.

8. A factory in Ukraine. Photo by the author.

9. Ukrainian coal miners. Photo by the author.

10. The author (*left*) with Viktor and Jenia in Kyiv, Ukraine. Courtesy of the author.

11. The author with the Ukrainian military. Photo by Dima Gavrysh. Courtesy of the author.

12. The author with detained Ukrainian protesters. Courtesy of the author.

is being tougea in the minas of the Ukrainian public. The people must overcome skepticism and take action to save the country.

Page 6

REGION

Moldova goes Red

With Communists sweeping the elections, some fear that Ukraine's neighbor may join Belorus in Moscow's orbit.

Page 8

WORLD

Bloody clashes

Security troops are trying to quell ethnic fighting in Borneo that has refugees fleeing the island.

Page 9

DAY & NIGHT

Gifts that wow

women with quality and style are tough to come by, but they're a necessary part of International Women's Day.

Arts and entertainment section on page 9B

KYIV POST

BUSINESS

Russian cash

has figured prominently in recent privatization tenders. Is Russia buying Ukraine piecemeal?

Venture capital

has helped a Sumy-area brick maker lay a foundation for its success.

Ready to rumble

Seven year-old Vova Radzuk waits with UNA-UNSO members as they are given their orders for the Feb. 25 protest. The nationalist party UNA-UNSO is largely responsible for protection at tent city, the camp constructed by the Ukraine Without Kuchma protest movement in downtown Kyiv. Katya Cengal's account of life in tent city starts on page 4. *(Photo by Dima Gavrish)*

Pollution mars life in Cherkasy

By KATYA CENGEL
Post Staff Writer

CHERKASY – "Azot is Life," reads a sign on the highway at the edge of town. In Cherkasy, however, the grim reality may be that Azot, along with another of the city's chemical plants, may be at the root of cancers and other life-threatening illnesses that have plagued residents for decades.

This chemical-manufacturing city 200 kilometers south of Kyiv has a history of pollution. At one time, the air was so foul residents were advised to keep windows closed.

"We couldn't even breathe," said Iryna Ionova, a doctor at the local children's hospital.

Ionova is no stranger to the mal-adies the city's plants have manufactured as a byproduct of their chemical fertilizers and synthetic fibers. During the 1980's, doctors at the hospital discovered many young patients suffered from acetone sickness, a liver disorder. The problem became serious enough that a special commission was

See POLLUTION page 2

New repor fails to say tapes real

By PETER BYRNE
Post Staff Writer

After stating in a long-awaited that it was highly unlikely that the rious Melnychenko tapes had been tored, the International Press Ins stopped short of declaring the tape and referred the case back to Ukra law-enforcement authorities.

"The technical experts expressed conviction that it is nearly impossi detect manipulation with a r absolute level of certainty," the Fe report said.

The report was a blow to Ku opponents, who were hoping an une ocal statement by IPI that the tap real would increase international pre on Ukraine's embattled president.

The IPI report did say that th almost no chance that Mykola M chenko, the former presidential se guard who allegedly made the tap guard who allegedly made the tap a large volume of footage.

"If the existing evidence had sisted only of the approximatel minute long recordings related [Georgy] Gonaddze case, one coul sibly imagine some manipulatic doctoring by a 'potential aggres wrote IPI Director Johann P. "However, as the total volur recordings available covers hundr hours of conversations over the of several months, it seems ha believe that such a huge amount o umentary evidence may have bee tored or manipulated."

With the report, IPI and its par

See TAPES

13. A copy of the *Kyiv Post* with the author's story and Dima's photos. Courtesy of the author.

Petaluman Katya Cengel currently lives in Kiev, where she works as a free-lance writer covering Eastern Europe. "I like the sense of history you get," she says.

14. The author in Kyiv in a U.S. article. Courtesy of the author.

15. The author's press passes. Courtesy of the author.

16. The author and Dima. Courtesy of the author.

17. Riot police in Kyiv. Photo by Dima Gavrysh. Courtesy of the author.

17 Darkness at Dawn

I should have seen it coming. I mean, how do you miss a revolution? A bus, an appointment, an anniversary—those are all things one misses. Not a revolution. There were signs: mass protests, secret arrests and trials, riot police by the busload. But they came later. In the beginning there were just rumors. We wrote them off as hiccups in the regular oppression. And if you look at it through the long lens of history, that is pretty much what it has all become. A short-lived shake up that, for all its noise and disturbance, left things pretty much the same as they had been before. A new leader was elected, but he ruled as President Leonid Kuchma had. And Kuchma followed the Soviet model, minus the perks of heated buses and a few extra hammers and sickles.

Still, the whole thing was an entertaining distraction from the usual topics of meddling oligarchs, impoverished pensioners, and glue-sniffing youth that occupied us as journalists. Later, after secret recordings implicated Kuchma in a massive cover-up in the case of missing journalist Gongadze, he took on the role of villain. Prime Minister Viktor Yushchenko filled in as hero. The heroine of the movement was Yulia Tymoshenko. She was a product of Eastern Ukraine, an area rich in coal, Russians, and politicians who took up politics after amassing large sums of money in the gas industry. Tymoshenko wore her tresses in thick braids wrapped around her head and held court from prison cells. She frequently went on hunger strike. Her unusual digs were a perk of her rising influence among the opposition and the tax evasion accusations that tended to follow such prominence. Not to say she didn't steal, just that no one seemed to care until she entered politics.

The Tymoshenkos of the system made money in the energy sector, but it wasn't trickling down to the villagers of Muisynska, where the energy started as coal. When I visited in the fall of 2000, it had been five years since there had been central heat or gas in Muisynska. Or water in winter. The heat was the first to go because it used waste heat from the steam turbines. It shut off when the local electric power station closed. (When the heat was turned on and off each year was not controlled by individual households but by local authorities. At least that is who I believe was in control; it was never exactly clear.) Without power there was no way to prevent the pipes from freezing in cold weather, so water service was stopped. Showers were not greatly missed. Without heat most people never removed more than their hat and shoes. I didn't even remove that much. The prosperous attempted to heat their homes with homemade metal ovens of a type not seen since World War II.

There were plenty of coal mines, but they were in such disrepair and so badly managed that it was questionable whether they were profitable. I tried to figure out how the system worked, but "who stopped paying whom when" was a convoluted mess. What was clear was that somebody was getting rich, some companies were getting free power, others were overpaying for the same service, and the coal miners were getting pickled tomatoes. That isn't a metaphor; they were actually paid in pickled tomatoes one month. Another month it was boxes of slippers. Coal miners' widows, of which there were plenty, pulled baby trams down the street, filling them with coal scraps they could exchange for food.

In the midst of this deprivation I tried not to complain when the lodging we found—I have trouble calling a building with no customers or services a hotel—lacked light, heat, water, and food. Sveta and I walked to a nearby kiosk in an attempt to warm ourselves through movement. Our failure to even quell our shivers inspired us to create a hotel room exercise routine that included jumping jacks, running in place, and waddle walks. At some point a very old woman appeared and offered to get us some hot water for tea. When she heard my American accent, she wrapped her arms around me and held on. She had never met an American before and was reluctant to let me go. Eventually she released me and went in search of the promised hot water. She was gone so long I was starting to worry she hadn't made it when she returned with a small container of lukewarm water. Sveta and I used it to make a single cup of tea each before climbing into our beds with our boots, hats, and gloves still on.

We woke up cold and hungry and already dressed. We ventured outside in search of food, almost colliding with a stumbling drunk at seven in the morning. The man offered a cheerful toast with an invisible glass before collapsing at our feet. Later in the trip we were served cognac shots at breakfast. The concept of it being too early in the day to start drinking was a moot point when no one ever stopped drinking. Drunkenness and misery were worn with pride, each person trying to outdo the next with how much alcohol he or she could consume and how much suffering he or she could endure. Neither the drink nor the suffering seemed to be in short supply in the region. Coal mining was the only real occupation in the area, and it was performed under primitive conditions. A single headlamp was shared by as many as a dozen miners, who used pickaxes in mines that hadn't been repaired for a quarter of a century. In the nine months before our visit, 261 people had died in the mines.

The miners haunted the region like ghosts, their raccoon eyes glowing in the dark when they emerged from their underground tunnels. I met with them above ground, spoke with their bosses in offices, and visited their wives in their homes. I read the news reports and studied the engineering maps. I knew the conditions underground were beyond deplorable and that danger and death were far more reliable than any paycheck. But to understand the situation in depth I felt I had to experience it; I had to see the broken-down shafts and the ill-equipped miners at work with my own eyes. I needed to feel the contradiction of each swing of a pickaxe that brought the miners both closer to survival and closer to their own demise.

I made my desire known whenever there was a lull in the conversation. "How many people died in your mine last month? Can I go down and have a look?"

Either Sveta wasn't translating or Misha wasn't listening. Misha was our guide, a suave little Kyiv government worker who had agreed to show us around the mining industry. He worked in the energy sector and liked to stand on low walls and other impromptu stages and rouse the populace with talk of salaries and safety. They in turn were full of questions. When would they have heat? When would they have water? Did anyone in Kyiv care about them?

Misha reminded me of what I imagined a Depression-era labor organizer would have been. He wore nice suits and his hair gelled to the side. Misha never said I couldn't go down a mine; he just never said I could. The local mine owners and managers he introduced me to were more blunt: women are not allowed below ground. They are bad luck. There did not seem to be an abundance of luck to begin with. I didn't think any potential additional bad luck would be noticed. I kept asking. And they kept answering: *nyet*.

The last guy to turn me down was a former miner who now owned his own mine. He was the one who served cognac at breakfast. He was an old pal of Misha's, and he was happy to show us everything at his mine except the mine itself. I saw the bunnies he raised to pay his miners. I am not sure what the conversion rate of rubles to bunnies was, but at least his miners were given something they could cook or at least cuddle. I saw the maps of the area that outlined the various mines and their depths. I was served a lot of dehydrated fish and toasted more strangers and strange things in two days than I had in the previous two years. I wasn't a fan of the food or the fanfare and kept asking to see the real thing, the work that went on underground.

He served me more cognac. I pretended to take a sip with each toast, but by the sixth one I could not even pretend to keep up. After a day of freezing cold the warm dinner food was making me sleepy, and I was tired of fighting to remain sober. I just wanted to go to bed. Strangely, the food was having the opposite effect on our mine operator. Suddenly he was asking if I really wanted to go down a mine. The answer, if I was being honest, was no. I wanted to go to bed. But I had the reputation of my sex to defend. So I nodded my head and followed him out into the cold, dark night. As we headed toward the supply shed, I noticed several forms lurking in the dark, miners having just gotten off their shifts, their faces smudged with coal, the whites of their eyes glowing with wisdom and suspicion like those of a cat. Then I caught the mine owner looking at me, testing me for fear, smiling at my discomfort. I took a headlamp from a cubbyhole in the shed and declared it fit after placing it on my head. He smiled at my naïveté. "Turn it on," he said in Russian. I tried. It didn't work.

I tried another. It also didn't work. The fourth offered a dim and sporadic glow that he declared "good enough." Then he slung a mask over my shoulder that looked like it belonged on the set of a World War II movie and handed me a water canteen and lunch container. We didn't need any of these—I hoped. We did need special clothes, thick layers that would keep us warm and keep the coal dust from ruining our regular clothes. Sveta and I piled on oversized ratty men's sweaters and pants and pulled caps over our hair until we looked like street urchins from a Dickens tale. Instead of socks we were given *portyanki*, kerchief-like cloth footwraps to wrap around our feet before slipping them into large rubber boots. Sveta and Misha tried to show me how to wrap my feet. But my sock wrappings kept coming undone, so Misha finally just did them for me. As he wrapped my feet, he looked at me for what I figured were signs of wavering, as if I would suddenly declare, "Okay, nice joke. I don't really want to go down a mine. Let's all go back and sleep." I think deep down we both wished I would say as much. I didn't utter a word besides *spasibo*, thank you.

We were the only ones on the bus that took us to the mine entrance. The next shift change wasn't for some time, so we enjoyed our short ride in quiet. We didn't have to walk far once we got off the bus, and all too soon we were cramming ourselves into a rickety little ride rather like the kind you come across at an amusement park. As we traveled ever so slowly down below, I tried to ignore the fear starting in the pit of my stomach and climbing toward my chest. I reached out and touched the damp earthen walls that closed in tight around our little train, cocooning us in what seemed an endless tunnel taking us farther and farther from light, air, and life. I held onto the back of Sveta's sweater, recalling all the wire reports that regularly came in about mining deaths. Back in the newsroom there was a morbid weekly game of betting when the next beheading would occur in the Middle East and how many mining deaths there would be in Ukraine.

That is how common they were. As if to prolong the torture, our little cart crept along slowly, threatening to stop every hundred feet or so. My knees were crammed into my face, and the surrounding walls were wet with I didn't know what. The farther we went down, the more scared I became, realizing that as slow as it was getting down, it would be twice as slow getting back up should we need to escape. And I knew there were many reasons why we might need to escape.

Finally the tunnel leveled off into a larger open space, and we climbed out. I could stand without hunching and extend my arms without touching the walls. But it still felt enclosed, small, dark, and lonely. I am a bit claustrophobic. I can handle pain, heights, and spiders, but closed spaces freak me out. I was secretly congratulating myself for having made it this far and wondering when we would be going back up when I realized the tour had only just begun. This was the easy part, the open area where the miners took breaks to eat, go to the bathroom, and drink before climbing farther into the darkness to work. I pretended to take notes as the mine operator babbled on about production and protocol, but my hands were shaky and my headlamp kept falling over my eyes.

Then he climbed up onto a ledge and started crawling forward on his hands and knees. Misha and Sveta followed. And then so did I. The walls closed in on my head and back, and the distance I could see in front of me and behind me narrowed to a sliver of light. I was sandwiched between two large slabs of heavy rock. I felt a fear and all-consuming weight in my chest and heart. The fear was less intense than parachuting but more enduring. Crawling is slow going, and the idea that if something happened I would not be able to run away terrified me. "Sveta," I whimpered. "Sveta . . . Sveta."

It was the only word I could utter, and I don't know why I said it, maybe just to hear a familiar and comforting sound in a very unfamiliar and uncomfortable setting. Each time I spoke, the voice was a little shakier. Sveta's response was neither Russian nor English but a strange noise that was more animal than human. We didn't need communication, just the sound of our voices to let us know we were both still in this together. We stopped after several minutes, and our mine operator actually started to give a speech he expected Sveta to translate and me to record. Sveta pretended to translate, and I pretended to listen. Then he hit one of the wood planks that was keeping the stone above from crushing our skulls. Sveta's mouth opened but no words came out.

"What is he saying?" I asked.

"These are the planks they don't have enough money to buy," she said.

We both started to note the wooden stabilizers holding up our stone roof. There weren't many. Sveta and I began to back out of the shaft, but Misha and our guide seemed content to stick around. It was probably the cognac. They struck at the coal seam with little chisels and picked up the bits as they fell around them. I was petrified. They were striking at the very thing we didn't want to crash down on top of us. The whole thing seemed incredibly precarious, a delicate balance that seemed to weigh more heavily in favor of nature than man. Still, that weird instinct that makes you believe you are going to live up until the moment the bus strikes you convinced me to slip a few handfuls of coal into my boots at the same time I was waiting to be buried alive.

I closed my eyes for a while on the ride up, just hoping time would pass and I would be somewhere safer when I opened them again. I must have still been white with fear and shock when we reached the dressing area because I sat motionless on a bench inside for quite a while before speaking or undressing. Misha finally came forward and pulled off one of my boots. A handful of coal tumbled to the ground. "The American stealing," he said in Russian.

I was too tired to stop him from taking off my other boot. More coal tumbled out. He laughed and handed me a larger piece of coal he had taken for himself.

A few weeks later a story came across the wire about two more dead miners. I saw it first and showed it to Sveta. "Isn't that the mine we went down?" I asked.

Sveta read the piece. It was brief, just an update on mining deaths. She finished it quickly and nodded her head. "Yeah that's the one."

We looked at each other. No words were necessary. We had been through so much together, and we would go through so much more together. It was a weird relationship. It was her country and she knew much more about it than I did, but when we worked together, I was the one in charge. And yet I relied on her so much: for translation, for moral support, for friendship. The stories I did were adventures, and without Sveta by my side they would have been overwhelming. With her they were fun. I don't know that she got as much out of the relationship. She would have liked to have continued teaching, to have married and had a family. Instead she had me.

Suddenly we both laughed.

Not long after, they found the headless corpse in the outskirts of Kyiv. No officials were talking about it. But everyone else was. The people didn't ask for answers like they had in Muisynska. They already knew the ending. It had to be the body of missing journalist Georgiy Gongadze.

The revolution had begun.

18 Radioactive Romance

We met on the bus ride back from Chernobyl. He was sitting a few seats away from me listening to his Discman. Someone asked what kind of music he liked, and he handed over an ear bud. I watched silently, gathering the courage, and the right Russian words, to do the same. I listened as he called his mother from his cell phone and told her he would be home late. His voice was sweet and gentle. At the time I thought his concern for his mother was a good thing. Now I tend to avoid men who talk to their mothers daily.

I had noticed him earlier in the day. He had been stalking a very large domestic cat in a town not far from the nuclear power plant. Ukrainian men don't smile. Dima was different. He smiled with his mouth and his wide-set eyes. He laughed with the joy and infectiousness of a child and joked that radiation had morphed the orange cat into a monstrosity.

The cat joined our group about halfway through the day. The tour began in Kyiv in pre-dawn darkness. It was the morning of the eve of the shutdown of the power plant's two remaining working reactors, and the government had organized a massive press trip. It had been planned for months and served as a convenient distraction from the unfolding Gongadze saga.

After a farmer discovered the headless corpse, officials maintained it was too decomposed to be Gongadze's. They insisted it belonged to someone killed long before Gongadze disappeared. But they made no further effort to identify the corpse, allowing it to further decompose in the local morgue without refrigeration. Frustrated by official ineptitude, Gongadze's colleagues visited the site where the body had been found and discovered jewelry they identified as having belonged to him. An X-ray of one of the hands revealed a shrapnel injury that matched one Gongadze possessed. The local coroner agreed to turn the body over to Gongadze's colleagues, but before they could collect it, the state prosecutor removed it for DNA testing. It took the prosecutor's office several more weeks to obtain blood samples from Gongadze's family.

In the meantime a political rival of Kuchma released tape recordings of alleged conversations between Kuchma, his presidential chief of staff, and the interior minister. The male voices on the recordings talked about ways to stop Gongadze: deport him to his native Georgia, prosecute him in Ukraine, or have Chechens kidnap him. The state security officer who made the recordings fled the country. The government's strange behavior, including an announcement that Gongadze had been murdered in a robbery attempt, only further aroused suspicion. A coalition of political parties called for Kuchma's removal. Small protests sprung up around the country.

Kuchma denied any involvement and was able to briefly distract the press corps and international community from the case with the Chernobyl shutdown. It was a huge production. In Kyiv there were buses to transport two hundred journalists from around the world to Chernobyl. But not Sveta. As a translator, she lacked the proper credentials. We pleaded, argued, and cried, but the officials wouldn't budge. Sveta couldn't come. I knew some basic Russian by this point but not enough to conduct interviews that progressed beyond name, age, and necessary questions like, "Do you have ice cream?" I tended to learn the words and phrases I needed most, and *shokolad morozhenoe* (chocolate ice cream) was one of them. "What will you do now that the nuclear power plant is closing?" was not.

Sveta assured me that with so many foreign journalists on board the announcements would be translated into English. Ten years later they might have been. But back then the government response still leaned more toward the Soviet model of *ne moya problema* (not my problem) than the Western model of accommodation. There were no translations.

On the bus ride there I solved the communication problem by sleeping. It was freezing, and the scenery was dark and dull. Snuggling into a tight ball and shutting one's eyes was the only comfortable option for enduring the two-hour ride. Even in my dazed state I was struck by the irony of the situation. A much-heralded line of buses was headed to an area no buses had traveled to since a somber procession had exited in secretive fashion fourteen years before. Back then the buses were loaded with survivors of the world's worst nuclear calamity. Now they were filled with journalists eager to cover the end of a story that had been forbidden to them fourteen years ago when it had begun.

Our first stop was the abandoned city of Prypiat, where many of the plant's workers had once lived. The tour organizers ushered us off the bus and encouraged us to take pictures and notes on the nothingness we found. I had been there before but had missed the slogans scrawled on the walls, like "Work will set you free." My Ukrainian colleagues had fun pointing them out to me. In the distance the power plant hovered over the city that had been created to house those who served it. I struggled to describe the eerie quiet and rushed abandonment of the place without removing my gloves. There was snow on the ground, and all I had on to keep my upper body warm was a long-sleeved shirt and a £10 (about $15) plastic jacket from London's Kilburn High Road. The jacket was silver and squeaked, and it was one of the only splashes of color in the photos taken in Prypiat that day. Later one of the photographers sent me several of his shots. I am not sure why he placed me in his pictures, but I wasn't surprised. To Ukrainians I was almost as much of an anomaly as the deserted town, a young, single American woman.

Our tour schedule, and the freezing weather, left little time for exploratory wanderings, and before long we were back on the bus and headed to our next stop. I had always been more interested in the people than the plant itself. But when we were taken to a view point a couple of hundred yards from the plant, I shivered at the thought of the damage it had caused—and still could. Civilians were not usually allowed so close, at least not without full body space suit gear. But this was a "special" day.

The plant was more ordinary than anything else, a rectangular industrial building with a crane sticking out the top. A scientist talked about the sarcophagus that covered the exploded reactor. His words weren't translated. I knew the covering was an imperfect and semi-temporary solution, which made the excitement shown by journalists and officials at their close proximity to the spot rather troubling.

Residents of Slavutych had a different reason to fixate on the plant. Slavutych was the new Prypiat: five thousand of its twenty-six thousand residents were employed at the plant. They had been relocated from the immediate vicinity of the plant after the 1986 disaster and didn't want to relocate again. Their relative proximity to the plant didn't seem to bother them. The loss of their jobs did. While President Kuchma held concerts in Kyiv to celebrate the plant's closing, the people of Slavutych gathered in their main square to protest. They waved banners demanding that their "social survival" be guaranteed.

It was estimated that one thousand of them would lose their jobs immediately. The others would be kept on to replace the sarcophagus that covered the ruined reactor and build a new heating system to keep the plant at a safe temperature. They had no idea who would have a job the next day and who would be let go. The government promised aid, but few believed it would follow through. Once the international attention and congratulations faded, they knew they would be forgotten, just as the victims of the disaster had already been. Fourteen years after the explosion, the government compensated just 10 percent of victims' medical care and rehabilitation.

A few residents joked they would move back to Prypiat. They sounded like the characters in *Fiddler on the Roof*, only they didn't sing as they talked about once again having to pack their bags and relocate. I was able to interview them thanks to a *New York Times* reporter. The reporter didn't speak much Russian, but he had a translator with him, so I made a point of introducing myself and convincing him to loan me his translator for some basic interviews. The reporter was from the *Times'* Moscow bureau, and he was as old, grumpy, and uninformed about the situation in Ukraine as I expected. My jealousy may have tainted my impression. He was a foreign correspondent for the *New York Times*. I hoped if I worked long enough and became sufficiently old and jaded enough, I might just be eligible for such a posting. Unfortunately, like the town of Prypiat, the position has all but disappeared into the hollows of history. These days foreign bureau jobs with newspapers are about as common as Chernobyl workers, the ghosts of a different era.

Slavutych was a gold mine for writers but a bit of a dead end for pho-tographers. They had seen their share of protest banners and were not greatly impressed. The cat held far more sway. I discovered a group of them huddled around it on the sidewalk in front of our bus. The way they talked and laughed I expected it to have two heads or at least an extra paw. But when I peeked inside their circle, all I saw was a large friendly cat. It had been a long day.

The whole closure was a two-day media circus orchestrated for the benefit of the West. President Kuchma had received international congratulations when he had set the December closure date back in July. Now he wanted to make the most of it. He downplayed concern about electricity shortages. They would probably be in villages, and the government was not overly concerned by regular blackouts in rural areas. Still, the same day we were touring, the parliament made a show of trying to postpone the closure, an empty gesture because it had no authority to do so. It made the life of journalists a little more hectic. I worked for a weekly newspaper that had yet to embrace internet updates, so I wasn't on any urgent deadline. The sole goal I set for myself on the trip back was to talk to Dima.

It was a brief conversation limited by my Russian, but before the ride was over, I knew his name. I asked what kind of music he liked and was given an ear bud. Listening to the same classical tune, I felt connected even though we barely spoke. He adjusted the volume for me and asked with eager eyes whether I liked it. I wasn't that crazy about it, but I smiled and said it was nice. He got off before me and I watched him go, hoping it wouldn't be the last time I saw him.

The next day Kuchma saw to it that the switch was flipped. He thought he would be known as the president who closed Chernobyl. I thought I had found the love of my life.

We were both wrong.

19 Children of Tomorrow

After meeting at Chernobyl we had to keep it epic. Our first date was on New Year's Eve—at the start of the new millennium. I thought I had celebrated the new millennium the year before, but in Ukraine it was celebrated at the start of 2000 and at the start of 2001. I hadn't much liked my first new millennium celebration with a silent date, so I was pretty excited to have a "do over" with a date that talked, even if it was in a foreign language.

Anya arranged everything. During our brief encounter on the bus, Dima and I had discovered we shared a friend, Anya. The paper had two Anya's, the annoying one and the arts writer who knew Dima. Focused, intense, and opinionated, Anya seldom made an appearance in the office. It was a week after the bus trip before I could corner her and ask if Dima had a girlfriend. He didn't. His last girlfriend had been needy, possessive, and lazy. Anya hadn't liked her.

Anya was not one to keep her opinions to herself. She was strong-willed, abrasive, and judgmental. There were a lot of people she didn't like and who didn't like her. I was not one of them. We didn't know each other that well, but I had a reputation for being independent, adventuresome, and athletic, all traits she admired and shared. She decided I would make a good girlfriend for Dima and was delighted to play matchmaker. She was holding a New Year's Eve party at her apartment. Her invitation to Dima included my phone number and a suggestion that he call. He called the following day.

He spoke in a sweet and patient tone, the same tone I had heard him use on the phone with his mother the day we met. People think of Russian as a harsh language, but it can also be gentle. When Dima spoke to me, he used diminutives and endearments that lent his words an added affection. Unfortunately it didn't help me understand them any better. Worried he would not want to date a woman who couldn't speak Russian fluently, I pretended to understand more than I did. I tried not to think about how we would make a relationship work long term when I couldn't express much more than basic pleasantries. There would be time to figure that out later. At present all I needed to know was where and when we would meet on the day of Anya's party so we could go together.

The metro stop he chose for our rendezvous was not one I usually used. It was near downtown and my apartment but none the less unfamiliar. I arrived a few minutes early and waited outside as Dima had instructed. I was dressed in knee-high black boots, plaid red tights, and a black skirt. On top I wore a wool sweater and my infamous silver jacket. It was a warm ensemble that I was convinced was also sexy. The comments I received on my walk to the metro reassured me of my attractiveness—and of the desperation of men not wanting to spend the holiday alone.

I was pretty pleased with myself. I looked good and had a New Year's date with a guy I liked. The warm and fuzzy feeling lasted about twenty minutes. Then my toes started to go numb. Next my fingers turned white and my legs began to tremble. My mood changed in direct proportion to my drop in body temperature. By the time my teeth were chattering, I had moved beyond frustration to fury. If he was going to stand me up, he could have at least been considerate enough to arrange a meeting spot inside where it was warm.

If I had known then how many times I would end up waiting for him in the cold, I might have walked away. But I didn't. I didn't call him, but I didn't give up either. I decided I would go to Anya's on my own and possibly see him there. I took an escalator down into the metro station. I was headed toward a train when I felt a tug on my coat. Annoyed at the interruption, I whipped around impatiently. Standing in front of me was Dima. His face was a mix of European and Asian that I couldn't resist, flat and round with almond-shaped brown eyes and light hair. His lips had a serious and intense set but at the edges hinted at a smile. He was about my height, with well-formed shoulders and athletic legs. I was furious and indignant that he had kept me waiting so long, but I calmed at the sound of his gentle voice.

"Where were you?" he asked.

"Here," I replied, with less patience and less pleasantness in my own voice. "Where were you?"

"Here as well," he said. "Which exit were you waiting at?"

"Which exit?"

I hadn't realized the station had more than one exit. Dima smiled at my confusion. It was then that I remembered the "extra words" from our earlier phone conversation. When he had mentioned the metro stop, Dima had mentioned a few things I didn't understand and so ignored. I figured the name of the metro stop was all I needed. Unfortunately those "extra words" had been an explanation of the metro stop's various exits, including the one he had suggested we meet at, which of course was not the one I ended up at. Later his mother would say it was fate that led us to each other. I knew better. It had been something far more practical. Dima recognized my silver jacket from across the station. Having not found me at the exit where he had suggested we meet, he had gone down into the station to look for me and noticed my jacket. He would later tell me how much he despised that jacket, the very reason we had been able to find each other that day. I liked his mother's version of events better.

I met her later that night. Having wasted an hour trying to find each other, I figured we would probably head directly to Anya's, but Dima had other plans. It was still early, only six in the evening, so he led me to the office of the wire service where he worked as a freelance photographer. He sat me down in front of the computer and proceeded to show me dozens of photographs. He was like a child seeking my approval, and I found it endearing, if a little strange and rather boring. He was a talented photographer, but there were hundreds of images, many of them series from a single assignment, and I struggled to think of something original to say for each one. I tried to imagine taking him to the *Kyiv Post* and making him read all my stories. I was proud of my work, but subjecting a potential partner to it on our first meeting seemed a bit much. Still I was disappointed that he didn't want to talk about my work, just his own. I had not prepared for an impromptu show of his work, and after uttering *klassno* (cool) and *krasivo* (lovely) half a dozen times, I had exhausted my Russian superlatives.

I thought I had been faking my limited knowledge of Russian pretty well, so it came as a slight surprise when Dima asked if I would rather speak in English. His English wasn't great, but it was an improvement over my Russian, and we were able to communicate slightly better. We seldom spoke in Russian again, and I became embarrassed to practice it around him. An hour later there were still plenty of photos to view. Worried we might miss the dinner at Anya's, I hinted we might want to leave. Dima consented.

But we didn't go directly to Anya's. First we went by his house to celebrate with his parents. I hadn't expected to meet his family on our first date, but there was no way he was getting out of celebrating part of the holiday with his mother and stepfather, and I was now included in this celebration. It was weird but also rather flattering, so I went along with it. Really I had no choice. From the outset it was clear this was Dima's country, and he would be the one to decide what we did and how we behaved. He was a cultured European. I was an artless American.

He lived in an apartment complex in the suburbs. We took a small, slow elevator up at least a dozen floors. His mother, Ludmilla, greeted us at the door, wrapping me in a hug before I got my coat off. She was short and round and rosy with slightly slanted eyes and a voice as soft and sweet as her son's. Ludmilla had been a doctor. She had two children, a daughter in Australia and Dima, her son and baby. She fussed and clucked at both of us, speaking in sweet, soft, and slow Russian that I could easily understand. I never met Dima's father.

Edward was as reserved as his wife was welcoming. He sat silently in the living room, leaving the talking and fussing to his wife. I never got to know Edward well. The main thing that defined him for me was that he had become sick after helping to clean up Chernobyl. He had been an engineer.

There were two bedrooms in the apartment, but that first evening we spent most of our time in the living room. To my dismay I discovered food had been prepared for us. I was still under the impression we would soon be eating a large feast at Anya's and did not want to fill myself up beforehand.

Dima and his mother assured me it was only a snack, a little something to help us welcome in the New Year. Shot glasses were filled and small dried fish and pickled vegetables were placed on the table in front of me. I nibbled on a carrot and avoided my shot glass.

"I don't really drink," I told Dima in English.

He smiled. "I don't either."

We didn't touch our shot glasses then or later that night. Now he jokes about getting drunk, but back then he was always sober. It is strange to think that he avoided alcohol all those years in Ukraine only to take up drinking in America. He has changed a lot since then in ways I never expected. I still don't drink. But I suppose I have changed in other ways.

Dima translated our conversation for his mother, and she used the word "fate" again. Then she filled our glasses with juice and offered a toast. It was still several hours before midnight, so I wasn't sure if toasting the New Year was appropriate. But I was not going to argue or keep Ukrainians from their vodka. Edward was largely silent.

Ludmilla did most of the talking of the sort that did more to fill the silence than advance a conversation. I smiled and sipped and added a few comments when I could. It was the same role I play with English-speaking mothers. They all love me at first. It is only later, when I talk more and they listen less, that they begin to regard me as something other than the perfect partner for their sons. They are probably right. It took Dima's mother longer to figure this out because we were limited by language. When I said goodbye that first night, she hugged me again with warmth. I both appreciated and distrusted her enthusiastic embrace.

It was nearly ten o'clock by the time we got to Anya's apartment. I was worried we had missed dinner. We had almost missed the New Year. I found Jenia and whispered in her ear.

"Did we miss dinner?"

"No. They haven't even started it yet."

"Oh good; I was worried it would all be gone by the time we got here."

I sat down next to her on the couch. Anya and her boyfriend were across the room, talking with Dima. A few other people I didn't know were mingling here and there. I could see into the kitchen, and no one was in there.

More important, there were no smells of food wafting from it. "Wait, you mean they haven't even started cooking dinner yet?"

Jenia's smile was the only answer I needed. I started to regret not having eaten more at Dima's house when I had the chance. Jenia and I decided to relocate into the kitchen and see if others would follow. Soon we were chopping vegetables with several other women. I was hopeful we might have something in our stomachs before the new millennium when Anya came in and announced it was time to go downtown for the celebration. The oven was turned off, the chicken cooking inside left to wait until after we returned. I was starving and in no mood to go outside and get cold again. But there didn't seem to be any other option. I couldn't stay behind with a half-cooked chicken to ring in the New Year solo. So I put on my scarf, hat, gloves, and jacket and followed the rest of the group to the metro stop.

The first train that arrived was so full that I figured we would wait for the next one. Instead I felt a shove from behind as Dima pushed me into the mass of humanity. No one seemed to mind. Most everyone was already drunk and singing and happy to be crammed together in a tightly enclosed space. I wondered if it would have been more enjoyable had I been drunk. At least I didn't have to worry about being cold. I didn't walk off the train so much as feel myself carried off by the people in front of and behind me. We got off downtown at Khreshchatyk and shoved our way through the crowds toward the main celebration. A decorative bridge had been erected across the street for the millennial celebration and a large firework display planned. But the only thing I remember noticing was where Dima was in relation to me. I had schemed with Jenia beforehand to make sure that among the mass of humanity I was near Dima when the clock struck. I wanted to get my New Year's kiss. It was quick and on the cheek. But it was a kiss. I was happy and ready to head home.

Instead we began the long march to the home of every random acquaintance Anya knew. We boarded buses and metros but mostly walked up and down the streets, entering apartment after apartment to down shots and wish the occupants a happy New Year. Most of the time I didn't know the people where we stopped, and neither did much of the rest of our crowd. But that never seemed to matter. Our hosts greeted us like old friends, always insisting we sit down and share a toast and a snack with them. Dima and I both grew tired of turning down the endless shots of vodka. Jenia was just plain tired. Toward the end I am not sure if Anya even knew the occupants whom we called upon. We never stayed in any home long enough to relax and rest, only long enough to nibble and greet and proceed with our task. It was exhausting, and my legs ached from walking in heels. I could tell Jenia and Dima were as tired as I was, but none of us knew how to extract ourselves from Anya's long march.

Finally around two in the morning we headed back to Anya's. Jenia and I crashed on the couch. Dima sat in a chair nearby. I was no longer hungry, just tired. I struggled to keep my eyes open and to maintain the semblance of a conversation with Jenia. Anya seemed to gain energy as the evening progressed. She floated around the apartment like a dancer, modeling some of the dresses she had made by hand. Food was finally cooking in the oven. Two hours later it was still cooking, and Anya was still dancing. I was more in the mood for cereal now than supper and nudged Jenia awake.

"Want to go home?"

"Yes, we can share a cab."

I turned to Dima. "I think Jenia and I are going to go."

"I'll come with you," he said.

It was starting to get light outside, but the snow-covered streets were still quiet and empty. It didn't take long to flag down a driver. Dima got in the front, and Jenia and I snuggled in the back. "Wind of Change" was playing on the radio. A new millennium had begun, but in Kyiv the chorus remained that of the Scorpions' *glasnost* hit. We listened silently to the anthem that commemorated the end of the Cold War: "Where the children of tomorrow share their dreams." I watched the quiet city streets pass by the window.

More than a decade later I heard the song playing in a gym in Yerevan, Armenia. It was the first time I had been back in the former Soviet Union since I had left Ukraine many years before. I still knew the lyrics and hummed along as I exercised. For a minute I felt as if no time had passed and I was back in Kyiv riding in a gypsy cab on New Year's Day. Back then I had thought I understood the meaning of the song. In Yerevan I knew better. I could appreciate the lyrics and be nostalgic for the melody, but I would never understand the children of tomorrow. Dima taught me that.

20 Wet Dreams

Dima had a childlike sweetness about him. He was two years younger than I and in many ways inexperienced. Now I recognize that some of what I perceived as a youthful genuineness may have simply been a result of his broken English. When your vocabulary is limited, it is hard to sound sophisticated. But there was also something else there. He may have helped support his family financially, but he was otherwise dependent on his mother. She cooked for him and packed his suitcase when he traveled. When he did something inappropriate, she would laugh it off as if he were still a child. I laughed with her. I thought it was cute that he liked animated movies—so long as he also played the role of the adult, the protector. And around me that is what he did. I guess I thought that was the role he would always play, not realizing that the reason he could play it so well was because he had his mother taking care of him at home.

I could take care of myself, but in Kyiv it was exhausting. Having someone there who could look out for me was appealing. I understood the reason I could travel the world on my own was because I made friends who became like family and watched out for me. Dima was as eager to please and as playful as a little boy, while still being as protective as a father. I liked that about him.

On our second date we went skiing, with Anya. There was plenty of snow in Kyiv, but I had never heard of any ski resorts. The place Anya took us was not exactly a resort, just a small hill at the bottom of which an entrepreneur had opened a ski rental. The whole place was overrun with new Russians, wealthy mafia types, and others with more money than taste. The women wore bright snowsuits, and the men wore dark jeans. They sped and tumbled down the hill in all directions, at all speeds, using all kinds of creative techniques.

Anya could actually ski. Dima had never been before. I fell somewhere in between, having spent more time skiing cross-country rather than downhill. I did have a vague sense that the usual way up a mountain was in a chairlift. This was not a mountain, and there were no chairlifts, just bars attached to a tow rope. Getting up the hill was the real athletic feat, and most of the women and children let go midway up, their partners continuing on without a backward glance. I held on tight, my hands burning, my palms blistering, my biceps throbbing. At the top I tried to ski down without hitting any Russians, a challenging objective because they tended to travel down the hill at random, following neither the rules of skiing nor, in some cases, the rules of gravity.

After two and a half hours of avoiding human obstacles while maneuvering down a small hill that took less than a minute to descend and about fifteen minutes to ascend, Dima and I were ready to go. We had run out of the tokens needed to use the tow rope and didn't want to pay for either more tokens or more time on our rented skis. Anya had her own skis and it seemed unlimited tokens, so we spent the next hour watching her ski. Finally she took pity on us and agreed to let Dima drive her home. There the New Year's Eve scenario repeated itself. We were trapped at Anya's, waiting for something to happen that never did. We all sat at her kitchen table in a silence punctuated only by Anya's voice. Finally Dima said something about needing to get home, and we politely excused ourselves. Back at my place Dima and I ran out of things to say and started kicking around a soccer ball. We were battling over the ball when I slammed my right foot against the wooden leg of a cabinet.

I crumpled to the floor in pain. Dima got a bag of frozen food from the refrigerator and placed it on my foot. He didn't seem to know what else to do, and I was in too much pain to know what to do with him. We sat like that for an hour or so, and then he started talking about dinner and being tired. I sent him home. I told him I would be fine. I thought I would be. Ice and elevation had worked with most of my other sports injuries. Dima helped me hobble to a seat by the heater so the rest of me would be warm while my foot was numbed by the frozen *pelmeni*. After he left, I hopped to my bed and attempted to sleep.

The *pelmeni* thawed and started to smell. As the numbness wore off, the pain became more noticeable. I was tired but in too much discomfort to sleep. In the States I would have had an ice pack or at least several packs of frozen peas to numb my foot long enough for me to fall asleep. I would have had a bathroom with a medicine cabinet stocked full of ibuprofen and other pain killers and a mother I could call on the phone for sympathy. In Ukraine I had only myself. Being alone and in severe pain in the middle of the night is a disturbing experience. Being in a foreign country makes it even more so. I began to whimper quietly, a habit I found slightly comforting if for no other reason than that it was familiar and produced a human noise, even if only my own. I had no idea what was wrong with my foot, but I was pretty sure whatever it was would require medical assistance. And in Ukraine I had no idea what that meant.

Somehow I made it to morning. I remember watching the clock, waiting impatiently for it to reach what I considered a reasonable hour at which to call Dima. He was still asleep at eight o'clock. His mother told me to call back later. A few hours later he was on the phone, worried and upset. He told me not to go anywhere, as if I could. He would come as soon as he was able. It was late afternoon before he arrived. He must have raced up the stairs because when I opened the door he was out of breath. "Katiusha, Katiushinka, I'm so sorry. Edward needed the car and then my mother needed . . ."

I let him rattle on, my only response my silence. It would become a familiar scene: his gushing apologies and my silent disappointment. At the time I half believed his excuses. I knew he had a lot to take care of and wasn't angry with him for keeping me waiting. I wasn't exactly pleased either. But I was happy that he was finally there and taking me to a doctor. He helped me hobble down the stairs to the car and then sped around town trying to find a clinic that wasn't closed for the holidays. New Year's had passed, but there was still Orthodox New Year's. I was starting to get the feeling that you are pretty much out of luck if you get sick or injured in December or January in Ukraine. The place that finally took us was on the third floor of a high-rise that lacked an elevator. I held onto the stair rail and started hopping. When I stopped for a break on the first-floor landing, I asked Dima how people in wheelchairs got to the clinic. "They don't," Dima replied.

The thud made by my good foot as I hopped up the stairs echoed through the building. There didn't seem to be anyone around. The waiting room was silent and cold. I was about to ask Dima if we were in the right place when a doctor appeared and motioned for me to follow him down the hall. I got up and started hopping. The doctor kept walking, not once glancing back to see if I needed help. Actually he did look back once, with impatience. At the end of the hall he turned right into what appeared to be an X-ray room. The machine was massive and ancient looking. The doctor manhandled my foot into the position he wanted and then went to flip the switch. No question about whether I was pregnant, no big comforting metal apron to shield me from excess radiation, just a bully of a doctor and a very imposing-looking machine. I worried about the radiation for a minute. Then I remembered I had been to Chernobyl.

There was no wheelchair or crutches to help me back down the hall to what served as an office. Dima was invited in to help translate. The doctor found a piece of paper with a diagram of a foot on it and pointed to a bone toward the top of the foot. He spoke for several minutes. Dima translated a single sentence. I had broken a bone in my foot. I never did find out exactly which one. The doctor kept talking. Dima offered a second sentence: I needed a cast. I was too exhausted from pain and hobbling to protest. The doctor directed us to another room to have the cast applied. The room was small and already filled. We stood outside looking in as a shirtless man lay face down on an examining table while two older women pulled at his arm. When one of the women spotted us, she motioned for Dima to come in. Not me, Dima. I watched in growing apprehension as Dima, a photographer with no medical training, was instructed to pull and prod the man's arm back into place while the women pushed on the man's back. There were a few pops and several screams, and then the man was sent on his way and I was welcomed onto the table.

My date had just pulled a man's arm back into place with nothing more than brute force, and now the women who had recruited him were ready to work on me! I was no longer convinced going to a medical clinic had been the right solution to my problem. Had I been able to run, I probably would have. Instead I let Dima help me onto the table. I was slightly comforted when the doctor came by to offer instructions. But it was not at all clear the women were listening. I don't believe they had medical training, but they seemed to think they were the ones in charge, not the doctor. They barked at me in rapid-fire Russian. "They want you to take off your pants," Dima translated.

I pushed up the right leg on my overalls instead. "I wore these baggy pants so they'll fit over the cast," I explained.

Dima didn't translate. He knew better than to argue with babushkas. I was pretty sure I was not going to win this one. If I had known Dima better, it might have been different. But we had only been on two dates. We hadn't even really kissed. Now I was being asked to strip down to my underwear in front of him. I avoided his eyes as I pulled off my overalls. I tugged my shirt as low as I could get it to go. My legs were pale and covered in goose bumps. I was grateful Dima kept his gaze focused on my injured foot.

I had suffered many sports injuries over the years. I had pulled, twisted, dislocated, and gouged various body parts, but until then I had never broken a bone. Casts were new to me, and I had no idea how they were applied. Watching the babushkas work on my foot, I wasn't convinced they did either. I lost further confidence in their expertise when they once again recruited Dima to help. The process reminded me more of a grade school art project than state-of-the art medical care. The women did not position my foot before they began. They simply dipped pieces of cloth in wet plaster and wrapped them randomly around my foot. When a piece of cloth failed to stick, they handed it to Dima, who wet it again and then handed it back. "How high is it going to go?" "Do I need to hold my foot a certain way?" "Does it have to be quite so wet?"

Dima answered all my questions in the same way: "Wait." I waited. I waited while the dampness from the cloth strips seeped into my skin and made me shiver. I waited while the strips were placed further and further up my foot. I waited for someone to dry my cast. When it became clear that wasn't going to happen, I started with the questions again: "Aren't they going to dry it?" "How am I supposed to walk out without pants?" "How am I supposed to walk?"

Dima ignored my questions. He was too busy thanking my captors, first the babushkas and then the doctor. I wasn't exactly pleased with their performance, but Dima understood the system better than I did. He paid them. Health care was free, but to ensure good service you paid. I didn't understand what Dima was doing at the time, but I would get more than enough practice in the months and years that followed.

The cast reached a quarter of the way up my right calf and covered my entire foot except my toes. I wasn't sure how I was supposed to walk out of the doctor's office without wearing any pants. I attempted to put my overalls on but I was having trouble getting them over my cast, and the babushkas were proving impatient to see me go. Dima grabbed my overalls and swung me off the table.

"Aren't they going to give me crutches?"

"Crutches?"

"You know, the things you use to help you walk when you're injured."

"They don't have those here."

"Do they have wheelchairs?"

"Katiusha, why would they have wheelchairs?"

I wasn't sure how to answer. A far more reasonable question in my mind was, "Why wouldn't they have crutches and wheelchairs?" I didn't ask it though. I was focused on trying to maintain a smidgen of dignity as I hopped bare-legged out of the place. Dima volunteered to walk behind me so no one would see my butt. I wasn't sure which was worse, having my butt watched by a guy I was trying to impress or by total strangers. I opted for the latter, telling Dima I needed to lean on his shoulder. When we reached the bottom of the stairs, Dima whisked me into his arms and carried me to the car. We were about the same height, but I was thin and he lifted me without much trouble. It was kind of nice being carried and might have even been romantic had my foot not been encased in wet plaster. Inside the car I draped my overalls over my exposed thighs, trying to pretend Dima hadn't already seen even more.

"How long do I have to have the cast on?" I asked.

"They want us to come back in a few weeks."

"And then they'll take it off?"

"They just said to come back in a few weeks."

"What am I supposed to do until then?"

"Rest."

I decided to hold off on revisiting the crutches issue. When we reached my apartment complex, I was so tired I let Dima carry me part way up. Once inside Dima settled me by the living room heater. My foot was damp and clammy, and my whole body was shaking with cold. He had bought me some pain pills earlier, and I took a few.

"It's so cold," I whined. "Can you please dry it?"

"Put it on the heater," Dima advised.

"I am, but it is still so cold."

Dima smiled: "I have an idea."

He disappeared into my bedroom and returned a minute later with a hair dryer, which he spent the next hour using on my cast. It worked on some of the outer layers, but the layers next to my skin were still frigid. I stopped worrying about how I was going to get around for the next few weeks and started worrying about whether I would catch pneumonia. With my foot encased in layers of damp cold it was nearly impossible to get warm.

In the morning my cast was still wet. I stayed in bed, too cold and tired to do anything. I was still there later that morning when Dima showed up to check on me. I asked about crutches. He promised to enquire. He returned again around dinnertime with bread and cheese. I had managed to get dressed by then, and we ate together at the table. Afterward I hopped to the door to say goodbye. Dima leaned in close and kissed me on the lips for the first time. I held onto the door for balance as I kissed him back, trying my best not to fall over. The kiss was awkward and brief, made even more so by the fact that I was balancing on one foot. If Dima's mom could see fate in our first meeting, I saw an imbalance in that first kiss, each of us relying on roles neither of us could maintain.

21 Home Remedies

The crutches were still MIA. It was three days before they made an appearance. By then my cast was just about dry, and I was just about to develop bronchitis. Dima was frustrated by my impatience. If I was injured, I should just stay home and get better. But I wanted to go back to work. I wanted to leave my apartment. I wanted to be able to move without having to jump on one foot. I wanted a pair of crutches.

The pair Dima finally secured belonged to an elderly aunt who was related in some way to someone in his family, possibly Edward. She must have been about a foot shorter than me. Even when the crutches were extended to their full height, I had to hunch over to use them. I was hesitant to voice any complaint, though, lest they be taken away, forcing me to wait yet another three days for a replacement. Apparently crutches were not an easy item to find in Kyiv. Even for the son of a doctor. Pharmacies, hospitals, and clinics didn't seem to have any.

The next challenge was finding something to wear. I had spent a lot of time in my pajamas over the last few days. They were warm and fit over my cast. Now I needed an outfit I could wear out on the street and at the office. I had a pair of pants and a pair of jeans that fit over my cast. The jeans just barely made it and required a good deal of careful tugging and patient maneuvering. No socks or shoes were large enough to cover my bandaged foot, leaving my toes exposed to the elements. Gloves were hard to wear while I was trying to grip crutches and scarves tended to become unraveled and tangled. I wore the jeans that first day and most of the days that followed.

It took me a good ten minutes to make my way down my apartment complex's stairwell. The stone steps were worn in the center and slippery. The lighting was dim. I rested on each landing. At the bottom I stared at the door, wishing someone would magically appear and hold it open for me. No one came. I held it open with my shoulder as I hooked my crutches over the ridge at the bottom of the doorway.

The cold air hit me at once. It had been several days since I had been outside, and I had forgotten how frigid it was. Fresh snow was piled on the side of the road, and the sidewalks were icy. My right toes tingled and my fingers stung. I had slung my work bag over my shoulder and across my chest, but it kept slipping down my arm as I hobbled along. Both the bus and metro stops were a downhill walk from my apartment. I proceeded slowly, careful not to slip on icy patches. Children pointed. Adults stared. The ten-minute route took me thirty minutes. The metro meant going down stairs, so I stuck with the tram. No one helped me when it was time to board. They jostled and pushed to get on, impatient with the efforts I made to ensure my crutches didn't give out on the two small steps I had to climb to board. An older man bumped my foot and a piercing pain shot up my leg. "Ow!"

I said it loudly, hoping my discomfort would be noted and other passengers would give me a wider berth. It garnered more stares but no obvious sympathy. The woman next to me asked in a rather accusing tone why I hadn't simply stayed home. It would have been easier, she said. I got the impression she wasn't talking about my convenience so much as her own. It would have been easier for her and her fellow passengers if they hadn't had to wait for me to board. "But what would I do at home for three weeks?" I asked.

She shrugged. What I did or didn't do at home didn't affect her. It was when I tried to go out that I inconvenienced her. That I enjoyed coming to work and was useful to my employer did not seem to have crossed her mind.

It was easier at the office. The American staff understood my need to work and helped fetch me water when I needed it. Sveta was happy to see me back. She was a good friend, but she was also completely dependent on me. If something happened to me, her job was in jeopardy and thus so was her reason for being in Kyiv. Maybe that is why she worried about me so much.

"I just know you are going to slip in the shower and hit your head and die, and no one will find you because you live alone," she told me.

"Thanks, Sveta."

"I'm serious; the tub is so hard and it is so easy to slip, and no one is there with you," she said. "I've heard of that happening to people. I just know it's going to happen to you."

"It's not going to happen to me, Sveta."

"It is. You should take baths instead. You could still slip, but it isn't as likely."

She freaked me out enough that I took baths, hanging my foot outside the tub as I washed. Even after I recovered, I continued to take baths when I could, forever scared by Sveta's fear that I would slip in the shower and die.

Dima promised to take me grocery shopping but he was busy, and I quickly realized I might starve if I waited for him. So I ventured by a few nearby shops on my way home, draping the shopping bags over my crutch handles. It was a miserable uphill effort getting home, the bags bumping into me, my work bag slipping off my shoulder, and my crutches slipping on the worn and icy spots of the sidewalk. At work there was an elevator, but at my apartment I had to climb six flights of stairs.

Two weeks passed. My foot no longer hurt, so I was hopeful I would be able to get the cast off soon. Dima took me back to the clinic. I waited expectantly as the doctor cut through the layers of plaster. Once my foot was exposed, he pressed down on the top of it. I yelped in pain. He shook his head.

"It needs more time to heal," he said in Russian.

"How much time?" I asked in Russian.

He ignored me and addressed Dima. He said we could come back in three weeks. Then he shooed us out of the office, pushing us toward the babushkas' torture chamber. I am not sure if my tears were the result of my fear of the old women or my unhappiness at being told I would be spending another three weeks on crutches. I cheered up when the babushkas seemed to take an interest in my athletic endeavors. Instead of just slapping on the wet plaster without so much as a hello, they asked if I liked to play sports. Dima translated their questions and (from what I later gathered) added some of his own insights as well.

"They asked if you like to run," he said.

"Yes, very much," I said.

There was more back and forth between Dima and the babushkas. I tried to understand what they were saying, but they were speaking too fast.

"They want to know if you do any other sports."

"I rollerblade, I play soccer, I like basketball, but I haven't played that much in Ukraine. I like to ice skate."

I would have continued but Dima cut me off: "Okay."

There was more back and forth. Dima did most of the talking, the babushkas nodding in unison like matching bobble heads. I smiled for the first time since the doctor had declared my foot unhealed. I was proud of my athletic background and was under the impression the babushkas and Dima realized how important it was for me to stay active. I thought all their questions meant they were trying to figure out a way to make a cast that would allow me to be more athletic or even to skip the cast altogether. My euphoria lasted until they started wetting the strips. The cast was going back on. Their questions now seemed a cruel taunt.

"Why did they ask me all those questions if they were just going to put the cast back on?" I asked Dima.

"So they would know how high to make it," Dima replied.

I realized too late that he was on their side, not mine. He had encouraged them to ask about my activity level. I thought this meant they would make accommodations for me as had sometimes been done in the States, where I was given air casts for strained tendons so I could still swim and bike. Instead they viewed my athleticism as an annoyance they would have to work around and conspired to find ways to keep me immobile. I watched in desperation as the papier-mâché creation crept ever closer to my knee. A trip to the clinic that had begun with so much hope ended with me in tears and with a cast that reached the middle of my calf instead of the bottom.

At work the next day I turned to Sveta for help. Sveta suffered from Soviet-era skepticism; she trusted no official or expert. She was not convinced my bone was broken or that I was in need of a cast. She knew a local doctor who worked at the pricey American clinic I couldn't afford and convinced him to see us that day. Dr. Kriel couldn't do much for me without taking off the cast, and I figured I probably shouldn't do that, but he managed to procure a pair of crutches that I could use without completely hunching over. I paid him for the loan of the crutches but not for the visit. He promised not to charge me if I came back in three weeks to have the cast removed. He had a machine that cut casts and said it wouldn't be a problem to remove it.

Sveta didn't have quite that much patience. She decided to play doctor a week or so later while we were on the road reporting a story about drug-resistant tuberculosis in jails. The trip had begun like most of our trips, on an overnight train. No matter how near or far, almost any city or town in the country could be reached by overnight train. You would go to sleep on a bunk and wake up at your destination. In order to make every trip last long enough for passengers to get about eight hours of sleep, this sometimes meant the train was idle for long segments of the night. It was always strange when I woke up and realized I was on a train that wasn't moving. But it saved on having to pay for a hotel or waste valuable daytime working hours traveling. Of course it also necessitated making new friends. We rode second class, which meant we slept in a tiny carriage with a window, a small table, and four plank beds, two on top and two on bottom.

The other two beds were always occupied. How much rest we got depended on who was on board with us. Our companions were usually male, and we did our best to ignore them, spending the hours before bed in the narrow hallway outside our room and those at night tucked silently in our bunks. But too often our companions were friendly businessmen who insisted on sharing their dinner and drinks, no matter how politely we declined. Then there was the fat American who was overjoyed to be able to speak to another American. He had come to Ukraine to marry and was traveling with his wife. We spent the night worrying he would break his plank bed and flatten his new bride. On one trip we were able to get a man moved from our cabin after he became so drunk that he couldn't walk or talk, but on other trips we had to endure plenty of tipsy middle-aged men eager to entertain young women.

That was when we could ride in style. Later, when I was trying to save money or second class just wasn't available, I rode third class. Instead of having to endure two or (if Sveta wasn't with me) three strangers, I was subjected to a long open compartment filled with dozens of men, women, and children I did not know and in most cases did not want to know. You slept with your clothes on and your bag tucked under your head so no one could take it. Someone was always eating some pickled concoction that left the most foul smell in the air, someone else was always drunk or on the way there, and several people were usually arguing loudly. Sleeping on the top bunk by an open window was about the only thing that made it bearable. In the heat of summer I was lucky enough to have such a berth and opened the window wide. The young woman sleeping across from me promptly closed it. I opened it. She closed it. I opened it. She yelled something in Russian about how her boyfriend, who had the bunk below mine, had a cold and the fresh air would make him very sick. It was close to ninety degrees, and the air inside the train was stifling and still. I was nauseous from the heat and the smells of my fellow traveling companions and their assorted culinary items. I told her I would puke if the window was closed. She closed it anyway. I opened it again—not all the way but enough for my fingers to fit in. I kept them there the entire night, assurance against the girlfriend's blocking my sole access to fresh air. She cursed me but didn't dare slam my fingers in the window.

On the tuberculosis trip we rode second class, and I don't remember having any memorable traveling companions. When we arrived, we headed straight to the prison. The doctor in charge explained the situation. He admitted that drug-resistant tuberculosis was spreading rapidly in Ukrainian prisons, including the one where he worked. There wasn't enough money for the proper drugs to treat tuberculosis and drug-resistant tuberculosis. There was little awareness about the dangers of not completing the full regimen of drug treatment and little follow-through to ensure that patients did so. After he filled us in, I asked to speak to a few of the sick prisoners. He agreed to let me, but Sveta refused to translate. I understood. She had parents who depended on her. She couldn't risk getting sick. But I felt I needed the patients for the story. I went on my own. We met in a small visiting room. They were seated behind a table, white surgeon's masks covering their mouths. I remained standing.

"Hello," I began in Russian. They smiled and greeted me in unison. I turned to the man seated directly in front of me and asked his name. After he answered, I asked his age. I asked his occupation and where he was from. I didn't know how to ask what crime he had committed. I knew most of the words but not the main one I needed: crime. I stumbled through several attempts at the question, none of which he could understand. I decided to move on but realized every other question I wanted to ask contained at least one word or phrase I had no idea how to say in Russian. I asked the other two patients their names, ages, occupations, and hometowns. Then I thanked them and left. I hadn't obtained much aside from exposure to drug-resistant tuberculosis. Frustrated we had come all this way and might not have a story, I asked to meet with the prison director. He wasn't much interested in talking about the prisoners' health, but he was eager to show us the hand-made boxes and fake money they made. The boxes were beautifully crafted traditional wood pieces with intricate carvings. They went for anywhere from five to thirty dollars, depending on their size and design. I hadn't come to the prison to shop but realized that was exactly what the director was hoping I would do. He ran his hand over the smooth lid of one of the boxes.

"The prisoners made this," he explained in Russian. He smiled, coughed, and smiled again. "And they made these too," he said, placing a handful of fake bills on the table in front of me.

The $100 bills had writing in both English and Russian. On the back were the words "In cool we trust" and on the front the word *dengi*, Russian for "money." A hooded rapper type flashing a street sign had replaced Benjamin Franklin.

"What do you do with the money?" I asked.

"It is just for fun," he said.

He coughed again, smiled, pulled out a handkerchief, and coughed into it. "Don't worry; I am not sick." Sveta and I exchanged looks and sat further back in our seats. "You must take some back to Kyiv," he said, pushing small boxes and fake money toward us.

He coughed again. We thanked him and declined. He insisted. We tried to explain journalism ethics. The boxes he gave us were of the smallest, cheapest variety, and the money he handed us had replaced the word

"God" with "cool." Accepting it wasn't going to change the way I wrote the story. It wasn't going to change anything; it was just going to get us out of his office and away from his hacking cough. We took the boxes and money and headed back to our hotel.

To save money we always shared a room. A spot on my right calf had been itching all day. I took out a pencil and tried to poke it down between my skin and the cast.

"I don't know why my cast needs to be so high," I complained.

"I don't either," said Sveta.

I had been able to jam the pencil down an inch or two, but I could not move it in a way that would relieve the itch.

"How do they expect me to scratch an itch with this thing?"

"They don't know anything," Sveta scoffed. "Why don't we just make it shorter?"

"Yeah, right; how would we do that?"

Sveta held up a pair of scissors. I am pretty sure she had packed them for this exact reason. There were no televisions in the hotels where we stayed. Cutting up my cast was probably the best entertainment option she could think of for the trip. I wanted it off, but I wasn't sure letting Sveta cut my cast lower was the smartest move.

"Do you think we should do that?" I said. "I mean they probably made it higher for a reason, right?"

"You think those babushkas knew what they were doing?" Sveta asked. She waved the scissors.

"Come on; we'll just make it a little shorter. It's your foot that's broken; why does the cast have to go up almost to your knee?"

She had a point. And a pair of scissors. I let her cut. It was slow going and crude work. If we hadn't been stuck in a hotel in a tiny town in winter, we probably would have given up. But as it stood, we had nothing better to do. So Sveta carved away, sawing off small pieces of plaster one at a time. After three hours she had hacked off maybe an inch or two until the cast was about the same height as the first cast the babushkas had given me. My leg still itched. And now the cast's jagged upper edges cut into my skin, causing me even more discomfort.

I had it removed a few weeks later. Dr. Kriel used his cool machine, which sliced it down the side in a matter of minutes. Dima didn't approve. I had gone against the doctor he had chosen. Sveta and Dima often disagreed, like parents with differing opinions of how to care for their American charge. Dima was a bit of a snob and looked down on Sveta for being from the provinces. Her parents were factory workers; his were scientists and doctors. Sveta was practical; Dima was status-obsessed. They weren't that different in age, but the collapse of the Soviet Union had hit them at different phases in their lives and forever separated them into two different generations. Sveta had already been working; Dima had still been a student. He looked forward; she was always looking back. They were my closest friends, and I became far too dependent on both of them far too quickly. After I broke my foot on our second date, I became Dima's responsibility, and he took my care very seriously. It was a burden; he was only twenty-two, but it was also a sign of manhood and maturity in Ukraine. I didn't make the task easy.

Not long after my cast was removed, I found out that the prison director had been fired. He had been profiting from the prisoners, selling the boxes to increase his own income. I also found out he had tuberculosis.

22 Paddington Bear Gets in a Brawl

While I was falling in love, Ukraine was falling apart. After breaking for the winter holidays, the anti-Kuchma folks resumed their campaign in late January. Their original protests had been sporadic and easy to ignore. Most people figured their disappearance over the holiday season meant they had given up. Instead the opposite proved true. After the break their numbers were greater, and so was their resolve.

Not that they were a very coherent bunch. They were a loose group of centrists, socialists, nationalists, and several dozen other political affiliations—plus some students and generally discontented citizens. They had in common only a dislike of their leader sparked by the Gongadze case. By this time Gongadze's widow had identified the body and the jewelry found with it as belonging to her husband. The authentication of the tapes was still in question, but sentiment leaned toward their validity. Theories and rumors were rampant, but solid concrete information was difficult to obtain. It looked increasingly as if the government had planned it that way, decapitating the body and dousing it with dioxin to further hinder identification.

The protesters vowed to make Kuchma step down. Their original "headquarters" was a makeshift camp on Freedom Square in downtown Kyiv. From there they relocated to a nearby stretch of sidewalk on the main drag of Khreschatyk. They pitched more than fifty tents just steps away from various governmental ministries. From the windows of the street's trendy shops and restaurants you could see the yellow and blue Ukrainian flags with which they decorated their camp.

Tent city became a popular hangout for citizens of all ages and backgrounds. Those who could not join the protest supported the movement in other ways. Women stopped by to deliver jars of raspberry jam, and pensioners handed out cups of tea. Employees from the nearby McDonald's donated burgers, and local university students served soup to the protesters three times a day.

People stopped to chat with them on their way to work in the morning and on their way home from the bars in the evening. I found myself making weekly detours to the camp. I would check in with the student leaders, fishing for news and feature story ideas. Most of the students were a smart, driven, and rather privileged bunch. They spoke excellent English and were around the same age as I was, making it easy for me to mine them for information.

I admired their passion and purpose and was slightly jealous of the role they might end up playing in history. They were determined to change their future and that of their country. They were people of action. By definition my role was passive. I was there to document activity, not be a part of it. I was a journalist and an outsider, roles I both loved and suddenly slightly resented. I knew I couldn't allow myself to become involved, but my emotions sometimes got the best of me. I was able to keep them in check partly because I still had trouble believing anything would actually happen. It seemed unlikely that a few idealistic youth and opposition leaders would be able to triumph over the deep-seated fear and apathy that gripped the rest of the country. In Kyiv there was electricity and warmth. Outside the capital there was darkness and despair. The Kyiv protesters demanded the government pay attention to them. The rest of the country wanted to be left alone. Corruption and cronyism had taught people to find their own solutions. They didn't trust that anything would ever change.

I understood their apprehension and had my own doubts about the level of engagement of the political leaders who had helped organize the protests. They lent their names and titles to the movement, funded the protest newspapers, and supplied the tents. That last part was the most important. The tents themselves belonged to parliament deputies whose property it was illegal for the government to remove. But I was pretty sure none of them slept in their tents in February, when the temperatures reached as low as minus twenty degrees Fahrenheit. To find out, I decided to spend a night in tent city.

The official reason I brought Sveta along was to translate for me. The real reason was that I didn't want to go alone. On my own it was intimidating. With Sveta it was an adventure. Sveta was no longer the timid provincial music teacher Sabra had introduced me to. The spunk that had always been there had bubbled to the surface. Sveta was the one who decided we should take kickboxing lessons—not girly kickboxing workouts but real lessons in a boxing gym where female students had not practiced before our appearance. She flirted with our married teacher. Sveta was becoming almost as much of a risk taker as I was. In a way she didn't have a choice. She had already lost almost everything she cared about: her career, her future, her dream of how her life would be. But she was too young to give up. So she kept living the only way she knew how, laughing as she went along.

Our great escapade began at my place on a frigid Friday afternoon in February. We had agreed to rendezvous there in order to pile on layers of warm clothes and pack supplies before walking to tent city together. I lay on my bed trying to pull a pair of jeans over two layers of tights and a pair of long underwear.

"Damn it, I can't zip them," I said.

Sveta wasn't concerned: "No one will notice. You'll never even take your coat off."

I sat up and looked at her. She had just pulled a hat over her recently shorn hair. With her layers of sweaters and tights, pixie haircut, and impish grin she looked like a street urchin. I didn't have to glance in the mirror to know I looked the same. In a city filled with willowy women wearing clingy clothing, we had transformed ourselves into sexless bundles. I made one more attempt to zip my jeans, then gave up and got off the bed. I hefted my backpack, in which we had packed extra tights and socks and some water bottles, and Sveta tucked a sleeping bag and pillow under her arms. If we got a chance to sleep, we figured we would take turns.

Outside I tried to hide behind my scarf, embarrassed that I might be mistaken for a beggar. But there were no snickers or stares. There was no response at all. We had become invisible, members of the faceless masses generations of Ukrainians had been conditioned to ignore. I was relieved and disappointed at the same time.

When we arrived at tent city, we stashed our sleeping bag in the first tent we found. The unemployed young socialist occupying the tent seemed a trustworthy sort. She kept her suitcase and purse nearby and talked about love. We excused ourselves as quickly as we could and went off in search of more noteworthy residents, like the Orthodox priest. With his beard and black robes, Volodymyr was easy to spot. He told us he had been excommunicated two days before. It was a symbolic gesture. His church had been closed since June, when armed police had interrupted his sermon to shut the place down. He spent six days walking to Kyiv with his six-year-old son, Vova. By the time we met him, he had been living in tent city for three weeks and had already married several couples. He wasn't the gentle religious soul I had expected but a brutish and cross man. Vova was a cute little guy in a floppy fur hat who had an annoying habit of calling people Communists and demanding money. He was like an evil Paddington Bear with red boots and a club.

The camp commander was more civilized and sympathetic. Yevhen was twenty-three, a law student, and the assistant to a socialist party deputy. He gave us a tour of the roped-off enclosure and its various amenities. I struggled to take notes with fingers gone numb from the cold. There was the canteen tent, a megaphone for announcements, and a collection box for donations. The central tents were occupied by Yevhen and about thirty or so core members of the organization who lived there full time. The rest of the residents came and went. Some stayed a day, some a week, some a month. Yevhen estimated that about five hundred people had cycled through at one point or another.

When I asked Yevhen if I could talk to his deputy, he pulled out a cell phone. An hour later a man in a long dark coat and leather gloves escorted Sveta and me to a car. The deputy was waiting inside. I dragged the interview out as long as possible, placing my hands over the heater vents whenever I wasn't using them to write. For a few minutes my teeth stopped chattering.

Back outside the air felt even colder as it crept toward evening, burning our chapped skin and hitting our lungs like punches. My toes were numb under my layers of socks, and I shivered as I asked questions. There were fewer people in tent city now. It turned out many of the students and ordinary people, most of them unemployed, went indoors during the night. Several of the political leaders had rented an apartment for the protesters to crash in, and others had friends or relatives they could stay with. The local ones simply went home. The few who stuck around lined up outside the canteen tent, where bowls of a thin potato soup were handed out. It didn't look appetizing, but I felt I needed to taste it for the full effect. It was also something warm to hold.

The soup was as bland as it looked—a weak concoction of hot water and tasteless potatoes. But it was hot, and for a few minutes afterward my midsection was briefly warm. It was during that time that I mustered the courage to explore the camp further. Sveta and I spent another hour walking around, observing and interviewing. When my fingers had become too cold to remove them from my pockets and our brains were too drained from the effort of keeping warm to formulate questions, we ran across the street into a friend's basement pub.

We warmed ourselves over bowls of mushroom soup and cups of tea while entertaining our less adventuresome peers with stories about the potato soup and rabble-rousing priest. I attempted to put on another pair of tights in the bathroom, but my fingers were still too cold to be of any use, and I gave up in frustration. Before we left, a few of our colleagues promised to stop by tent city later to check on us. It was a Friday night and most of them had been drinking for several hours. Diana left early, sober.

"Maybe she's pregnant," someone mused.

"That would explain those baggy overalls she's been wearing," someone else added.

"And not drinking," the first continued. "She didn't drink at all tonight, and she hasn't been drinking for several months now."

I didn't venture an opinion. Diana didn't look as if she had put on much weight. And because I never drank, I hadn't noticed that she had recently cut back. The only person I was really thinking about was Dima. Our romance was a hurried one, snatched moments together amid the chaos of a crumbling country. We were a couple after our second date, both of us assuming we were together without ever really discussing what that meant or what we wanted out of it. He saw beauty in images and spoke about his work with passion, excitement, and pride. We shared that. I thought that meant we shared more.

Dima was unlike the other Eastern European men I had met and dated. He had female friends. He was playful and sensitive. He smiled and wore colors other than black. All of this made him more trustworthy in my eyes— and more attractive. I liked his tender qualities. But I also liked that he could protect me. That evening he sent several texts. His broken English making them all the more sweet and childlike. He was worried about me. I told him everything was okay.

But back outside things were getting sketchy. At midnight the street lights shut off, and the only residents who hadn't gone indoors were the guards. Sveta and I kept walking around the tents, fearful of stopping and attracting too much attention. When I spotted a guard who looked more sober and friendly than the rest, we approached him.

"Can we talk to you for a minute?" Sveta asked in Russian.

"How much will you pay me?"

"Nothing," Sveta and I replied in unison.

He laughed and looked us slowly up and down. Then he spit on the sidewalk in front of us and walked away. That was one of the more polite responses we received. The guards were different from the rest of the protesters. They belonged to an extreme right-wing group from Western Ukraine known as UNA-UNSO. They wore army fatigues and boots and hid their faces behind black bandanas. They marched twice a day in front of the tents, wore red armbands, and carried clubs. Most didn't look much older than teenagers, but aside from pimples and peach fuzz there wasn't much innocent about them. They were crude and bigoted, and I had no doubt that if given a chance, they would gang up on us.

We made a point of checking in with our young socialist camp commander every fifteen minutes. I wondered if he could control them but tried not to imagine what would happen if he couldn't. Luckily they were preparing for the next day's protest and didn't have time to harass us more than in passing.

At three in the morning I decided we should decamp to my apartment for an hour or two of rest. With all the UNA-UNSO drunks walking around, sleeping in tent city was out of the question. We slept at my place, too tired to remove our boots or jackets. As it was beginning to get light, we returned to our adopted home, refreshed by a few hours of sleep and warmth. Our priest was on the megaphone commanding the troops. Porridge was being ladled in the canteen tent. In the light of day we felt safer. The students were back, and the UNA-UNSO militia had been transformed from shadowy thugs to marching boys. Sveta and I were interviewing a young woman in her tent when a familiar face popped through the opening.

"I brought you guys some hot chocolate," Diana said, holding a thermos toward us.

"Oh my God, thank you," I said.

Diana entered the tent and sat down. "How was it?" she asked. I waited until I had a cup of hot chocolate in my hands and had taken the first warm sugary sip.

"Very cold," I said. "The porridge wasn't half bad."

"I can't wait to read the story you write," she said.

She stayed a few minutes longer. In the warmth of the tent, over mugs of hot chocolate, during the first stages of a revolution, she told us she was pregnant. She wanted us to know before the rumors got out of control. We congratulated her. And she congratulated us for surviving the night. I was relieved that she left before the protest march, suddenly concerned about a woman who for the first time since we had met had been truly kind to me. I didn't want anything to happen to her or her baby.

23 Atonement

Kuchma's "trial" was held on February 25, a traditional religious day of reckoning on which people atone for their sins. No one expected Kuchma to absolve himself of anything. The version of him on "trial" was a cardboard cutout, the trial a mock-up of a real event that would probably never happen. It was all part of the larger protest movement, a planned action held the day after the night we spent in tent city.

The protesters used a megaphone and marched up and down Khreschatyk, parading the cardboard Kuchma around in a handmade wooden jail cell. The government organized concerts on the sidewalk adjacent to the street the protesters marched down, the music competing with the megaphone. The crowds listened to the concerts for a while and then walked with the protesters, disconnected from both causes but happy to take part in free entertainment of any kind.

Early in the day I watched UNA-UNSO militia strap on fresh red armbands and cover their faces with black bandanas. The bandanas were decorated with the Russian word for truth surrounded by barbed wire. (Later I tied one around one of my stuffed animal toys). The wooden clubs the protesters passed out were less endearing. The socialists explained that the clubs were a precaution against the amnestied prisoners it was rumored the government planned to unleash on them. I don't think the socialists believed that any more than I did, but I didn't press the issue. If UNA-UNSO types wanted to walk around with clubs, they got to walk around with clubs. It was understood that without UNA-UNSO's muscle the more peaceful elements of the movement would be crushed. It was only because there were hundreds of young men walking around with bandanas over their faces and clubs in their hands that the student protesters could peacefully strum their guitars and sing songs of hope.

Thousands showed up for the demonstration, although some among that number may have actually come for the government concerts. It was hard to tell. It all ended peacefully enough. Opposition politicians called it a success. UNA-UNSO complained that it lacked action. I was happy it was over and I could finally go to bed.

But that was just the beginning. A week later the protesters had fragmented and multiplied, and little actions were taking place all over the city. At work we followed rumors from one neighborhood to another, waiting to see where people would gather next. We would show up outside a government building looking for a disturbance and find only journalists in attendance. We would whip out our cell phones, calling editors and sources, looking for advice on what part of the city might erupt next. I would often run into Dima at the protests, and we would update each other on where the action was occurring. It wasn't the place to talk about anything else.

His past came to me in pieces. As I mentioned, his mother had been a doctor and had been relatively well compensated and well regarded during Soviet times. I don't know what his father did or when or why he left. I believe he was also a doctor of some status but am not sure. Dima and I shared that: the missing father. We didn't talk about it, but it was always there between us.

There were other losses. Dima had grown up privileged; his family had been members of the elite. They could listen to banned music and had enough money for Dima to buy everyone in his class ice cream on special occasions. They were sophisticated and cultured in a "classless society" where class was everything. That was until the system that had supported them abandoned them. The demise of the Soviet Union had been hard on his family. His stepfather had been a high-ranking television communications engineer. Now he stayed at home with Dima's mother. They were relics of the past, uncertain how to negotiate the new world. Dima's older sister had married an Australian and moved away.

Dima was left in charge, a child in some ways and an adult in others. He helped support the family financially, but when we took a trip, his mother packed his bag. She cooked for him, cleaned for him, and did his laundry. Later she would do mine as well. In dating Dima I had found a family to care for me while I was far from my own. They were a stable force in an unstable country.

Over time the protesters and their causes began to blur. A young woman who had previously spoken out against the atrocities being committed in Chechnya started hanging out with UNA-UNSO and garnering more press coverage than she had ever had before. On one occasion she tied herself to a railway track. I was there and so were many other reporters. I don't remember what she was demanding, but I remember there were red roses on the track beside her. We watched for an hour or so until someone untied her and we all went home.

A few days later I spotted her on the roof of a low building at another anti-Kuchma protest. I was with a group of journalists pushing to get closer to the line where protesters and police met. She was threatening to jump, for what cause or reason I am uncertain. No one stepped forward to stop her. She jumped. The crowd was so thick and the building so low that she landed without incident or injury. We paid her little attention, having judged her heroic acts more theatrics than daring.

After weeks and months of teasers the press and public seemed in the mood for real action. It was like the buildup before Christmas. Whether one worshipped or despised Kuchma, everyone seemed equally excited for something, anything, to happen. The mood was expectant. Each side was preparing for the other to strike. Police were bused into the city and practiced maneuvers and drills in squares and quiet neighborhoods. They would line up with their riot shields and helmets, anonymous walls of armored silence. A few people would gather to watch and then the crowd would grow, and soon pensioners in scarves and men in work jackets would be throwing stones and trash at the mass of authority. Watching one such gathering, Sveta and I sympathized with the troops at first, their shields raised to create an umbrella to protect them from the onslaught. They were young outsiders defending themselves from the citizens of a city where they could only dream of living.

Then they dropped their shields and pushed into the crowd. It happened quickly, a blur of movement and noise that was over almost as soon as it began. The protesters fled, and the street was silent again. It was hard to know if anyone was ever seriously injured during these confrontations. There were rumors of injuries, but they were just that, rumors. The truth was hard to discover. Often injuries happened after we had gone. The few witnesses that saw them were usually too scared to talk.

The time we got closest to a major confrontation occurred after a protest outside the presidential office during which protesters hurled rocks, snow, fences, and even several Molotov cocktails at the police. Despite the onslaught, the police remained still behind their riot shields, and the protest ended peacefully enough—or so we thought. But later that day calls started coming into the *Kyiv Post*. One of my editors asked if I had seen the police attack the crowds. She was hearing reports that things had turned violent once the camera crews and media had left. I hadn't seen anything, but I started making calls of my own.

The official version was that several police had been injured during the onslaught and those thought to have been responsible, 217 people, had been arrested. Force was used only on those who resisted arrest. I got the unofficial version from various sources, including a man who had worked in the United States as a police officer. That man said he saw plainclothes police abuse several handcuffed captives at Olympiysky stadium and then shove them onto a bus. Inside the stadium the man saw riot police slam the face of a handcuffed captive down on the concrete and club several others.

One of the largest roundups occurred at the Ukrainian Conservative Republicans' party headquarters, where out-of-town UNA-UNSO members were staying. When I visited the office afterward, few of the doors had handles, one window hung crookedly, and the floor was littered with chair arms, wood planks, and documents. Out-of-town students reported being held captive by the police. Families spent several days searching for their loved ones in various hospitals.

Sveta and I visited one of the hospitals where we had heard a UNA-UNSO member was being treated for severe internal bleeding and a broken rib. Viktor (the photographer) joined us. We made it into the hospital and to a unit where new arrivals were being treated. Guards stood outside the rooms, keeping us from approaching the patients inside. Several family members sat waiting in the hallway, and I approached them tentatively. They told me that their father, brother, husband—for the victims were always male—had been at the protest. They wouldn't give me their names or the name of the family member in the hospital. A few started talking about their loved ones' injuries, but then they would catch the eye of the guard stationed outside the door and suddenly grow quiet. When that happened, I knew the interview was over. They were nervous and scared, fearful of what they had already risked.

The guards never stopped watching. Something had happened. I stood in the hallway watching the guards watch me and wondered how I could report the abuse I knew had occurred. My sources so far had either refused to give their names or been far from impartial. Then I noticed the doctors racing in and out of the rooms. The doctors had seen the evidence on the bodies. As trained professionals, they could be relied on to provide official impartial information.

"Sveta, the doctors," I said.

"You really think they'll talk to us?" she asked.

"They might," I replied. "We have to at least try."

The first doctor we approached walked away before Sveta could even finish her question. The next was equally unresponsive, shouting back over her shoulder as she continued down the hall that she didn't have time to answer questions. Besides, she said, we needed official approval to ask anything of anyone on the premises. This was our cue to get moving; we probably had ten minutes before she called some bureaucrat to escort us out. "We better go," Sveta said.

Viktor and I followed her lead toward the exit when another doctor stopped us. He had overheard us talking to his colleagues. When his unhelpful colleague saw him pulling us toward a corner to talk in private, she shouted at him in a threatening tone.

"What did she say?" I asked. It took Sveta a minute to translate. "She told him he will be fired if he talks to us," she said.

The doctor nodded, understanding by Sveta's tone and my sympathetic look the meaning of Sveta's translation. Viktor shook his head and yanked me away from the doctor. "You can't interview him," he said in Russian. I pulled away from his grasp. I didn't like being told what to do. "This is a time of oppression," Viktor continued. "Ask Dima."

I didn't need Dima to tell me what I already knew. I might have been American, but I wasn't living in a hole. I knew what Viktor was saying was correct. I knew it was a time of oppression. I understood the risk the doctor was taking by talking to me. And I felt it was the doctor's decision to make, not Viktor's. "If he wants to talk, it is my job to listen," I told Viktor.

Viktor shook his head again and looked at me with a mix of disgust and annoyance. He stepped closer, his face right in mine. He was about to launch into another lecture when the doctor's steady voice cut him off. "I know I will be fired," the doctor said in Russian. "But I want to talk." We were all silent, even Viktor.

"The injuries I am treating are consistent with beatings. People need to know that."

I asked about the type of injuries he had seen and why he thought they were the result of beatings. He described broken ribs, concussions, and injured kidneys in detail and the method by which they had most likely been delivered: batons. It all added up to only one probable conclusion. He believed they had been beaten. I asked his name and how long he had worked at the hospital. I asked about the guards at the patients' doors and whether they had arrived after the most recent protest. He answered all my questions. Then he went back to treating his patients for as long as he would be allowed to do so.

24 Justice

One of the few pictures of Dima's I keep from that time was snapped in the calm before a group of protesters and police collided. The image shows a line of gray metal softened by pink blossoms. The protesters were armed with carnations, the police with riot gear. Most of the faces are in profile, eyes hidden from the camera, but one boy has turned slightly toward Dima. He is shorter than the rest and looks lost among his taller companions. He regards the camera with curiosity, as if asking, "What are we doing here?" It is the same question I saw in the eyes of a young man whose shield I almost decorated with a flower earlier that morning. And the same one I believe he saw mirrored in my own.

It happened the day the action came closer to my world than it ever had before, just a five-minute walk from my apartment. Sveta had to take the metro to reach the site. I just walked to the park down the street. We met up on the edges of the gathering and pushed our way through to the front where the protesters were placing flowers in the policemen's shields. Someone handed me a carnation. I was about to stick my flower in a young grunt's shield when I felt a hand on my wrist. "You shouldn't do that," Sveta said. "You're a journalist, you can't get involved."

I knew she was right, but I also wasn't sure what that meant anymore. I wasn't siding with the protesters or the police, just adding a splash of color to the harsh gray metal barrier separating them. I looked at the round, childish face above the shield. A smile played at the edges of his mouth. The flowers had broken down a barrier. He was no longer a policeman, and I was no longer a journalist; we were just two young people caught up in something bigger.

Then the crowd started pressing forward against the shields. The police pushed back. A camera was smashed. Like when you are trapped in a rip tide, I swam not out to sea or toward shore but at an angle, pushing my way to the side of the action. The police were using clubs now to keep the protesters back. The change had happened so fast. One minute I was looking into the eyes of a young man thinking we understood each other. The next I was shielding my head from the blows raining down on those around me.

I spotted Dima near the action with a bunch of other photojournalists. They had to be close to catch the perfect images. Writers had the luxury of standing back and describing it all from a distance. I wasn't sure where I should be. I wanted to make sure Dima was okay and that he didn't risk his safety for a picture. I started pushing my way toward him, but when I got near, he shoved me back. "Get out of here Katiusha," he said.

He couldn't take a picture, protect his camera, and look out for me. I stepped back. It was easier now to find space. When the clubs had come out, the majority of the protesters retreated. I filled the void they had left, watching those who remained get beaten back. I was no longer completely on the sidelines. But I wasn't fully in the fight either. It wasn't my country. It wasn't my cause. I wondered where Dima stood in it all and where exactly that put me.

Tent city was torn down so fast and unexpectedly that most of us missed it. It happened early on a snowy and cold morning. Hundreds of police descended on the encampment. The protesters linked arms and refused to disperse. But they were outnumbered and outmuscled and easily pulled apart. The lucky ones escaped. The rest, about forty of them, were thrown into paddy wagons.

Sveta and I arrived in time to see the last of the paddy wagons drive away. Like everyone else, we had heard about the standoff too late to observe it. By the time we got there and the last wagon had gone, the street was quiet and still. There were no tents, no priest, no Vova, no UNA-UNSO thugs. In their place was a void far larger than the space the protesters had occupied.

Off to the side I noticed a man kicking at a leaflet on the ground. He kept dialing his cell phone, talking into it for the briefest of moments, and then dialing again and talking again. He was dressed too nicely to have been a tent city occupant but seemed too frantic to be an uninvolved observer. Sveta and I approached cautiously. We asked if he knew what had happened. He told us his story in short bursts in between his brief cell phone conversations.

His name was Vadym, and he was a parliament deputy for the Socialist Youth Congress. He had arrived on the scene a few minutes before we had, too late to prevent his comrades from being taken away. Now he was working his network, trying to find out where the protesters had been taken. He looked about thirty and had a plump and friendly face. Sveta was straining to eavesdrop on his latest phone conversation when he suddenly slammed his phone shut and started walking away. He called back to us over his shoulder. "I think I found some of them." Sveta and I hurried to catch up.

"Where are they?" I asked.

"We think they might have been taken to a nearby jail," he said.

He spoke English to me, Russian to Sveta. There would be no time to call the paper and get advice on how to proceed. My best lead to the story was about to disappear. "Can we come?"

He stopped for a minute and regarded us, two eager young women in jeans and winter jackets willing to follow a total stranger for a story. I think he understood. After all, he was following a tip that would likely lead nowhere. "Sure, but we have to go now."

I called Greg from the backseat of Vadym's car. I explained I was with a parliament deputy headed toward a police station trying to track down the missing protesters. Greg told me to be careful and keep him updated as to where I was. Vadym drove fast, talking on his cell phone the entire time. He regularly changed directions at the last minute. He kept getting new information about the protesters' whereabouts from contacts who called his cell phone. It was a weekday, but I remember the streets being quiet and lazy like a Sunday morning. There must have been people hurrying about. Their actions probably seemed slowed by the urgency of our mission.

The distress was real. As long as no one knew where the protesters were and no one was there to observe their treatment, the government had free reign. The authorities could do what they wanted with the protesters and deny they had anything to do with their fates. There was no need for any of us to mention Gongadze.

We stopped at the first police station for only a matter of minutes. I barely had time to get out of the car. Vadym asked the guard out front if any protesters had been taken to the station. The guard said no. We all got back in the car. Vadym was on his phone again, steering with one hand and holding the phone with the other. Between his first and second phone conversations I caught his attention.

"How do you know that guy wasn't lying?" I asked.

"I don't," Vadym said. "But I don't think he would risk lying to a deputy."

Vadym went on to explain that if no one important was watching, the authorities might keep the protesters. But if asked directly by a government official, he believed they would not lie. It seemed a strange distinction to make, but then I knew far less about the inner workings of corrupt governments than Vadym.

The story was the same at the next station and the one after that. I decided I wouldn't even get out of the car at the fourth stop. Vadym received another call just before we arrived. The phone still glued to his ear, he swung the car around in a quick U-turn, skidding slightly on the icy road. He was talking excitedly now, and Sveta struggled to keep up so she could inform me of what he was saying. "They're not in the jails," she said. "They're in the courts."

The government was trying to sentence the protesters before anyone found out. Vadym was determined to at least witness the injustice. We went to three courtrooms that afternoon, each more absurd than the last. The first "courtroom" was in a dingy basement that smelled of urine. The building was so decrepit that I hesitated before entering. I was certain there must be some mistake. Official trials could not be held in a building that looked as if it had been condemned. As we walked down a dark hallway, I voiced my concern.

"I don't think this could be the right place," I said.

"Neither do I," said Sveta.

"Just wait," said Vadym.

We followed him to the basement. I wished I had told Greg exactly where we were going. I wished I *knew* exactly where we were. I hoped I had been right to trust Vadym. Looking around, I wasn't convinced I would escape from this unscathed. Half the overhead lights didn't work, and the heater was broken. One of the benches was little more than a heap of broken wood. Vadym was on his phone trying to halt things or at least get a lawyer. But there was not much he could do; the trials were already under way. I took a seat and watched as protesters who had been held for hours without food or water were brought in, sentenced, and fined in five minutes or less. There were no lawyers, and the stenographer drew pictures while the judge rubbed his eyes. When I looked at Vadym, he shrugged his shoulders and laughed. "Ukrainian justice; it's a joke," he said.

The fines were not large and the sentences mostly for time already served, but the injustice remained. The protesters had not been allowed to defend their actions or prepare for trial. As they were being escorted back to the holding cells, Vadym slipped one young protester a candy bar. They were officially "free," but none were released. Vadym seemed to trust that because there had been witnesses, the protesters would eventually be let go. After observing the farcical trials, I didn't share his confidence.

At the next court we were taken into a holding cell where fifteen protesters were being kept. The "cell" was a small unheated room. The protesters still had their coats and hats on. Many of them were students. They told us that they had been locked up for disturbing the peace. They had been given no information as to whether they would be charged, when they might expect to be released, or whether anyone had been informed of their situation. They didn't seem overly concerned. I am not sure if this was because they were too young to know better or because they were old enough to know there was nothing they could do about it. Out of view of the guard I snapped a photo of them, their fingers raised in Vs, for victory or peace I am not sure.

They were called from the cell one at a time and asked to sign a document that said they had been arrested at eleven in the morning, two hours after they had actually been taken. If they signed the document, their passports would be returned. If they didn't, they would have to wait for a trial. No one signed. A lawyer arrived just in time for the trial. They were taken before the judge one by one. I am not sure if it was the lawyer's presence or our own, but the trials were brief and simple. No one was found guilty. In the end they were all released.

There was no lawyer at the final court. When the first protester brought before the judge demanded one, he was locked back up to "reconsider." Those who followed went ahead with the proceedings and accepted the monetary fines that were leveled on them. It was dark by the time the last protester was tried. We had been chasing protesters all day, never stopping for food, knowing the longer we took to get to a location, the longer the protesters would be at risk.

The whereabouts of ten protesters were still unknown when we quit searching that evening. I learned later that they had been taken to yet another courtroom where they were fined and released. Not everyone got off so easily. The muscle of the movement was struck a stronger blow the day of the carnations. Six thousand police had been deployed to the park to protect Kuchma, who was to make a brief appearance. The ensuing clash between police and protesters resulted in nineteen arrests, all of them UNA-UNSO members.

Seven months later they were still behind bars awaiting prosecution. With their leaders locked up, the group began to splinter into warring factions. There were rumors that the schism had been created by the government in order to destroy UNA-UNSO. Others blamed the anti-Kuchma protesters, claiming they had used the organization for protection and then sacrificed it. Both were believable, but it was also possible that the group had simply destroyed itself. UNA-UNSO had volatile roots. Founded in 1989 in the midst of another revolution, the organization's first leader was the grandson of Roman Shukhevich, a founding member of an earlier group that assassinated Poland's interior minister Bronislaw Pieracki in 1934. Both of these nationalist groups had their enemies, but they also had quite a few defenders.

UNA-UNSO's current champion was an outspoken woman with short hair and an impatient manner. Tetyana maintained that her clients' prosecution was being delayed because there wasn't enough evidence to charge them. She was happy to meet me and talk about the case and even agreed to let me watch her in court. She believed her clients would probably be charged with assaulting police officers and causing damage, but she was largely operating in the dark. Trials were routinely delayed, rescheduled, and moved at the last minute. The day I followed Tetyana to court, I found out only the night before that she would be there. She drove me to the courtroom in her clunker of a car, talking the whole time about the horrible and wonderful country in which she lived. When we arrived, she hurried into the courtroom, and I followed directly behind. She was already across the room when the guard at the door stopped me. The room was overcrowded, he said. No one else was being allowed in. I pulled out my passport and started talking in English. He shook his head. I kept talking in English. He glanced at the picture in my passport and then at my face. I smiled as sweetly as I could. He continued to shake his head. But he stepped back a bit, allowing just the smallest space for me to pass through. I took it.

The noise and heat hit me first. People were everywhere—in seats, in the aisles, approaching the judge. And all of them were shouting to be heard. The defendants were enclosed in a raised cage. Women clung to the bars, sneaking kisses with husbands and boyfriends they hadn't seen in months. I was too cramped to remove my coat, and I was roasting from the heat and dizzy with the confusion of it all. I was nowhere near Tetyana, and there was no way I was going to reach her. I gave up and settled for trying to see the proceedings. Everyone seemed to speak at once: the judge tried to call things to order, and the lawyers attempted to get a word in over the shouts and laughter of the prisoners, who called out to friends and family in greeting. Five minutes of utter chaos and then it was all over. The judge declared that a larger room was needed. The hearing was postponed yet again. The prisoners were taken back to prison and the rest of us let out for air. I caught up with Tetyana on the street outside.

"What happened?" I asked.

"Nothing," she said.

And that is pretty much what continued to happen: nothing. There were more hearings and more postponements. I tried to keep up, but after a while I got tired of attending trials that never happened and stopped going. The rest of the population seemed to lose interest as easily, and before long none of us knew what was going on with the UNA-UNSO prisoners. Tetyana kept with the cause until she herself was charged—with what I don't know, and in all likelihood the government doesn't either.

It was a fascinating lesson for me. Had I been Ukrainian, it might have inspired fear in me. But I was American, so it was more of an adventure than a warning. I could leave. Dima couldn't. The more time I spent with him, the more I started to see it differently. I began to understand, if not feel, the fear that was always there lurking beneath the surface. I caught the worry in his voice, the urgency in his actions, and the frustration at the small daily injustices.

He was always running around, harried, frantic, and short-tempered. When I argued with him about the promises he was unable to keep, he would bring up worries about his stepfather's illness, his mother's pension, the apartment. I believed him. He may have been telling the truth. He may have just known how to make me back down.

Back then we were too busy to see each other much. Both of us were caught up in the energy and excitement of the protests. We would text and talk to let each other know where we were and what was going on. I would steal kisses from him in the stairwell at work. Not long into our relationship he was hired as a photographer at the *Kyiv Post*, where his salary increased considerably. He left me waiting more times than I care to remember, and I forgave him more times than I should have. We had both grown up too fast in some ways and too slow in others.

The first time I slept over, his mother made us dinner. The meat cutlet she served me was cold, fried, and tasteless. I left half of it on my plate. In the morning it was still there. I couldn't leave the house until I finished it. I felt like a child. The night before she had loaned me an old-fashioned nightgown and fixed a bed for me on the pullout couch. Dima stayed at my place once a week, so she knew we were sleeping together, but when I was in her home, I always slept alone.

At the office everyone knew we were dating. There were plenty of couples on the staff, so it wasn't much of an issue. Diana was the only one who made a big deal out of it, drawing attention to it whenever Dima stopped by my desk or called me on the phone. It irritated me, but I tried to ignore it. I remembered how sweet she had been that morning in tent city when she told Sveta and me she was pregnant.

She wasn't the one who told us the baby died. He survived seven days in a Hungarian hospital. He had been born too early. She had little memorial cards made, and I keep one in my scrapbook next to the picture of me in a jail cell with the protesters.

25 London Calling

We were in love with the idea of being in love. We walked with our arms linked and referred to each other by affectionate diminutives. I was Katiusha, Katiushinka, or Katinka. He was Dimka or Dims. We used each other's full names only when we were mad at each other, which was happening with more and more frequency. We wanted to be close, but the closer we became, the further we pulled each other apart. Dima liked gestures and images. I wanted reality, something I could count on.

He spotted the pale blue daisies on a day when I was wearing pale blue pants. A man outside our office had a bucket full of them. Dima bought the lot, minus the bucket, and thrust them into my arms. I was not pleased. A bouquet is one thing. A garden full of daisies without anything to place them in is another. I was at work and not in the habit of finding ways to keep large quantities of flowers fresh.

"What am I going to do with them?" I asked. "How will I get them home?"

Dima smiled. "That's not my problem," he said.

He kissed me quickly and left. I tried to keep my professional and personal lives separate. The armful of daisies was a glaring reminder of my failure. Back in the office I located an empty trash can that was big enough to hold them. I put some water in the bottom before placing the daisies inside. They sat at my feet the rest of the day, a tripping hazard every time I got up. I hadn't expected Dima to return to the office. But at the end of the day there he was by the side of my desk, fixing me with a stare so intense and angry it bordered on hatred.

"I buy you beautiful flowers and you throw them away?"

"It's all I could fit them in."

He remained silent.

"I put water in there."

He still didn't speak.

"I told you not to buy so many."

"They looked so nice with your pants."

"I just don't know how I am supposed to get them home."

Neither of us said anything more. He went home to his place, and I went home to mine. The flowers stayed in the office, a reminder of our argument. They wilted a few days later. Dima forgave me before then. I let him, forgetting I had also been mad.

It was hard to stay angry at a boyfriend who bought you balloons and flowers, even though a part of me knew they weren't really for my benefit. For Dima it was all for show. His purchases were impractical and unwanted, like the time he bought me a balloon as big as a small child. It had no string so I had to hold my arm above my head in order not to bump into anyone or anything. At least he bought the balloon on a weekend. We had been strolling along a downtown street when he spotted it. As a foreigner, I usually tried to blend in. With the balloon I was on full display, children running after me, couples smiling, and shopkeepers pointing. Dima even had me pose for a photo. In the image I look tall and thin and a little embarrassed, a shy half-smile conveying that I had accepted the situation even if I didn't understand it.

And I didn't understand it. I thought our arguments were the usual thing between men and women. I didn't realize it wasn't biology that set us apart but culture. We were both of European descent. I assumed our values were similar. But decades of lies had created a culture in Ukraine that had trouble grasping the truth. Even those who knew they were in the right sometimes fell for the deception. Maria was one of them.

She was seventy-six when I met her, a small woman with a deeply wrinkled face and a fading memory. She had recently been invited to tour Germany and recounted how every windowsill had a flower box in it. When I pressed her about the German people and whether she had forgiven them, she clammed up. She had been a slave laborer, one of a hundred thousand Ukrainians forced to work in Munich during World War II. She got to be a tourist as an old woman because she had spent her teenage years enslaved. I had come to interview her about the trip, organized by Kyiv's sister city, Munich.

The first time the Germans came to Maria's village in the summer of 1941, Russian soldiers beat them back. When they returned the following year, there was no one to defend the village. Maria and other single villagers were forced to sign a document saying they agreed to go to Germany. They had no idea what would happen to them there.

For three years Maria cleaned military shells in the basement of a factory. She was escorted to work by three guards and their guard dogs and watched at the factory by another set of guards. At night she slept on a bunk in a wooden barrack. She was fed only a thin slice of bread for an entire day and later survived on worm-infested white beets. She was so hungry that she risked beatings just to dig potatoes from under a garden fence. She was eventually freed by a group of American soldiers and sent home. But back in the Soviet Union her ordeal continued. "We were treated as if we were guilty, as if it was our fault we had to work in Germany," she said.

She was denied a passport and other official documents. She was turned down for jobs. She was not to be trusted, so no one trusted her. She survived, and then the Germans returned to offer her a different kind of experience. She enjoyed her second visit, but that is all it was to her, a visit. She neither dwelled on the time she spent in Germany in her youth nor questioned the way she had been treated upon her return to Ukraine as a young woman. It had happened; apologies now would mean nothing. That her country never gave her one seemed beside the point. She hadn't expected one.

I had trouble understanding her lack of emotion. I wondered if it was because she was old or because of what had happened before. Maria would have been alive during the famine. She would have understood the insignificance of her suffering. What was half a lifetime of discrimination, of being shunned and denied opportunities, when you had watched humanity feed upon itself? And that is precisely what happened during the artificial famine of 1932–33, when an estimated five to seven million Ukrainians starved to death.

There was food, but the farmers never saw it. Imports to rural areas were stopped after the farmers were unable to reach the impossible production quotas and unfathomable taxes placed upon them. The government took all the crops. Houses were searched for hidden food. Farmers were not allowed to reside outside their villages and so lacked the proper documents needed to leave. They starved to death en masse while grains rotted in silos. There were no cats or dogs on the streets. Doors were left open so the dead could be found in the morning. Out of desperation some resorted to cannibalism, including Volodymyr's neighbor.

Volodymyr's first memory is of dead bodies being carted to mass graves. His second is of police arresting his neighbor for killing her baby. The year was 1933, and he was four years old. After his neighbor was taken away, his father showed him her home. There were a few dishes and what was left of the baby. Just a few days before the woman had tried to lure Volodymyr into her home with candy. His grandmother had whisked him away at the last minute. Volodymyr's wife, Lyidia, lost her three older siblings during the famine. Her mother had to dig their graves with her hands because she was too weak to use a shovel.

Their countrywoman, Galina, remembers it differently. She was eleven when her father moved the family from Russia to the region in order to "quiet the nationalists." She recalled people eating birds, tree bark, and turtles but insisted there was enough food if you didn't spend your money on drink. I asked her why she thought her neighbors ate bark and birds. "Sometimes people are strange and eat strange things," she said.

I wondered whether she knew and was just lying to me or if she genuinely believed that was what happened. It was possible to deny the famine. Those who survived remained silent during Soviet times. Their stories are some of the saddest never told. What they saw was mass murder. It is hard to blame an old woman for being lucky enough to have not known what her father was overseeing. She must have decided to remain blind to the obvious so that no matter what was said, she never had to confront the reality she couldn't handle.

Maybe it's the same with love. You talk yourself into the parts you can handle and hide from the ones you can't. Some people are better at it than others. I had no experience of betrayal. Dima had whole generations. I didn't know how to be anything but myself in love. He didn't know how to be anything but the person he felt he had to be. I don't think either of us knew who that was.

That spring I invited Dima to go to London with me to meet my family. Later, when we were separated by distance and I suggested meeting in London again, he insisted we go somewhere else. He had seen London; what about Paris? I wanted to see him, not the place. But then I had seen so much more than he had. I had family in Paris as well as London, so it really didn't make that much of a difference to me. We met in Paris in spring; the sole romantic moments were those displayed by couples Dima captured on his camera. It wasn't the first time I resented the apparatus that put distance between us. Now I know the camera was just an excuse. Dima kept a barrier between us on purpose. He loved that I was tall and looked like a model. He loved that I was driven and worldly and knew how to get us both work. I'm just not sure that he loved me or if he even knew how to.

Chernobyl had brought us together. That was my Chernobyl story. Dima's Chernobyl story was different. It started with loss, that of his family and his country. Chernobyl was the beginning of the end for the Soviet Union. And the end of the Soviet Union is what took the family he knew from him, replacing his professional mother with a woman without work, his sister with letters from Australia, and his stepfather with the shell of a man. His mother was working in a lab the day of the disaster. She didn't know why all her cell cultures suddenly died. A few days later, still unaware of the risk, she let her daughter, Masha, march all day under a cloud of radiation in the May Day Parade with thousands of other children. Dima's stepfather, Edward, crawled underneath the reactor core, installing and organizing monitoring instruments. When I met him, Edward was one of the few from the cleanup supervising staff still alive.

As word of the danger spread, Dima was sent to live with family by the sea in Odessa. He was away from home for months. Later he would understand it was for his own safety, but as a child he saw it as banishment from his family. It was one of the few things he told me about his childhood—being sent away. I offered another escape and, more important for Dima, another family. His family wanted him in America, just like they had wanted him far from Chernobyl after the accident. It wasn't for me that he would later move. It was for them.

England was the first country Dima had ever visited outside the former Soviet Union. He packed greasy meat, bread, and dollar bills—the same things he packed when he traveled inside Ukraine. When he walked into the kitchen, he asked why there was a role of large toilet paper on the counter. He had never seen paper towels before. He was surprised to learn he couldn't use dollar bills everywhere and even more surprised to learn that British currency was stable. He had never known a world where you could count on the money you used to maintain its value from day to day and for food to be readily available wherever you traveled.

He was so awed by London that he forgot to be a snob. He wanted photos in the famous red phone booths, he couldn't get enough of the fish and chips wrapped in newspaper, and he read every word at museum exhibits. Later, in America, he would declare things provincial and inferior, the people fat and ugly. But back then he was too green to hide behind snobbery and Eastern European sophistication.

Still, there were hints of the biting criticism that would come. Most of them were directed at me. My jeans weren't tight enough, my shoes too masculine, my dresses too dull. In London he told me my black midcalf leather boots were ugly. I believed the boots made me look sophisticated, but Dima was unimpressed.

I had worn my boots on the flight over, stashing what money I had been able to save inside. September 11 had not happened yet, and you could still pass through security without removing your shoes. The first time I removed my boots since putting them on in Kyiv was at the apartment in London where my parents were then living. A little less than a dozen $100 bills fluttered out. My sister laughed. My mother stared. I collected the bills and handed them to my mother. The banks in Ukraine weren't trustworthy, so my mother had agreed to take the money I brought her in London and put it in my bank account back in California. But now, when I held the money out to her, she hesitated.

"Remember you agreed to put it in my bank for me?"

She nodded but did not speak.

"So . . . this is the money," I said.

She still didn't take it.

"It's mine," I said. "Why are you looking at me like I stole it or something?"

"You had $1,100 stashed in your boots," my sister said. "Don't you think that's kind of weird?"

Actually I didn't. It made perfect sense to me. I wasn't about to carry that much money in my purse, where a customs agent might find it. I knew no one would look in my boots, so that's where I stashed it. It felt safer there, close to me and unknown to anyone in authority. Of course I hadn't declared it. My mom was a military brat; she lived by the rules and respected authority. Once when she found ten dollars on the sidewalk, she made a point of putting it in a spot where its owner could locate it. Later she realized the bill had actually been hers. She had tried to raise me the same way. But I grew up in Berkeley, not on navy bases, and I was now living in a former Communist country where only the foolish trusted those in uniform. At the airport later that week when I needed to know where to go for our flight, I walked right past a uniformed official and asked a regular-looking person. The person was clueless. "Why didn't you ask the official?" my mother asked.

I hadn't noticed him before, but even now that I had, I knew I still would have stuck with the regular passenger. I wasn't sure why, and I couldn't explain it. It was just what I was used to doing. My mother also noticed that I now ended most of my sentences with a question. I am not sure how to explain that one either except that maybe that's what they were.

26 A Western Town in Ukraine

The rain came with Pope John Paul II. If I were religious, I would have said it was a sign. But then it rained in Lviv as well, not just Kyiv. And the Pope was welcomed there. He was welcomed everywhere in Western Ukraine. It was in the capital that he was greeted by protests.

In the months leading up to his visit old women in Kyiv spouted such venomous statements that I had trouble writing them down. It was difficult for me to understand their hatred. In America some question those that focus on the effects of slavery, which we see as having happened in the distant past. But slavery in the United States had occurred relatively recently compared to 1045, the date when the Catholic and Orthodox churches split. And yet Kyiv's true Orthodox residents could recite every wrong that had been done to them since the breakup. Now the head of the Catholic Church had the audacity to enter their country. It probably didn't help that John Paul II was from Poland, and so represented the West, while the Ukrainian Orthodox church is tied to Russia and the East.

In Kyiv the Pope's appearance was greeted by empty stands. I tromped through the mud, dutifully trying to find the rare spectator. The showing was so dismal that I convinced Greg to allow me to go to Lviv to cover the Pope's appearance in Western Ukraine, which I assumed would be more eventful. Sveta and Jenia came with me.

It was the first time I had been to Western Ukraine's largest city, and I was surprised by the contrast. Kyiv has domes and grand monuments. Lviv has courtyards and outdoor cafés. It also has a lot more Catholics.

The Pope's beatific image beamed down from billboards. Street traders hawked papal postcards, coins, and rosaries.

The Pope's main appearance was to be at a hilltop cathedral, and we headed there soon after our arrival in the city. The rain had yet to hit here, the dirt road was dusty, and for some reason buses and cars were not being allowed to traverse it. We joined a bedraggled group of pilgrims tromping along in the sun and resting in the shade. The hike took us what seemed like several hours but may have been more like an hour. The air was humid, and we were nervous about reaching the location on time. We weren't sure we were on the right path until we finally spotted the cathedral and the crowds in the distance. It was like an outdoor rock concert: seas of rowdy spectators standing and shouting and straining to catch a glimpse of their hero.

When the Pope-mobile made an appearance, the crowds went crazy, and I found myself joining in, pushing forward and leaning to the side to catch a glimpse of the famous man and his ride. It was an image I had seen often in newspapers and on television but never expected to see in person. The strange white vehicle with the little guy standing in the back looked as comic up close as it did from afar. All I could think was how weak he looked. His shoulders were hunched, his movements labored. I hoped I wouldn't have to write a news story about his demise. I actually prayed, asking God to keep the Pope alive at least until he left Ukraine. That's when it started to rain.

The Pope's speech ended before we got a chance to sit down and rest. I didn't understand most of it and I didn't understand his followers' devotion. But I understood the tradition, ceremony, and symbolism. Standing among the wet and weary pilgrims, I felt my own little euphoria at the wonder of the world and the people in it. As a journalist, I got to attend historic events, and while not really a part of them, I was able to feel a little of the wonder you can't get through a television screen or newspaper. That sense of awe ended when I realized we had to hike all the way back to our hotel in the rain.

The train to Kyiv didn't leave until the following night, so we spent the next day hanging out in the city. It was rainy and cold. We ducked from one café to the next, buying the cheapest drinks we could in order to stay inside. Our bladders were filling and our money was running low when we struck on the idea of watching a movie. Sveta had seen a theater a few streets away and led us to a small shop with a banner outside announcing movies. The woman selling tickets seemed surprised, and a little annoyed, that she had customers. She told us there was only one movie playing, and it would begin shortly. It was nothing any of us had ever heard of, but it only cost a few kopeks, so we decided to try it.

The woman led us to a dark, dusty storage room. The place was crammed with old furniture. The floor was bare concrete, and wobbly wooden chairs were stacked halfway to the ceiling. I had long ago given up on the idea of popcorn, but I had been hoping to find a seat. Jenia pushed her way among the junk and managed to find a chair that was not broken or holding up another item. I found another several feet away, and Sveta found a third. We sat down and waited. Nothing happened. I was pretty sure there weren't going to be any other moviegoers so figured our presence was all that was required to start the show.

"Do you think she forgot us?" I asked.

Jenia shrugged her shoulders.

Sveta laughed: "Maybe it's a trick, and the mafia is going to come for us now."

"Wait, I hear something," said Jenia.

We were all quiet. A flicker appeared on the wall in front of us, and an image came into focus. It was grainy, black and white, and half blocked by upturned table legs and desks, but it was a film. It looked like an American made-for-TV movie from the 1980s. It was hard to be sure because parts skipped, the sound was jarring, and it had been dubbed into Ukrainian. Neither Jenia nor Sveta spoke the best Ukrainian, and I picked up only the first English word of every conversation that could be heard before the dubbing took over. It was cold and damp in the room, and we walked out before the film ended. When we saw our ticket taker, she told us we would not be getting our money back. We assured her that was okay. Then we headed to the train station early.

The next morning we were back in Kyiv and the Pope was back in

Rome—or on the road to some other country. Jenia and I finished our various stories. Both of us were doubling up; she was writing for the *Kyiv Post* and a religious wire service. I was writing for the *Kyiv Post* and the *San Francisco Chronicle*. I needed stories that would hold the interest of both Ukrainians and Americans, something Kuchma was making easy. Gongadze's disappearance had focused international attention on the issue of press freedom in Ukraine. Reporters without Borders featured Kuchma on one of its posters and the Committee to Protect Journalists ranked Ukraine seventh on its list of the ten worst enemies of the press. In just the first two months of 2001 there had been thirty-three reported cases of Ukraine's obstructing the rights of journalists. The *Chronicle* agreed to take a story on the dangerous lives of Ukrainian journalists.

The editor of an independent weekly told me he no longer kept track of the number of threatening phone calls he received. The steps outside his apartment building had been bombed, his office phones disconnected, and his building raided. The paper's bank accounts had been frozen by tax inspectors five times in the last few years, and his reporters were routinely denied accreditation. When I met him, the lease on the paper's office was up, and he was worried it wouldn't be renewed. A Russian journalist based in Kyiv had had a knife held to her throat. She managed to escape but insisted she was still being followed.

"Have you reported it to the police?" I asked.

"The one journalist who told police he was being followed was Gongadze," she said.

I met Andry in a hospital where he was recovering. I could barely understand the mumbles he made through his clenched jaw. It wasn't wired shut, but it probably should have been because it was clearly broken. Andry covered politics for a small Kyiv paper. He had been attacked by four men in what authorities were calling a "random incident." Andry's phone had been disconnected before the assault, and the police found his name and phone number among the belongings of a man recently accused of murder. I saw him first in the hospital hall, shuffling along and holding his rib cage. When he got closer, I saw that his cheeks were swollen, his nose was displaced, and the skin around his eyes was purple. I was pretty sure most of his teeth had been broken or were missing. I couldn't tell if he had been good looking. All I knew was he wasn't anymore.

Looking at him, trying my hardest to decipher what he was saying, I was scared. For the first time I realized something could happen to me. The *Kyiv Post* was regularly subjected to tax and other inspections. We would snicker and laugh as the "inspectors" toured our office. Their fear tactics were wasted on us. We had American backers. They could fine our publisher and even detain him at the border. But they couldn't really harm us. At least that is what I thought. Now I wondered if there was anything stopping them from beating one of us up and blaming it on a "random act of violence." Or from hurting the locals at our paper, like Sveta, Vitaly, and Dima. I didn't want to lose any of them or spend the rest of my life with false teeth or a bashed-in nose. I was not obsessed with my looks, but I was rather fond of them. I wondered if I had been Ukrainian if I would have been brave enough to report for the independent papers like Andry or if I would have played it safer and reported for one of the government-backed dailies. "The press is the same as society," the editor of one such daily told me. "It is not able to be better than society."

He didn't send his reporters on dangerous assignments, he said, because it wasn't worth risking their lives. I wondered, though, if he was risking something else, something inside them that could end up just as damaged.

27 An Internal Attack

I had to get out of there. Needle tracks covered my forearms. My flesh was a tender purple-and-blue mess, my breath foul, my saliva thick and ropey from lack of water and teeth brushing. I was frail and unsteady on my feet. I hadn't eaten in at least a week and was thinner than I should have been. I cradled my injured arms and took it a step at a time, resting every few feet. I cringed at the sight of people, not wanting to risk reigniting the pain in my arms by brushing against them. My apartment was only a few blocks away, but it took me an hour to reach it. A week later I was in an emergency room in California in danger of heart failure, an ill-fitting emerald ring on my finger.

I had celebrated my twenty-fifth birthday two months earlier. My sister's birthday card to me included a note about not putting confetti in the envelope so it would be less tempting for postal workers to steal. I had a problem with mail disappearing, especially magazines and cards. Dima's mother signed her card to me in Russian. I understood the part where she said she loved me. She definitely enjoyed having me around. I like to think it had more to do with my personality than my passport. But I'm not sure. I do know that my limited Russian and tendency to smile made me come across as incredibly sweet and innocent. Her even more limited English and mothering habits made her seem gentle and nurturing. She treated me like a member of the family almost immediately, and I in turn looked to her as a replacement mother.

I remember her insisting I accompany them on a family picnic even though there clearly was no room for me in the car. I ended up sitting on

Dima's lap, squeezed among baskets of food. They thought it was sweet. I thought I would die if we got in an accident. We were headed to their country cabin outside Kyiv. With a *dacha* in the picture I felt like a true Ukrainian. When we arrived, Edward went fishing while Ludmilla prepared dinner. Dima and I swam, hiked, and otherwise acted like children. When we returned to the beach, we found Ludmilla in tears and the picnic table empty. A wild dog had run off with the meat.

Dima and I broke out laughing, but his mother wouldn't stop crying. I suggested we eat what was left, enjoy the bread and vegetables and cheese. But Ludmilla was inconsolable. It was all ruined, and there was nothing to do but head back to the city. We drove back to Kyiv in silence save for the rumblings of our stomachs. We never returned as a family. I learned not to raise the topic with Dima's mother, whose sadness seemed extreme in comparison to the loss. But when you don't feel it yourself, sadness always seems extreme and unexplainable. It is only when it is your own that you understand its depth.

Sadness wasn't something I thought a lot about back then. It was too early in my relationship with Dima for disappointment to transform itself into despair. We were still giddy with infatuation. He laughed with me, not at me as he would later, irony ruining his humor. He wanted to share everything with me. When he bought a bike, he convinced me to buy a matching one so we could ride together. They had to be the best. Appearances meant everything to Dima. When we went on a ride with another couple, Dima posed for the group photo by throwing himself dramatically on the ground in mock exhaustion. The picture ran in the newspaper the next day, Dima on the ground, I and another woman standing nearby. It was Latvia all over again. Only this time I wasn't referred to as "happy girl." I wasn't named at all.

The pain started a month or so later. It pulsed in my upper legs, back, and abdomen. It was so sharp that I thought I had appendicitis. It was evening, and I was lying on my back in my bed, my legs curled to my chest. My cell phone was in the hall, and it hurt too much to move, so I didn't call for help. Stomachaches had always been a part of my life. But this pain was stronger than any I had ever experienced. I waited until morning before calling Dima, using all my strength and concentration to move myself the short distance to the hall to retrieve my cell phone. It was even harder when I had to get up to let Dima and his mother in an hour later. Once they were inside, I immediately went back to bed. They attempted to coax me out, but I couldn't move. I refused water and food. I was nauseous and worried I would throw up. When Ludmilla tried to touch my midsection, I whimpered in agony. It hurt too much to let anyone near me.

Ludmilla shook her head and made tsk-tsk noises. Then she spoke to Dima in Russian too hurried for me to follow. I couldn't concentrate anyway. The pain took all my energy. They decided I needed to go to the hospital. I told them I would never make it down the stairs. Dima must have carried me because I don't remember walking out of my apartment. I remember the car ride and how I tensed in anticipation of each bump in the road and each sudden stop. The hospital they had chosen was only a few blocks away, but each jerk and turn of the car rattled my body, increasing the pain tenfold.

The hospital was bigger and busier than the place where I had gone for my broken foot. Patients, doctors, nurses, and family members wandered the halls. Light shone in through large open windows. It was not unpleasant, at least not early in the morning before the summer heat baked everything inside. Dima found a seat for me. I sat doubled over, clutching his hand for comfort. His mother returned with a nurse, and Dima did his best to translate her questions. There wasn't much to say. I had eaten *pelmeni* for dinner and been in excruciating pain ever since. Dima's cell phone rang halfway through the intake interview. "Katiusha, it's work; I have to go," he said, extracting his hand from my viselike grip.

I didn't have the strength to formulate the words that would make him stay. So instead I raised my head slightly and fixed him with my eyes, large with pain and fear. "I'll call soon," he said. "My mom is with you."

Then he left. I watched him walk away with panic growing in my chest. Dima was more than just my boyfriend; he was my translator and advocate. Without him I had no idea what they would do to me.

Ludmilla squeezed my hand. She had been a doctor and knew better than Dima how to secure treatment for me. But the only English she had ever spoken to me was, "I love you." Even in her slow and simple Russian I sometimes missed the meaning of what she said. I clung to my cell phone, my link to Dima and everything I understood. I texted him throughout the day, my messages the only thing that seemed to make sense in the chaos that followed.

No one explained to me what they were doing or why. Or maybe they did and I just didn't understand. I remember Ludmilla leading me into a room where a number of patients were already waiting. Several old women voiced protests as I was whisked past them and into a smaller room that led off the larger waiting room. They had probably heard the simple way Ludmilla spoke to me and thought the special treatment was because I was a foreigner. But that wasn't the reason. Ludmilla had been a doctor and still held sway with her colleagues. Dima probably also had slipped someone some money.

In the smaller room a man in a white coat, which I assumed identified him as a doctor, gestured for me to open my mouth wide. I was still standing when he sprayed my throat with something that made it slightly numb. Without waiting for me to swallow, he began to shove a huge tube down my throat. I gagged and choked. I bent forward and Ludmilla held me to keep me from falling. Tears of pain sprung from my eyes. With the little strength I had left I reached for the tube, attempting to tear it from my mouth and end the pain. But Ludmilla wrapped herself around me, forcing my arms down. I was too weak to fight her and collapsed in her grasp.

She cooed softly in my ears: "Katiushinka, Katiusha, *spokoino, spokoino*." Quiet, quiet.

The tube was shoved deeper into my stomach. My gag reflex never left me the whole time the tube made its way down. It hurt just as badly when it was pulled out a few minutes later. Even after it was gone, I couldn't stop gagging. My throat was raw and my eyes stung. Ludmilla kept whispering in my ear and stroking my back. I felt betrayed by the softness of her words. She had tricked me into trusting doctors who had hurt me badly. I knew there was nothing else she could have done. Had she been able to tell me what really was going to happen, I would have run. It was better this way, but I couldn't help resenting her a little all the same. Later I had a similar procedure done in the United States—under full anesthesia.

As I was ushered out of the smaller room, the babushkas who had clucked about my having cut in line just a few minutes before uttered quiet encouragement. I was no longer a foreigner receiving special treatment but a young woman crying like a child.

There were more tests, none as painful as the first. Eventually I was taken to a room and shown to a bed by the window. There were half a dozen other women in the room and no curtains to provide privacy. The door was left open and so were the windows. The air was stifling. There was no air conditioning, and the air outside was still with the heat of summer. My roommates lay motionless. There was no television or radio, and none of them seemed interested in reading. They didn't talk either. They just lay there and watched me with their eyes as I settled in. The majority were older or at least looked past middle age. One girl who appeared closer to my own age cried almost continuously. Another woman moaned.

If I had had any energy, I might have been frightened or disturbed. But it was all I could do to keep upright. The pain had not gotten better, and I was confused and exhausted by all the tests. I wanted to lie down, close my eyes, and disappear from everything that had happened. But first my bed had to be made. The sheets the nurse provided had faded red marks on them. There was no blanket. But then none was needed. Ludmilla tucked the sheets in, and I curled up on the bed and shut my eyes. If I didn't see the hospital, I thought maybe I could pretend it wasn't there. I didn't sleep. I just lay there like the other women. Ludmilla sat on the edge of my bed waiting. There were no chairs for visitors.

In the afternoon a doctor with a large following of assistants stopped by. I heard their presence before I saw them and struggled to sit up. The doctor asked me how I felt. I could answer that easily enough in Russian: *ochen plokho*, very bad. But I had questions for him myself that could not be voiced in Russian.

"Do you speak English?" I asked in Russian.

"A little," he answered in English.

"What's wrong with me?"

"I think you are having a pancreatitis attack. You need to rest your system. No food or drink."

His English was good, my anatomy less so. I had never heard of pancreatitis and wasn't entirely sure what a pancreas was. When I asked for further explanation, he turned away from me and addressed Ludmilla in Russian. I watched them anxiously, wanting and at the same time not wanting to know what they were saying. I knew Dima's mother was a doctor, but it had never been explained to me exactly what kind of a doctor she was. I also knew I was in a country where educated people believed fresh air could make you ill. What kind of treatment they thought I needed and the diagnosis itself were not things I felt I could blindly trust.

I texted Dima: The doctor says I have pancreatitis

He texted back: ?

I don't know. Pls come

I needed him to tell me what was going on, to lie to me and tell me it would be okay. Instead he called and asked to speak to his mother. They spoke too fast for me to follow. When the phone was returned to me, all Dima said was, "I'll be there later." Then he hung up. The doctor was already gone. Ludmilla took her leave a few minutes later, saying I needed to rest and she would return in the evening with Dima.

I was alone. The pain in my midsection had eased slightly, which had the unfortunate effect of leaving me with energy to contemplate my situation. Mostly I thought about the new pain in my throat, which felt as if it had been rubbed raw with sandpaper. I shut my eyes, hoping to keep out the other occupants, but their presence intruded by way of their moans and cries. It was too sticky and hot to sleep.

It was dark when Dima and his family returned. Edward didn't venture out much, so I knew I was in bad shape when I saw him. I had texted Dima earlier, asking him to bring me a book to read, and he now handed me Bill Bryson's *A Walk in the Woods*. A hiking adventure wasn't really what I had in mind, but it was the first book Dima had found in my apartment, so it was what I got. Ludmilla brought a bag of supplies. She placed a roll of toilet paper under my bed and a lightweight camisole and boy shorts on my lap.

"I don't need all this stuff," I said. "I'm going to be out tomorrow or the next day."

No one spoke.

"Right?"

I looked at Dima. Dima looked at his mother, then back at me. Their silence and the supplies told me what they couldn't. This wasn't going to be a one-night stay. I changed into the new underclothes. I had become a body more than a being and didn't even hide myself from Edward or my roommates. I wore nothing else the rest of my stay, which lasted more than a week. I never showered, brushed my teeth, or washed my face. I never used the toilet paper because I only used the bathroom once.

A nurse approached and handed Dima's mom a list of medicines she needed to buy for me downstairs. Dima and Edward stayed with me until she returned. Before they left, I asked Dima to email my mother. "I will," he said. "What else should I do?"

I shrugged my shoulders, afraid if I spoke the tears forming at the corners of my eyes would turn into sobs. I shut my eyes so I didn't have to watch him leave. I opened them to find a nurse at my side preparing an IV. She punctured my vein and got a drip going. I had no idea what was in it and was beyond caring. It was agonizingly slow. I watched for the entire two hours it took to empty the bag. There was nothing else I could do. My bag was hooked not to a wheeled hanger like in the United States but to a cord above my head, the same cord my roommates' IV bags were hooked to. When I moved, I jiggled the cord and thus their bags. When they moved, they jiggled the cord and my bag. So we all remained motionless. I tried to read my book, but reading about hiking is hard when you are too weak to turn pages. I have heard *Walk in the Woods* is a great book, but I have never been able to finish it. Every time I pick it up, I am back in a Ukrainian hospital, alone and more scared than I imagine a run-in with the bear on the book's cover could ever make me feel.

28 A Chance Engagement

It was too hot to sleep. A nurse returned in the night and removed my IV needle. I took this as a positive development, believing it meant I would not be receiving any more IVs. I had been hospitalized before and knew if they planned to give you regular IVs they left the needle in so they wouldn't have to continuously restick you. At least that's what they did in the United States. I had no reason to believe they would do it any differently in Ukraine.

I kept my phone in my hand. Every once in a while I would bring the screen to life and stare at Dima's good night text. I felt less alone with the phone in my grasp, Dima's words accessible on the screen. I was ready for when he called or texted. This was before everyone had smart phones, so calls and texts were all the phone could do. I was also ready for the thieves I had been warned about.

In the morning the nurse returned before Dima and his mother. Without so much as a greeting she reached for my right arm and repricked me in the same tender area where she had stabbed me the night before. I winced but let her continue, figuring this had to be my last IV. I watched the bag slowly drip into the tube and then into my arm. Whatever medicine was going into me seemed to be helping because the pain in my abdomen, back, and legs had eased.

Dima texted: he wouldn't be able to come until afternoon. I waited. An hour after my IV finished, the nurse returned to remove my needle. I lay back down and tried to read. The Appalachian Trial seemed an impossible undertaking. I could barely sit up and had trouble remembering that I had been able to walk and run just a few days before. The everyday events of living were absent from my existence. I didn't go to bed because I didn't get out of bed. There was no breakfast, lunch, or dinner. No work or play. I tried to remind myself that work wasn't always fun, that just because Dima was free to come and go didn't mean he was having a good time. It didn't work. I still resented him his freedom and the emptiness I felt waiting for him to visit.

At midday the nurse returned. She was carrying another needle. I realized that it had been no mistake that my earlier needles had been removed. They didn't have the kind that stayed in. They weren't done giving me IVs, which meant they weren't done sticking me. But I was done being stuck. As the nurse approached, I withdrew into myself. She reached for my arm.

"*Nyet, ne nado* [No, there's no need]," I said, yanking my arm away.

"*Nado* [There is need]," she said.

I did not need more pain. I hugged my arms to my chest and refused to let her pry them away. In time she gave up. But when Dima and his mother came later that day, she pulled them aside to talk to them. Afterward Dima sat on the side of my bed and held my hand.

"Katiushinka, you need the medicine," he said.

"It hurts too much," I said.

"I know, but it is helping."

I shook my head no. But when the nurse came back, I let her prick me again. With my other arm I squeezed Dima's hand as hard as I could.

My mother called my cell phone that evening. I tried to explain what was happening, but I didn't really know. I let myself collapse at the sound of her voice, whimpering like a scared child.

"Mom, it hurts real bad; they keep resticking my arm."

"Hang in there," she said.

We were both silent for a minute.

"Katya, listen to me. What are they saying is wrong with you?"

"Pancreatitis."

"Pancreatitis?"

She knew something I didn't: pancreatitis is usually suffered by overweight alcoholics. It wasn't something a young teetotaler was supposed to get. "Can you have Dima get me a doctor?" I sent Dima off in search of the doctor and told my mom to call back in fifteen minutes. When she did, I handed the phone directly to the doctor. "It's my mom in America. She wants to know what is wrong with me."

I don't know what my mom asked, but she didn't let the doctor do much talking. I heard only several "yeses" and "nos" and "not sures" on his end. He held the phone gingerly and gave it back to me as quickly as he could. Then he scurried off to another patient. I felt bad for him, having to endure my mother's questions and defend her unspoken prejudice against what she thought were less than first world standards in a language he didn't fully understand. I wanted reassurance from my mother but recognized by the high pitch in her voice that she needed it even more than I did. I let Dima do the work for both of us, assuring me and my mother that it would be all right, that he would do everything he could to make sure I got better.

He looked exhausted, overwhelmed, and a little panicked. His mother urged him to go home. I knew she was right, but I hated to be left alone in that place. When they left for the night, it would be more than twelve hours during which I wouldn't hear from or see Dima or his family. I imagined them driving home and sitting down to dinner at their kitchen table. They could leave the nightmare behind, sleep in their own beds. I was trapped, by the hospital walls, by my own body.

The days passed slowly but never as slowly as the nights. During the day there were distractions. I could watch my IV drip. I could attempt to read. I could check my cell phone for texts from Dima. When they came, they were almost always a disappointment. He was on assignment and would come after he was done. I would wait eagerly until I figured enough time had passed for him to have finished his assignment, and then I would text for an update. He would apologize and explain that he had been sent to another assignment. It was usually evening before he was able to visit.

Diana and Greg came during the day. Word had spread quickly at the office. It was my third day in the hospital. I was wearing the undershirt and boy shorts Dima's mother had given me. I made a half-hearted attempt to cover up, shaking the sticky sheet from my sweaty legs and pulling it toward my chest. Greg looked around the room nervously, raising his eyebrows when my roommate moaned. Diana handed me a bottle of juice.

She said something about my needing to drink it to put on weight. They stood behind the bottom of my bed, wiping sweat from their foreheads as they tried to think of cheerful things to say. They joked about the stories my colleagues were writing, the latest government gossip. I felt more alone in their presence than I had before. They were a reminder of my former world, one I didn't have the strength or energy to think about.

After they left, I handed Dima the juice. I still wasn't allowed to eat or drink. All my sustenance came from IVs. It didn't seem like enough, but after days of not eating my stomach had shrunk, and I wasn't so hungry anymore. The card they left behind was a better gift. In it Diana wrote that I was taking investigative journalism too far by testing the hospitals. Greg joked about official sick days. There weren't any. Everyone knew that if you were sick, you stayed home. When you were healthy, you went in. Greg didn't expect me to come back until I was better; if that was in a week, great; if it was in a month, so be it. But he did advise me to run if I started feeling better and the hospital staff wouldn't let me go. I don't think he expected me to take him seriously.

My Ukrainian colleagues wrote different versions of the same message, the gist of which was that everyone knows better than to get sick in summer. They joked I should time it better in the future. They didn't visit. The heat drew out the smells of sickness and sweaty bodies. The patients tangled themselves in damp sheets, exposing swollen limbs and red skin. The doctors and nurses moved slowly. Dima brought me a fan that I placed in the window by my bed. The other women cheered. But the fan just pushed around the warm air. It was also noisy, so I turned it down. The other women hissed at me to turn it back up. The fan was no longer mine.

There was little I could control. Days would pass without a doctor visiting. I was given medicine but had no idea what it was called and what exactly it was treating. When I asked Dima's mother for an explanation, she would show me the list of medications, a hand-scrawled note written in Russian. Every day a nurse would give Ludmilla a new list, and every day Ludmilla would go to the pharmacy and buy the medicines and supplies I needed for that day. Sometimes she would come back with needles, other times with gauze and vials. The nurse would take only what she needed right then, and Ludmilla would hide the rest away, my private hospital stash. It was the same for the other patients; their families were the ones who followed up on their care and kept them supplied. I tried not to think about what would have happened to me if Dima and his family hadn't been there. Even after the supplies had been delivered and Ludmilla had attempted to get an update on my condition from a doctor or nurse, she would still stay. We would talk briefly in Russian, and then I would lie back down and shut my eyes, not knowing how else to respond to her presence. When I opened them a few minutes later, she would be gone.

On the fourth morning my right forearm was so bruised and tender that I cried when I saw the nurse. I didn't even bother with Russian. "No, please no," I said.

I tried to pull my arm away when she reached for it, but I was too weak to fight. She turned it over, exposing the soft bruised underside. She stroked the tender skin ever so gently, cooing to me like she would to a child. Then, instead of stabbing me, she gently released my arm and walked out. I had been saved. I wiped my face with my sheet. She returned a few minutes later with a pile of rags. Slowly and very gently she wrapped them loosely around my right arm, protecting the injured tissue from further damage. I almost smiled. It felt like the first gentle thing that had been done to my body since I had arrived. I was so relieved that I didn't notice when she reached for my left arm. She stabbed me before I could protest.

A few days later the nurses were wrapping both of my arms. They would unwrap each before setting up the IV, trying to determine which was the less bruised. Then they would poke that one, evening the score until next time. I understood now the fruitlessness of fighting and lacked the energy to mount any protest beyond tears. Those I let fall freely.

After a week I was worse off than when I had been admitted. The doctor insisted my pancreas could not handle food or liquids. The only nourishment I received came by way of a small IV bag three times a day. I knew my body, and I knew that wasn't enough. I was six feet tall with a fast metabolism. I needed a lot of liquids and calories. If I waited much longer, I realized I might be too weak to help myself. I made the decision to leave. It wasn't that I didn't agree with the doctor. The diagnosis made sense, and so did his order to rest my pancreas. What I had trouble with was the way I could feel my body slipping from me. People die without water, without food. I didn't want to be one of them. Something inside told me if I stayed in that hospital, I might just not wake up during one of those long, lonely nights.

The summer dress I had worn when I arrived was even looser than it had been the week before. As I was walking down the hall, an administrator stopped me and asked where I was going. I told her I was leaving. She told me I couldn't go without being released by a doctor. I asked when a doctor would be coming. She didn't know. I said goodbye. She begged me to at least call someone and have them pick me up. I relented. I walked back to my room and texted Dima. An hour passed, and he didn't arrive. I waited another hour.

Then I got up. I could take nothing with me. Both my arms were bandaged in rags and hung uselessly at my sides. I left the fan for my roommates and figured Dima would pick up the plastic bag I had stuffed with my book and camisole when he finally showed up. The woman who slept across from me called after me, telling me to wait for Dima. They all knew his name. There was no privacy there. I didn't stop to answer; I just kept walking.

Outside I was almost knocked over by the bustle of the living. People rushing places, life happening; it was all so much more overwhelming than what I had grown accustomed to in the hospital. A month ago I was one of them, healthy and thoughtless about the energy it took to do something as simple as walk a few blocks. Now I felt every step, measuring distance in buildings rather than blocks. I hugged myself to protect my arms and because I was scared and overwhelmed by how quickly I had lost all I used to define myself, my ability to work, my athleticism. The flights of stairs in my apartment building were the final injustice. I fought them and then collapsed on my bed too tired to even cry. I was still there two hours later when Dima arrived, a ball of fury.

"I go to the hospital, and they say you are gone? That you left?" he spat at me. "I was coming for you; why didn't you wait?"

"I couldn't stay there any longer."

"It was just another hour or two."

"I couldn't do it."

He looked at me then and saw something that made him understand. Or maybe he just realized there was no fight left in me. Either way the anger left his voice. "Katiushinka."

He lay down next to me. I took his hand in mine and held it close to my chest. "Don't leave me," I said.

He didn't answer. We both knew it was me who was slipping away. I tried hard to get better, to get stronger. I thought yogurt would go down easily and attempted to eat some the next morning. My stomach was like a rock, clenched shut against food. Every bite I took was torture. It was as if my body knew food would bring back the pain and treated it like the enemy, taking away my appetite and ability to eat. Even water was difficult to get down. I didn't throw up, but I worried that I would.

Somehow I managed to get myself to work. I stayed seated the whole day, too tired to move. I wasn't eating or drinking, so I didn't need to get up for food or to use the bathroom. Work distracted me a bit. But I could see the worry in my colleagues' eyes. They would joke about how skinny I was and how I needed to eat. The laughter that followed was nervous, uncertain. Their anxiety was finally what convinced me I had to leave. My mother had suggested I come to California for treatment, but I didn't want to be seen as a spoiled American who went home at the first sign of trouble. I realized by the way they looked at me that no one thought that of me at the paper; they just thought I was going to die. I'd seen the look before, when I was a child and very ill. Now I saw it again. I noticed the way they distanced themselves, as if preparing for my absence from their lives. It was natural—something we do without even knowing it. And it was that more than anything that convinced me to leave. I didn't want to die in Ukraine. There had been two times in my life when I had been in serious danger of dying. I remembered what it felt like, and I felt it now.

I was lying in bed when Dima came to take me to the travel agency to buy my airplane ticket. I planned to come back, but I didn't know when that would be. The ticket would be one way. Dima sat down on the edge of my bed. It was unusual for him to rest when we had something to do, and I propped myself up a little to look at him. "I want you to have something Katiusha," he said.

He reached in his pocket and pulled out a ring box. I sat up and popped the little gray box open. Inside was a gold ring with an impressive-sized green stone. "It's beautiful," I said. "Is it an emerald?" My birthstone is an emerald and my favorite color is green. "I think so," he said. "It's from Masha and the rest of the family."

Masha was his older sister. She was married to a jeweler in Australia. It made sense that the ring would come from her. But by saying it was from Masha and the family, I wasn't sure if it was a present from them or from Dima. I tried to clarify. "Which finger do I put it on?"

I didn't wear rings and wasn't sure exactly which finger was my ring finger. I also wasn't sure if that was the finger Dima wanted me to wear it on. Dima pointed to what I was pretty sure was my ring finger. I slipped it on. It was a little big, but then my fingers were thinner than usual after the hospital stay. I smiled at the ring and then at Dima. We were both still smiling as he drove me to the travel agency. I kept glancing at the way the emerald glimmered on my finger. I was more accustomed to seeing splints on my long fingers than jewelry of any kind, especially gold. I twisted it back and forth, trying not to think about what would happen in California or how long it would be before I was back in Ukraine. Finally I asked the one question I needed answered. "Dima, is this an engagement ring?" He was silent for a minute. I wondered if I had made a mistake. Then he spoke:

"Do you want it to be?"

"I don't know; do you?"

"I think so."

"Then I think so too."

When I arrived in San Francisco, my mother and stepfather took me straight to the emergency room. The nurses looked at the bruises on my arms. My mother stared at the ring on my finger. My veins were like ropes. I was so dehydrated my heart was in danger. My mother tried to distract me. She pointed my new ring out to the nurses. She told the doctor I was a reporter in Ukraine.

"Ah, you live in Russia," he said.

"Actually, Ukraine," I corrected.

"It must be interesting in Russia," he continued.

I didn't correct him again. I spent the next week in and out of hospitals, seeing different doctors and experts. If I had had a pancreatitis attack, it was now over, the damage done. There wasn't much more they could do for me or tell me. If it happened again, they could test my enzyme levels while it was happening and tell me for sure. Otherwise, unless I wanted them to do a complicated and expensive procedure to look inside my pancreas, there was no way to know. The thing to do now was to get me back to a healthy weight. My mom did her part by buying me frozen yogurt and milkshakes. She wanted to keep me longer. But she also recognized that the ring on my finger meant I wouldn't be staying. She insisted it was an engagement ring. I still wasn't sure. In my mind I went over Dima's exact words. They didn't tell me what I wanted to hear. He had said the ring was from his family; they all wanted me to have it. But did he? Before I flew back I called him.

"Dima, are we engaged?"

"You want to be, right?"

"Yes, if you do?"

It was about as clear as our original conversation. My sickness provided the reason, his family provided the ring. I didn't notice until later what was missing—a proposal. Dima never actually asked me to marry him.

29 Ukraine Accidentally Enters the War on Terror

I liked being engaged. It was a promise for a future I didn't have to deal with day to day. When I returned to Ukraine, Dima and I talked abstractly about when we would get married—a year, two years. I had never been one of those women who had sketched her wedding dress as a child, made guest lists on scrap paper in high school, or chosen her bridal colors in college. Now that it was a reality, I imagined a small and simple ceremony. I didn't picture which country it would be in or who would attend. All I knew was that I wouldn't wear white. White was what every other bride wore. I wanted something with color. My mom started looking for a dress. My cousin offered the loan of her wedding shawl. I wore my emerald ring and left it at that.

I was enjoying the present, something I seldom did. Being sick has its advantages; once you are well, your priorities shift. It doesn't last long. But for a while, and in combination with being in love, I was able to enjoy living without worrying about the goals I had set for myself. Just being able to walk to the tram stop, to eat without pain, and to play soccer on the weekend were all accomplishments. I let Dima and his mother worry and sunk into the safety of a second childhood, feeling protected and cared for in a way I hadn't since I was small. It was peaceful and pleasant. Just thinking about Dima made me smile.

We decided we would spend Christmas together in the States. I needed to have more medical tests done, and Dima wanted to see America. We didn't talk about where we would live after the wedding, if we wanted children, or how we would support ourselves. The whole thing was in the future, far off. In the meantime there were other distractions. My editor, Greg, and his girlfriend returned from their vacation in Crimea to find their apartment had been broken into. The protesters marked a year of unrest by arranging a trip to the site where Gongadze's body had been found. Ukraine celebrated ten years of independence with a parade of military might, tanks rolling down the streets, war planes flying overhead, and soldiers walking where protesters had recently marched.

Our lives might have stayed that way for some time, occupied with daily life in Ukraine. But then there was my pancreatitis and the revolution. And the day the planes crashed into the Twin Towers. We watched the last unfold on the newsroom television like a movie: buildings crumbling, people fleeing, distraught and tearful television anchors. When a caller first told Diana a plane had crashed into the World Trade Center, we laughed. We thought it was just another newsroom hoax. It was the end of the day, and we all wanted to go home. I didn't even know what the Twin Towers were. But the phone kept ringing. The emails streamed in. The wire reports piled up.

Diana was the first to turn on the television. The anchor was flustered, talking about events as they unfolded on the screen behind her. It looked like dozens of other scenes I had seen played out in disaster movies—the panic, confusion, and helplessness. I laughed. It didn't seem real. Ukraine had chaos and confusion, not America. Not my country. It was growing dark in Kyiv, but on the television screen the day was just beginning. It was all happening in a different world, on a day that had already passed in a place I didn't know.

"It isn't real," I said. "Is it?"

"Be quiet," Diana said.

She turned up the volume. Another plane crashed into the building. The images kept being replayed. I couldn't tell what had already happened and what was still happening. The whole newsroom stopped and watched the television. The Ukrainians kept quiet, glancing at Greg and Diana as if for clues on how to react. We had always commented on the tragedy of life in their country; now the situation was reversed, and no one was sure what role to play.

An American named Ben, a friend of a friend, was staying with me. He was a Latvian-based stringer for the *Wall Street Journal*, and he was in the office that day to meet with our publisher, Jed. Ben watched the television and talked to anyone who would listen.

"What's going on? I need to know what's going on."

"I don't think anyone knows," I said.

"Our office is there. That's our office," he said.

"Jed is from New York, isn't he?" someone called out.

"Yeah, he might know more," someone else offered.

I sent Ben to Jed's office. Later Jed came into the newsroom to tell us what we already knew. America was under attack. From the reports we were receiving it looked as if everything was happening in New York, but no one was sure. There was no point trying to get a phone call through to the States. Even in the best of times the Ukrainian phone service was spotty. Now everyone would be attempting to call family and friends in America. I emailed my mother in California and my sister in Rhode Island. I was pretty sure they were fine, but I waited anxiously for confirmation. It was an hour or two before I heard back that everyone was okay. Dima came over to my desk. "You still want to see America?" I asked.

He didn't answer. His dream had always been to go to New York City. September 11 didn't change that. It just changed his ability to get there. Not to visit, but to live. We didn't know that then, but Ukraine would end up on a list of countries the United States was watching more closely when it came to immigration. The block on which the U.S. Embassy was located in Kyiv was completely closed off by the next day. It had always been hard for ordinary Ukrainians to access the U.S. Embassy. Now it was almost impossible.

That night Greg sent me and my colleague Roman to expat bars for a reaction story. I couldn't find many Americans, but I got several Brits. They kept asking the questions instead of me. I was the American, and even though I was the reporter, I was now also the subject. It was a strange turn of events and one I wasn't entirely comfortable with. Finally I got to go home and watch the news from America dubbed into Russian and Ukrainian. Ben paced my living room and tied up my phone line. I didn't mind. Everyone I knew was safe. It was his friends, family, and colleagues who were in danger. At one in the morning I fell asleep with the light of the television shining through the glass doors of my bedroom and to the sound of Ben's anxious voice uttering again and again, "This isn't happening."

But it was happening, and the next morning everyone was walking around in a daze. Ben had decided overnight that he was done living abroad. He was packing it up and going home. He promised to pass on his contacts at the *Wall Street Journal*. I went to work. All the Ukrainians I encountered offered their condolences. I was embarrassed by their sympathy. I hadn't lost anything. The attacks hadn't changed things for me, or so I thought. What none of us realized then was that the attacks changed everything.

Far from home we were slower to understand this than most. We did our reaction story, and Peter focused on the many conspiracy theories, but otherwise we continued on as we had before. I went to Uman, Ukraine, a few days later to write about Rosh Hashanah, the Jewish New Year. The original plan had been for me to write two versions, one for the *Kyiv Post* and one for the *San Francisco Chronicle*. I assumed that was what I was still doing. After all, it was a good story.

Every year tens of thousands of Hasidic Jews, most of them from Israel and America, make a pilgrimage to Uman in order to pray at the grave of their founder, Rabbi Nachman of Breslav. They had been making the annual pilgrimage since Nachman's death in 1810. There are few Jews left in Ukraine, so seeing a small central Ukrainian city overrun with men in yarmulkes is a rare opportunity. During the holiday, only residents, reporters, and pilgrims are allowed in the city. Police with guard dogs man neighborhood barriers to keep everyone else out.

The residents who hadn't already rented their homes to pilgrims lurked in the shadows, trying to broker deals for sums that would support them in the months to come. They begged me to help, wanting me to serve as a translator in the negotiations. What they didn't understand is that while I spoke the same language as most of the pilgrims (English), I could communicate with them no better than the Ukrainians could. When I approached the men—for they were all men—they ignored me the same way they ignored the locals. They didn't need to understand the locals, and they didn't want to understand me.

In just a few hours they had transformed the city into their own. They strolled along the cobblestone streets, stopping to chat with each other without so much as a glance at the locals huddled on the street corners. Most didn't know Ukrainian or Russian or anything about the country beyond that their founder was buried in this little city. I was fascinated by their devotion, their tradition, and how easily they had taken over a place that didn't belong to them. I wanted to ask them about their journey, their faith, and what they thought of Ukraine. But whenever I approached a group of them, they avoided my eyes and closed their circle more tightly, offering me only their backs.

My questions in English, a language I knew almost all of them understood, hung unanswered in the air. In desperation I sent my male translator, Bruno, to ask questions for me. By afternoon I was told women were no longer welcome in the streets. I hid with Dima and Bruno in a field, trying to watch the pilgrims from afar. Several were swimming in a lake. It was peaceful and idyllic, like a scene from long ago. Then a cop found us and forced me to leave. Dima and Bruno were incensed that a woman was being treated so badly in their own country. The policeman was sympathetic. A woman who lived in Ukraine should not be pushed aside for a group of foreign men, especially Jewish men. Anti-Semitism usually trumps sexism in Ukraine. I wasn't a fan of either, but I found myself comforted by the way the Ukrainians had treated me as one of their own instead of as a foreigner. I was beginning to fit in, in large part because my fiancé was Ukrainian. Still it felt nice to be accepted, to be protected.

When I returned from my trip, I found an email from my editors at the *San Francisco Chronicle* saying they were no longer interested in the story. They would pay me, but they wouldn't run it. It took me a few more story attempts before I realized they weren't going to run anything that didn't have a link to September 11. The United States had turned inward, and foreign correspondents for U.S. publications around the world were finding the topics they could write about narrowing along with their country's interests. To make a living I needed to find stories related to terror. Ukraine, always obliging, helped out once again by shooting down a Russian passenger jet over the Black Sea.

Ukraine denied it at first. The Russians insisted it was an act of terrorism. The United States tried to ease fears by saying it was a mistake. In the office we tended to side with that assessment. The Ukrainians probably had shot down the plane, but we figured it was more out of ineptitude than malice. We were right. The whole thing was an accident. Just like how the Ukrainian military had accidentally hit a Ukrainian apartment the year before, killing several people. That was the last time the military had fired a missile during defense exercises. The next was when it shot down the Russian plane shortly after September 11. That the plane happened to be carrying passengers from Israel was an unlucky coincidence. Seventy-six of them died on their way to Russia.

I was attempting to report about Ukraine's incompetence for the *San Francisco Chronicle* when the power went out. It returned a few minutes later. Then cut out again. I worked on the same sentence for three hours as the electricity cut in and out. It seemed fitting. It all culminated with a loud pop and poof when Roman's computer exploded and started steaming. The entire office smelled like a bad perm. We turned all the computers off. It would be several hours before it was safe to turn them on again, so most people headed to cafés and bars. I stayed where I was, eager to finish the story for the *Chronicle*. I scribbled what I could by hand so I would be ready as soon as I could type it in. I finished just as it was morning in California and headed home to rest. An editor at the *Chronicle* called me that night to tell me the paper wouldn't be taking my missile story. America had bombed Afghanistan.

30 Shallow Graves

They found the bones before the snow came. Workers piled the shoes in a mound near the deep holes in the ground where they had unearthed the bullet-riddled skulls. Most of the shoes were rubber boots, their wearers likely murdered in autumn. Occasionally at such mass graves slips of paper are found in a shoe, receipts given to political prisoners when they entered confinement. The slips of paper were one of the few clues left as to which group of prisoners the footwear and accompanying bones had once belonged. The card I crumpled and left at the excavation site was more revealing, a business card with my name and number. None of the workers would talk to me. But I hoped someone might take the card and call later in a private moment when he or she wasn't being watched.

It was one of the coldest winters on record. And it began in October, the same month they had unearthed the bones. During the day temperatures hovered around minus five Celsius. At night they crept down to minus ten. We never took off our hats or coats. The heat had yet to be turned on due to an electricity blockage. Bills hadn't been paid, and there wasn't enough coal. The government promised it would remedy the situation soon. Sveta assured us it wouldn't. In her native Kaniv and in most of the rest of the country, electricity was not a given to be taken for granted but a treat that was doled out for short periods of time, just like running water. Sveta warned that soon it would be like that in the capital as well.

I wasn't sure I would be able to handle it if that happened. It was the coldest it had been in one hundred years. I rarely showered, reluctant to take off my clothes. One day I simply stayed in bed, too cold to move. I knew that was how old people died and that if I spent too many more days like that, I would do the same, simply surrendering into the warmth of eternal sleep. I got out of bed after that. The heat came on not long after. And that is about when they found the bones.

The reports were sketchy and unconfirmed. Someone had seen a large group of men digging in the Bukyvnya forest outside Kyiv, a site known for its mass graves. I grabbed Bruno and took a company car to the site before Greg had time to stop us. When we arrived, we found many men digging deep holes in the shade of the forest. At the edges of the holes we saw skulls, bent combs, and mounds of shoes. The shoes came in all sizes, weighty reminders of the lives that had been taken. Bruno and I approached several workers, but no one would talk to us. They kept their mouths shut and their shovels in the ground. I watched them gingerly dust off bones and old cups in silence, their eyes directed downward. My crumpled business card was a last-ditch attempt to discover something. One of the workers had briefly lifted his eyes in our direction, glancing from side to side to make sure no one noticed before mentioning the name of the person we should contact.

"Give me your card," Bruno whispered.

"What for? They aren't going to take it," I said.

"Crumple it and drop it by his feet," Bruno instructed, using his head to gesture toward the worker who had briefly acknowledged our presence.

I did as I was told. Bruno used his toe to push the crumpled card toward the worker. We didn't wait around to see if he picked it up. The murders had occurred more than half a century ago, but the silence that had allowed them to happen had not been fully broken in Ukraine. I wasn't scared to break it because I hadn't lived through it. I wasn't alive in 1971, when Soviet authorities had dug up some of the mass graves in Bukyvnya forest and declared them victims of the Nazis. I was watching a cartoon rabbit interact with humans in the movie *Who Framed Roger Rabbit?* in 1988, when authorities quietly admitted what Ukrainians had known all along: the Soviet secret police had killed and buried from twenty thousand to a hundred thousand political prisoners in the forest from 1937 to 1941. It was one of the largest, and first, mass graves in Soviet Ukraine. Prior to Bukyvnya, political prisoners had been killed in smaller numbers and buried in ordinary cemeteries.

Before admitting their guilt in 1988, Soviet authorities unearthed and reburied at least six thousand bodies from the forest. Simple plaques with a name and two dates—birth and death—decorated the pine trees. One had to look for the flowers, scattered at random in the dark and quiet forest, some tied to trees others left at their trunks. It was only after pressure from the Polish government that Ukrainian authorities agreed to conduct the new excavations I stumbled upon. I learned all this later, after Bruno and I went to the office of the man in charge whom the worker had mentioned. He told us only the basics. He was fearful. Upcoming parliamentary elections made it a tense time, he said. Political leaders, especially those in the Communist Party, didn't want attention drawn to the issue. The elections were months away. I had trouble believing him when he told me that he had planned to tell the media about the unearthing in November, after the excavations were finished.

Historians and scholars told us more. Their only fear was that the incidents would be forgotten, the perpetrators forgiven, the victims lost once again. But it was the fear of the ordinary workers who were digging up the past that told me what the officials and experts couldn't. Their silence let me know that the bones hadn't been buried as deeply as anyone thought.

I should have known as much. I did know as much. But I still needed reminders. The *Kursk* tragedy had been one of my first. Almost a year before, I had traveled to the Crimean port city of Sevastopol to report on the fourteen families there who had lost sailors when a Russian nuclear submarine exploded in August 2000. Sevastopol is home to the Russian Black Sea Fleet, and the homes I visited were filled with reminders of the sea: anchor picture frames, sea coral decorations, photos of children in sailor hats. It was no surprise to any of the families when their sons became sailors. That was what boys did in this southern Ukrainian seafaring town of 390,100. The fathers understood the danger because they had chosen the sea before it chose their sons. They knew how death came aboard a submarine, how death had come to all 118 on board the *Kursk*. Without oxygen the sailors became faint and fell asleep, never to wake up again. The families spoke of the unpredictability of the sea, of destiny.

But the *Kursk* had not been doomed. After being rocked by two explosions on August 12, at least some of the sailors had survived. Two crew members wrote letters to their wives after the explosions, letters that, when I visited Sevastopol half a year later, the wives had still not received. The letters were part of the official investigation as to what had gone wrong. International help was offered on August 14, two days after the explosion. It was another two days before it was accepted. By then rescue attempts were unsuccessful, and on August 21 Russia declared all on board dead.

Only one body was returned to Sevastopol. The other thirteen families who had lost sons mourned the single sailor brought back as if he were their own. They comforted each other, trying to piece together their sons' last days from the snippets they shared. The government remained silent, telling them little. One mother learned of her son's death through a television report, another from a neighbor. The secrecy that surrounded the catastrophe fed conspiracy theories and comparisons to Chernobyl. I thought it a fitting analogy. Pride would not allow the government to admit its mistake, sacrificing its sons for an honor that no longer existed. Individual lives meant little in the Soviet system. Ideals were what counted. Chernobyl had taught us that. The *Kursk* episode taught us how little "democracy" had changed things. After 9/11 this was lost in the focus on a bigger enemy. But the families of Sevastopol didn't forget it. And I couldn't either.

31 Homeland

Dima's sister Masha was flying over the Middle East when her plane's engine died. The pilot asked permission to land in Oman, a country that supported Afghanistan. The plane was from Australia, a country that supported America. The pilot circled in neutral territory, waiting for an answer. After fifteen minutes he told the passengers they might not make it. The plane went silent.

Then the answer came. They had permission to land in Oman. Armed soldiers escorted the passengers off the plane, taking them to a hall to wait. Two hours later a new aircraft was secured, but it was too small to fit all the passengers, and forty-five of them were left behind. Those forced to wait for another aircraft wrote their names and addresses on slips of paper and pressed them into the hands of those who boarded the first plane, just in case the second plane never came. In the end it proved an unnecessary precaution. But the drama of the action left Masha wondering the entire flight whether the passengers they had left behind would make it. She landed in Kyiv safely, but for days afterward she kept reliving what might have happened had Oman responded differently.

At first I thought her explosive temper was a result of what she had been through. Then I realized it was just Masha. She was an older sister out of the same mold as my own. On the day we met, she threw Dima's wallet across the room after he interrupted her to show her his press pass. She spent several minutes berating him in Russian, during which time Dima made little effort to defend himself. Dima was physically larger than Masha, but Masha was about a decade older than he. She was relatively short and slim, with an efficient and authoritative manner that lacked the softer touches of youth Dima still possessed.

When Masha was around, Dima's role in the family was reduced to that of Masha's little brother. She criticized the way he dressed, the way he acted, and the way he treated me. The fact that I didn't have a proper winter coat somehow became Dima's problem. I wasn't going to argue; it was better to have her mad at Dima than at me. After all, she was his sister. Her solution unfortunately involved taking me shopping. I am not a big shopper. The idea of shopping with Masha did not exactly make the excursion any more appealing. But saying no to Masha was not an option. We were downtown trying to find a coat shop when her temper flared again. "What is this? All these signs are in Ukrainian," she said.

She glanced up and down the sidewalk trying to spot a store sign she understood. Frustrated by her failure, she turned to me, pointing at a nearby billboard.

"What does it say? You have to read it for me; I don't speak Ukrainian."

"I don't either, Masha," I said.

In Kyiv you could get by with Russian, a language I was getting better at daily. Ukrainian was similar enough for me to guess sometimes, but usually I simply avoided anything I didn't understand. Because the two languages were so close, I figured Masha, who was fluent in Russian, had a better chance of understanding Ukrainian than I did. But she couldn't see this. She identified as Russian, not Ukrainian, and did not understand that the country she had left so many years before no longer existed. In Ukraine the change had been gradual, but for Masha it had been instantaneous. She gave up before we entered a single shop, insisting it wouldn't work because she couldn't understand several signs. We went back to the family apartment, where she could speak Russian and pretend nothing had changed.

Masha had come to Kyiv for medical treatment, trusting the underfinanced Ukrainian medical system to work where the Australian system had failed. As an American living in Ukraine, I understood the desire to go home for medical treatment. I just hadn't figured that someone raised in a less developed country now living in a more developed country would choose to return to the less developed country for treatment. But I guess when it comes to trust, comfort plays more of a role than logic. That may help explain why we had spent a frantic evening the previous month driving around Kyiv trying to buy medicine to ship to Masha in Australia. From what I could understand she had some sort of toothache, a condition that was rarely brought up once she was in Kyiv.

She seemed healthy enough whenever I saw her during her three-week visit. Dima spent as much time as possible with her, and I tagged along occasionally, like when we all went to buy me a coat. My first few choices were vetoed by the siblings, but eventually we found one at the packed outdoor market that both Masha and I could agree on. I am not sure what kind of an impression I made on Masha, but it must have been okay because if it hadn't been, I am pretty sure the relationship would have been over. What Dima did back then was largely dictated by the women who had raised him, his mother and Masha. I came in third; even after we moved to my country, he still trusted their word over mine.

When things happened with Dima's family, they were always dramatic. Masha's toothache required international travel. Edward's cold could lead to hospitalization because he had helped clean up Chernobyl. A stomachache was a reason to stay home from work, a headache a sign of something larger. Leaks became possible floods, misunderstandings a reason to break friendships. It seemed extreme to me, but then in Ukraine the probability of a small sickness becoming a large one or a little problem turning into a catastrophe did seem more probable than it did back home. Things were just that much closer to falling apart. So when Dima canceled on me because he had to attend to a family emergency, I believed him. I still do, I think.

The thing is, there was always something, some reason he couldn't stay at my place more often or couldn't meet me for dinner or couldn't spend a Saturday bike riding. The conflict that seemed to come up most often was staying over. He stayed at my place maybe once a week. I didn't stay at his place because his parents lived there, and we couldn't share a bed. It was also far from the center of town. He made excuses, finding reasons why he couldn't stay over. The bed was uncomfortable. His mother needed him. I let him off easy, but I worried about what it meant. If he couldn't manage spending a few nights a week at my apartment, I wondered what it would be like when we were married. Where would we live, or would we even live together, sleep in the same bed? I didn't ask him this. I should have, but I didn't want to hear the answer. And he definitely didn't want to give it. Instead he brought up marriage. I was surprised to learn that he wanted to get married as soon as possible. It was flattering—and terrifying. I wanted to be with him, just maybe not so soon. I didn't want to lose what we had, but I also wasn't quite sure what that was.

I thought taking him to visit my country might help him understand me better, and we planned to spend Christmas in California. I tried to prepare him for the trip by hinting at some of the differences between our two countries. One snowy day as I watched the speedometer creep toward the high double digits as he drove us around town, I introduced him to the idea of a speed limit.

"On California freeways you usually can't drive faster than sixty-five miles an hour," I said.

"What? That's what I drive on city streets in Kyiv," he said.

I had been in a car with him often enough to know he was only slightly exaggerating. His young man's tendency toward reckless driving was a bit of a necessity on Ukrainian roads, where speed and improvisation dominated. It was not uncommon to see cars towing other cars with what looked like a long cloth rag. The car being towed would swerve around on the road. If you drove fast enough, you might just miss it when the rope broke and the car being towed swung wide. Fast driving could be an asset in Ukraine. In the United States it could get you in trouble.

"If you drive that fast in California you'll get a ticket." I said.

"What's that?"

"You know, they'll make you pay."

"What if I offer to take the cop's picture?"

I laughed. He didn't.

"No," I said.

"A really nice picture?"

Sometimes I forgot how foreign my world was to him. I had been living in the former Soviet Union for several years by then and managed to slip between the two worlds relatively seamlessly. Dima had never been to the United States. When a colleague threw a Thanksgiving party, he wanted to bring a pineapple. I tried to explain why that wasn't appropriate. I probably shouldn't have bothered. At dinner all the locals put cranberry sauce on their ice cream.

The war on terror made things even more difficult. I was trying to introduce Dima to a new country, a new way of thinking, but even as I helped him navigate it, the world around us was changing. America was at war, and the whole world was affected. His sister's plane had almost gone down over the Middle East. Envelopes with white powder had been sent not only to U.S. addresses, but also to six newspapers in Kyiv.

The letter to the *Kyiv Post* arrived a few weeks before our trip. Our publisher, Jed, said the cops were taking care of it, but if we felt our health was at risk, we could go home. Most of us stayed. It turned out not to be anything. But everyone was on edge. There were terrorist drills on the metro and a number of murders of officials and their bodyguards. The latter probably had little to do with terrorism, but they were disturbing none the less, especially when one selfish guy used a little girl as a shield. They both died.

On the flight to America Dima took pictures of everything. He photographed the airplane wing out the window, the clouds in the sky, and the tiny specks of land below. During layovers he took pictures of waiting passengers, of the airport art exhibits, and of the armed guards. It was all familiar and unimpressive to me, except for the guards, who wore black and had large guns and protective gear. They looked more like the men I sometimes saw on the streets in Kyiv than anything I had ever encountered in the West.

Our first stop was in Rhode Island to see my sister. We were so jet lagged we had to link arms to keep each other upright. I didn't notice the flags until the next day. Every car had a God Bless America bumper sticker, every house had a flag, and every suit had a stars and stripes pin. I had never seen such patriotism. I had witnessed the attacks from afar and had received news about the aftermath in limited bursts. I didn't know that the Boston airport we flew into was the same airport the doomed flights had flown from. I didn't realize how each part of the country had been touched. From the outside it had appeared to be a single event in New York City. Inside it was far more vast, touching every person and place we visited. Later, when we flew into the San Francisco Bay Area, I was surprised to see flags in Berkeley, where it had never been cool to be patriotic. As my mother drove us from the airport, a song came on the radio about the heroes who had tried to divert the planes.

"How long has it been like this?" I asked my mom.

"It started the day after the attacks," she said.

"This isn't how it always is," I told Dima. "This isn't the country I remember."

I began to understand a little what Masha must have felt when she visited Ukraine and found the familiar signs of her childhood in a foreign language. When you return from living abroad, the changes hit you at once, highlighting all that you have missed, all the ways you no longer belong. I wanted Dima to know the country I knew. But I wasn't sure how to show it to him.

Dima was taking pictures the morning I went to the hospital. My gastroenterologist wanted to run more tests to determine if anything besides my pancreas was causing my digestive issues. The pictures of my insides were not good. My stomach lining was thin and worn like that of an old woman, and the flap that was supposed to keep food down at the top of my esophagus didn't shut properly. The gastroenterologist told me if the attacks continued, I would eventually need a pancreas transplant. She believed the problem was in the way I digested fat and prescribed pancreas enzymes and a low-fat diet. The enzymes were expensive but cheaper than another attack.

Dima assured me it would be okay. It was one of the first lies he told me. I knew he couldn't fix my health any more than he could fix his country or mine.

32 Disappearing Acts

When we arrived back in Kyiv, I discovered I had left my orthodontic retainers in California. Like many in my generation, I had sifted through my share of restaurant trash cans in search of misplaced retainers over the years. Having left the ones I wore at night in my mother's home in California did not seem much of a predicament by comparison. But then, I hadn't figured on the Ukrainian health minister getting involved.

Receiving packages in Ukraine is never a simple matter. It involves waiting in long lines, paying money for what I am not sure, and a lot of random slips of paper. I figured FedEx would be less complicated and asked my mother to FedEx my retainers and some ibuprofen, an over-the-counter drug I had not been able to locate in Kyiv. A few weeks later I was sent notification that I had a package from my mother. This was similar to how the normal mail worked. Packages were never delivered. Slips of paper arrived letting you know you had a package, and you would go to the post office to pick it up. But this time the slip of paper listed an additional step. I needed a letter from my mother saying the package was for me. It was quite considerate of the authorities to allow my mother this chance to change her mind. But she had been certain when she addressed it to me that the package was for me.

She wrote the letter anyway. I took it, and Sveta, with me to retrieve the package. A company car took us to a small "customs tower" that wasn't a tower at all. After a short inspection my notification letter was stamped.

"That's it?" I said, surprised it had ended so quickly. "Now we get my package?"

"No," Sveta said. "Now we go to customs."

"I thought that's what this was?"

"It was."

"So where are we going now?"

"I already told you, to customs."

It took twenty minutes to get to the second customs office despite short cuts that took us onto the sidewalk and over what should have been double yellow lines. We walked down the building's dark hallways until we found a babushka moving a stick with a damp dirty rag over the floor. She led us to a door outside of which a group of men and women was gathered. During the half hour we waited, no one entered or exited the room behind the closed door. Finally I walked up, opened the door, and went in. Sveta ran in after me. "*Izvinite* [Apologies]," she said trying to excuse my rudeness. The room was empty except for a small man sitting behind a large desk with four rotary phones. After looking over our papers, he told us we needed another letter. I had my office fax us a letter, and the officer issued us our stamp. But not my package; for that we had to go to another address.

FedEx was in a small modern building. In the front room a dozen women were unpacking a box of champagne, sitting on their desks, talking on the phone, and making long toasts while chomping on chocolates.

"What's going on?" I asked.

Sveta took a quick look around. "New Year's celebration."

"But it's mid-January. Even Orthodox New Year is over."

Sveta shrugged her shoulders and cleared her throat. A hefty woman fixed us with a stare. Sveta handed her our papers. The woman looked them over and then said something that required a great many sighs.

"She says you have to have a prescription for this ibuprofen," Sveta explained. "You also need a note from your doctor saying why you need this medicine and an explanation of your medical history in Russian."

"But it's not a prescription drug," I said.

Sveta ignored my protests. "Dr. Kriel would probably write it."

Dr. Kriel was the Ukrainian doctor at the American medical center who had helped me when I needed crutches. "Okay, forget it; I don't need the ibuprofen. I just want my retainers."

"I already told her that," Sveta said. "She can't separate the package."

"But it's my package, and I'm telling her she can."

"It would be easier to have Dr. Kriel write a prescription."

One look at the FedEx woman's hairy mole and spiky, dyed red hair, and I was in agreement. I called Dr. Kriel and convinced him to fax me a prescription for a non-prescription drug. After it arrived, the woman took us to another room. A boy whose pimples were just being replaced by peach fuzz sat at a desk twirling a pen. We gave him the papers, and he produced my package. He pulled out a small pink plastic container and thrust it toward Sveta.

"*Chto eto* [What's that]?" he asked

"My retainers," I said helpfully.

The child officer, Sergei, pulled my retainers away and took my package back. Then he launched into a long lecture in Russian.

"What's going on?" I asked Sveta.

"We need to get the health minister's permission and his stamp of approval."

I laughed. Sergei wasn't smiling.

"You're serious?" I said, looking at Sveta.

"Yeah," Sveta said. "He says the health minister has to approve your retainers before you can have them and wear them."

Ukrainian children were dying of Chernobyl-related thyroid cancer. Tuberculosis and AIDS were spreading rapidly. Typhus was still a problem. And the health minister needed to decide whether it was okay for a foreigner to wear orthodontic retainers at night.

We drove across town, trudged up three flights of stairs, and were told the health minister's secretary was busy. We went in anyway. The secretary had a champagne glass in one hand, a chocolate in the other. She and another woman in the office were celebrating. We were into 2007 by now, according to my count. The health minister was on vacation.

"When can we come back?" I asked.

"Whenever you want," was the reply.

"No, I mean when can the health minister see us?"

"They don't know when he'll be back," Sveta said. "They say we can call every day, and then, when he is back, we can fax our request. If he has time and wants to, he will contact us."

We went back to FedEx and waited outside Sergei's closed door.

"Maybe you should bribe him," Sveta suggested.

"Think twenty dollars would be enough?" I asked.

"I think so."

We stood pondering the situation a few more minutes. Then I told Sveta to go. I could risk trouble, but Sveta was local, and I didn't want to put her at risk. She squeezed my hand and left. I crumpled twenty dollars in my hand and walked into the room. I spotted my package in the corner, grabbed it, put the twenty dollars in its place, and ran. The security guard caught me halfway down the hall. Sergei came storming after me. "Take your money," he spat in Russian, throwing the twenty-dollar bill at me. "Give back the package."

Twenty dollars hadn't been enough. I handed the package over but not before taking my retainer case out and slipping it into my pocket. It didn't work. Sergei spotted my deception and demanded the retainers. With my hand in my pocket I slid the retainers from the case, carefully closed the case again, and handed it over. He was furious. "Give back the contraband!" he shouted in Russian.

Contraband! Now that was something my retainers had never been called; disgusting, yes, but contraband? By now everyone in the office had gathered round. Even the head of FedEx wanted my retainers. My orthodontist could have done great business in Kyiv. Amid the ruckus a slim young woman with long brown hair, leather pants, and stiletto heels stepped forward.

"My name is Tanya. What is yours?"

"Katya."

It seemed a strange time to be getting acquainted, but I clearly wasn't going anywhere. "Katiusha, you know they are going to call the police," Tanya said. I nodded. They had been nice enough to repeat that five times. "They are going now to call," Tanya said, pointing toward the head of FedEx, who was walking to the phone. "You will have to stay overnight in the jail because it is late and your embassy cannot help you until tomorrow."

She was right; no country could save you after five in the afternoon. It was six. Suddenly the security guard pushed me aside, and two fully armed officers entered. They scanned the crowd, looking for the culprit. Sergei pointed at me. "She has contraband goods," he said in Russian. The police officers looked at me, a young woman with a baby blue hat with a little tassel on the top. They looked back at Sergei. "You must take her or make her give back the contraband," Sergei said in Russian.

The police officers nodded as if they understood. Then they moved closer. I was starting to catch on that these people weren't bluffing. "Hand over the contraband," the first cop said in Russian. The second fiddled with a pair of handcuffs. "Jail here is not so good," Tanya said.

I pulled my hand out of my pocket and held out the retainers. The police officer gingerly took the two little pink plastic pieces decorated with tiny red hearts. Tanya patted me on the shoulder. "If you want them, you refuse the package, and it is sent back to your mother. Then she gets them to you in another way."

I followed her advice. A friend of a friend smuggled my retainers in her suitcase a few months later.

33 Taken

When my cell phone was stolen, I didn't involve the police, I just called my number from Sveta's phone.

"Hallo," a male voice answered.

"You have my phone," I said. "I want my phone."

I didn't bother with Russian. I just kept talking to him in English until he hung up. I called back, again and again. He hung up every time. Then he stopped answering. Cell phones weren't that expensive in Kyiv, and my phone card was almost used up. But it was my phone, my number, and now it was in someone else's hands. I couldn't cancel the number like in the United States; I had to get a whole new one. It seemed simpler to get my phone back from the robber, who I was pretty sure had lifted it from my bag while we were all jammed together on the metro. I had spoken to him; I knew his voice. There was a link to my phone that made it seem reasonable I would be able to recover it.

But it turned out the phone was as lost to me as the money that disappeared from the magician's hand in Moldova. That act was performed with the help of a room full of accomplices, leaving me bereft of both my money and my faith in humanity.

Moldova was the last stop on a reporting trip I took just before the winter trip to the States. And the first if you subscribe to the borders Moldova claims. But in Trans-Dniester no one follows Moldovan rule. A strip of land bordering Ukraine on one side and separated from Moldova by the Dniester River on the other, Trans-Dniester is one of several "breakaway" republics established in the wake of the Soviet Union's demise. It is officially part of

Moldova but leans east while the rest of the country leans west. It declared independence after Moldova made Romanian the official language in the early 1990s. A brief war followed, and a schizophrenic understanding has kept the peace ever since. Moldova insists Trans-Dniester is part of Moldova, while Trans-Dniester maintains its own government, laws, and currency. Complicating the matter is a large cache of weapons and ammunition stored in the region by the Soviet Army—and a lot of Russians, some of whom formerly belonged to the Soviet Army.

It was the weapons cache that attracted me. At least that was the excuse I gave my editor, Greg, for wanting to investigate. Really I was just fascinated by the element of make-believe. It was as if a child's game of create-your-own-kingdom had become reality. I wanted to know what it was like to live in a country that didn't exist.

A visiting Trans-Dniester government official made the arrangements. Sveta and I met him in the lobby of a fancy Kyiv hotel. He introduced himself as Grisha, and Sveta and I followed suit, offering only our first names. Later we discovered Grisha was vice president of the country. Sveta was mortified she had spoken to him so informally. I reminded her that while Grisha might be a vice president, the country he served didn't really exist.

We began our trip in the night, as Grisha had advised. It was a matter of practicality, not subterfuge. Overnight transportation saved on hotel costs and meant no day time was wasted in traveling. I had convinced Greg to let Dima accompany us, and I felt a little safer with him by my side. I had been hoping for a coach with reclining seats but settled for the back bench of an overcrowded bus. I tried to sleep by leaning on Dima's shoulder but went flying upward whenever the driver hit a pothole and forward whenever he stopped, both frequent occurrences.

We were awake but fuzzy with sleep when several uniformed men boarded the bus in the early hours of the morning. Armed officials frequently inspected buses in the region, so I was not immediately alarmed. Panic didn't come until they disembarked with our passports. I looked at Sveta and Dima, questioning them with my eyes instead of words. I was the only foreigner on the bus and had gone to a lot of trouble to sandwich my blue U.S. passport between Sveta and Dima's red ones. I was reluctant to ruin the deception by revealing my outsider origins with my accent. The guard who reboarded the bus a few minutes later had no such qualms. He waved my distinctive blue passport above his head.

"Who does this belong to?" he demanded in Russian.

"*Eto moy* [It's mine]," I replied.

He made a motion with his head for me to follow him off the bus.

"She is a foreigner; let me come with her to help translate," Sveta said in Russian.

"*Ne nado*," he said.

He took a hold of my arm. As I hurried to slip on my boots, Sveta whispered in my ear: "Just pretend you don't understand."

It wasn't hard to do. I was half asleep and found their official jargon unrecognizable. There were no lights visible on the road or in the fields that surrounded it. I was led to a little hut and told to sit. The man seated across from me turned each page in my passport slowly, pointing to a visa every once in a while and asking what it was for. He was not accusatory so much as curious. I wondered if he had ever seen an American passport. I wondered if he had ever seen an American. I didn't ask. Instead I focused on the bus outside, as if by keeping my eyes on it I could will it not to leave without me.

"Where are you from?" the seated official asked in Russian.

This was a tricky question. I decided to keep it simple by answering, "Kyiv."

"Why do you want to go to Trans-Dniester?"

Again a complicated question, especially because I wasn't sure if I was at a Moldovan or Trans-Dniester checkpoint. He had used the word "Trans-Dniester," so I decided he was probably not Moldovan. I did not point out that officially Trans-Dniester was in Moldova. Or that technically he didn't have any authority because he was employed by a country that didn't exist. If you have weapons, that is the only authority you need, and he and his men had weapons. So I told him the vice president had invited me to the country that didn't actually exist.

He handed me back my passport and told me to go. The guard who had taken me off the bus escorted me back onto it. The other passengers watched silently as I made my way to the back. They didn't look at me, and they didn't ask questions. They didn't want to know why I had been pulled off or why I was back on. They just wanted to go.

"What did they want?" Sveta whispered.

"I don't know."

"You were there half an hour; what do you mean you don't know?" said Dima.

"I think they liked looking at my visas."

I shut my eyes and lay my head on Dima's shoulder. Sleep was always a good way to escape a conversation I didn't know how to have. I was back on the bus and I had no intention of revisiting the fear I felt as I sat in that remote border post far from everything and everyone I knew. Unfortunately the experience was repeated once more before I made it to our destination. I believe this time it was Moldovan authorities that took me off the bus, but I am not positive. All I know is that every time we reached a border, or a spot where someone had declared a border, everyone remained seated while I was escorted off the bus and questioned like some sort of criminal. I kept my boots on the rest of the night and never slept more than an hour or so at a time.

It was daylight when we arrived in Tiraspol, the capital of Trans-Dniester. The station where we got off didn't seem that different from a Ukrainian bus station. The people spoke Russian, and the buildings were of the same uniform Soviet style. But the man who met us at the station made no pretense of being anything but a KGB secret police type. He took us to our hotel, where they immediately demanded double the price on seeing my American passport. I was getting a bit tired of the special treatment. It happened in Ukraine as well. I argued my case the same way I did there, explaining that I was living in Ukraine, not the United States, and while I was making more than most locals, I was not making anything close to Western wages. The price was lowered and I was headed toward the room to freshen up after a night spent on the bus when a bark from the receptionist stopped me.

"What's going on?" I asked Sveta. "Why can't we go to the room?"

"We aren't allowed to stay here until after we register with the police," she said.

"Register with the police? Have we done something wrong?"

"Not if we register with the police."

I didn't ask for further explanation. I had heard of police states; I just never thought police supervision was quite so obvious. In Ukraine the SBU (KGB successor) was sometimes heavy footed but never so direct. I heard the clicks that meant my home phone calls in Kyiv were being recorded, but I never actually spoke with anyone on the other line. When I briefly forwarded my email to my mother's email account during a trip back to California, someone attempted to hack into it. Her provider later traced the hack back to the Ukrainian phone service.

I knew I was being watched in Ukraine, but it was semi-discreet. In Trans-Dniester it was blatantly obvious. The man who followed us wanted us to know he was watching. When Dima took a picture of a poster hanging on the wall of the police station, two officers immediately surrounded him. They demanded he erase the shot. He did as he was told, deleting the photo of wanted criminals. I was glad he would not be added to the list and relieved when we were ushered to the front of the long line at the station before Dima could find something else to photograph. At the counter we showed our passports and were given a slip of paper. The fee we were supposed to pay was waived. Those waiting behind us looked as if they wanted to break our arms, but no one grumbled about our cutting in line or our lack of payment.

Our next stop was a money exchange. It seemed odd for a four-thousand-square-kilometer piece of land to have its own currency, but it did. If we wanted to buy anything, we needed to use it. With money and our registration we were able to return to the hotel and rest for a bit until the handler came back for us. On most trips I arranged the meetings and itinerary, but in Trans-Dniester no meeting was made without government permission, so it was Grisha who arranged everything and the handler who made sure we followed through. It was nice not having to work the phones but unnerving not being able to control what I saw and did.

I had asked to meet with the country's president, Igor Smirnov, but was only half expecting the interview to happen. Our handler liked to keep us in the dark until the last minute, so as a result the local television crew that filmed our meeting with Smirnov was better prepared than I was. I didn't see the newscast that ran later, but I am pretty sure my smiling American face did a lot to bolster the president's propaganda machine. He kept calling me Katiusha and asking about my Russian connections. I knew he was playing me, but I couldn't help enjoying the attention. He had one of those oversized personalities that are pure pleasure to be around when you are a welcome guest. He was a big man with bushy gray eyebrows that arched upward like an owl's and a trendy goatee and mustache. His was a carefully construed image that was displayed on the currency, on the cover of the country's official history, and on the walls of most government buildings. It was a classic cult of personality with an ironic Russian twist, as if Smirnov knew the whole thing was absurd.

When I asked about the Soviet weapons cache, I was told it was gone. It had disappeared during the chaos of the fight for independence following the Soviet collapse. When I brought up the issue of smuggling, Smirnov laughed good naturedly and changed the subject. I asked again. He offered me some of the best tea I had ever tasted. I wasn't going to get anything substantive from him with the cameras in the room. I enjoyed my tea and decided to find my answers elsewhere.

As Sveta and I fished for information in other meetings around town, she marveled at how the buses were still heated and the hotel had hot water, like during Soviet times. I noticed the Lenin statue outside the parliament building, billboards with hammers and sickles, and phrases like "Together we are stronger." Soviet passports were still in use, and the only foreigners we came across were a group of teenage handball players from Belarus, another Soviet wonderland ruled by a fellow egomaniac. It was the closest I would ever get to the USSR. It was a make-believe kingdom operated by a single man in a time warp under which the Soviet system had never collapsed. Smirnov's rein ended in 2012, but the illusion lives on. At his successor's inauguration the only foreign dignitaries present were Russian.

Dima headed back to Kyiv that night. Sveta and I planned to travel to Moldova in the morning to meet with a government official. We spent our evening searching for the tea Smirnov had served us. The local people went out of their way to help us track it down, escorting us to shop after shop until finally we found two boxes of it at a small kiosk. I noticed our tail the entire time and at one point was tempted to ask him for help finding the tea. He was so nondescript that I can't recall his name or anything else about him, but there was something about the way he moved and watched us that let us know it was him.

I think his presence is what kept the beggar girl from getting too close. She stood near us but kept her mouth closed, extending only a small dirty hand. I seldom gave money to beggars in Ukraine; the older ones were usually drunk and the younger ones at the mercy of an adult who took anything they were given. But there was something so desperate and gentle about this girl that I couldn't walk away without doing something. I bought her a tin of peanuts from the kiosk. When I placed the tin in her hands, her face lit up with pleasure. A few more children crept out of the shadows, and she shook the tin in excitement as if it were a toy. I thought they would all now demand a tin of their own, but neither the girl nor any of the others asked for anything else. They kept laughing and shaking and eating. We left them there, children for a brief moment of time. When I was robbed the next day, I kept thinking about how many peanut tins I could have bought for those children with the money that was taken from me.

In the morning we took an ancient bus bound for the Moldovan capital of Chisinau. In less than half an hour we were at the border. I was escorted off the bus once again. This time my interrogation was more intense. The Trans-Dniester border agents kept questioning the legality of my stay in their "country." Only after I produced the slip of paper I had been given at the police station did they allow me back on the bus. They warned me that I would have three hours to pass back through Trans-Dniester on my return before I would have to register again. No one asked to see Sveta's police registration or that of anyone else on the bus.

There was no Moldovan checkpoint because officially we had been in Moldova all along. I was getting a little confused as to whose laws I should be following. The scenery was rather beautiful, forests giving way to hills dotted with vineyards. The city was less welcoming. It was crowded, noisy, dirty, and chaotic. In Trans-Dniester the people had looked Russian; in Moldova they were darker and spoke Romanian instead of Russian. Street vendors were far more frequent than in Ukraine, and I noticed the lack of mafia wealth I had grown accustomed to in Kyiv. In comparison to Chisinau, Kyiv suddenly seemed civilized and cosmopolitan.

We pushed our way through the streets trying to reach the government building where we had arranged to meet with an official. The interview was brief. Moldova was engaged in an economic blockade of Trans-Dniester, stopping shipments from entering or exiting it. I had hoped our host would offer us tea and cookies, but no such pleasantry was extended, and Sveta and I went away unfulfilled both intellectually and physically. We hadn't eaten since morning and were hungry, but we were having trouble negotiating the intricacies of foreign currencies. When I tried to use my Trans-Dniester money to buy crackers at a kiosk, I was laughed at. When I tried to exchange it, I ran into a different problem. The money changer agreed to speak with me in her limited English but was less flexible in other areas.

"What is this?" she asked when I handed her a few of my Trans-Dniester bills.

"Money from Trans-Dniester," I replied.

"You mean Moldova."

"Yeah, kind of, but they have their own money."

"There is no such thing."

I wasn't sure how to explain that there was in fact such a thing and I was holding proof of it. In Moldova they were playing the same game of make-believe as the people of Trans-Dniester. I was getting a little tired of it. I wanted some food. I had money to pay, money I had used just the day before several miles away. But no one would accept it, and no one would change it into any other currency. The only other money I had was a $100 bill, and I didn't want to break it. That was a lot of money, and I didn't trust it to the sidewalk money changers. We went hungry a while longer. Our train tickets back to Kyiv weren't until the next day, but neither of us wanted to spend another night in Moldova, so we went to the station to see if we could change them. The answer was no. But we could convert them to bus tickets for that night and receive a coupon for the difference. The coupon was basically worthless, but the tickets had been cheap, and Sveta and I were desperate to get home.

The bus wasn't leaving for several more hours, so we decided to change money at the station and get something to eat. But the money changer was closed. An old woman approached and offered to help us. Sveta told her how much we had, and she said she couldn't exchange that much. Later Sveta would tell me that she started to get a weird feeling about things after talking to the woman. We were both uneasy and didn't like carrying around so much money, especially now that a local woman knew how much we had. Outside the station we stopped at a hotel to try to change the money. If we could break it, we could then spend a little of it and have a little less on hand to worry about. The women at the hotel told us the money-changing booth was closed. But when a man approached and said he worked in the booth, they didn't contradict him. As he pretended to open the door to the change booth, he asked to see the bill. I didn't like his attitude or having to show him the money. But I was stuck. I needed to change it. And it was in a legitimate hotel, and the people in the hotel did not deny that he worked at the change kiosk.

I looked at Sveta. She shrugged, as if saying what choice do we have. I showed him the bill. He grabbed it from my hand and started speaking rapidly in a mix of Russian and Romanian I couldn't follow. He held the bill in front of my face pulling it back and forth in his two hands as I grabbed at it. When I finally pulled it away, I realized too late it was not the bill I had given him. I was holding one dollar, not one hundred. He was gone by then. I ran out of the hotel and asked the men standing outside which way he had gone. They didn't answer me. I stormed back into the hotel, furious that everyone had been in on the trick but Sveta and me.

"Where did he go?" I shouted in a mix of Russian and English. No one met my eyes. No one answered. "You saw him; he took my money, where did he go?" They just stared at me.

"Someone knows where he went; you knew him," I said.

Sveta tugged at my sleeve. "Come on; they're not going to help."

"No," I said, shoving her away. "They saw it. They have to tell me where he went."

I stood there glaring at the people in the hotel, hoping I would make them uncomfortable enough to do something. But they did not seem to feel guilty. I threw down my bag, kicked the change booth, and stormed out.

Sveta picked up my bag and followed me as I ran down the street glaring at every man I passed trying to determine if he was the thief. I shoved past people as I went, the anger in me escaping in physical exertion. I walked into a bar where several men leered at me. I ignored them, intent only on finding the face of the man who had robbed me. After an hour and a short tour of that section of the city I gave up and crumpled on a set of stairs. I had just lost a hundred dollars, almost half of my rent, a huge sum of money for me at the time. "I hate this fucking country; I hate these fucking people," I said to no one and everyone.

A few young men snickered as they passed by. Another looked as if he might approach. I glared at him, and he scurried off. I knew I was creating quite a scene, but I didn't care. I never planned to return to Moldova, and I was too miserable to think about what I was doing. Someone must have called the cops because two nice young officers who spoke passable English showed up and asked me what happened. In between sobs I told them. They were sympathetic but said they wouldn't be able to do anything until morning. I told them I was not staying another night in their country.

Sveta and I walked back to the train station in silence. It wasn't fair, but I blamed her for encouraging me to change the money. Sveta was older and more familiar with this part of the world than I was, and I think I expected her to take care of me. She usually did, but Moldova was as foreign to her as it was to me. She had been with me and had fallen for the same trick. Only it was my money, not hers; I was the one who was out a hundred dollars. We started talking again on the bus ride back to Ukraine. A man sitting nearby who had overheard our story offered us his sandwich.

"This is not a good country; I do not like it," he said of Moldova.

"I hate it," I said.

He laughed: "Yes, Ukraine is better."

Later in the night I woke up to find his coat draped over me. I nestled under it, happy I was headed home.

34 The Missing

The woman I needed lived in a little village several hundred miles southwest of Moscow. She didn't have a phone, and she didn't answer the telegrams Sveta and I sent her. The only way to reach her was to go to her home. We took a train to Moscow and then another to Nizhny Novgorod. From there we took a car to the village where Yelena lived. We stood on her doorstep on a January day so cold that my metal pen stuck to my tongue when I briefly placed it in my mouth.

"What if she doesn't want to talk?" Sveta asked.

"She will," I said.

What I really meant was that she had to. I had convinced *Marie Claire* to commission me to write Yelena's story and those of women like her. I couldn't return to Kyiv without it. I had promised Sveta one hundred dollars to translate for me on the trip, a salary I couldn't pay if I didn't produce a story and get paid myself. Dima was with us as well, and he would receive no money for his photos if the story didn't run. I had already paid for all of our train tickets and several small meals. Yelena simply had to talk.

We had interviewed other women for the story, fearful souls who were reluctant to give their full names and whose trips to Chechnya in search of their missing soldier sons had taken place years before. Yelena was the only one I knew of who was still searching. She had been to Chechnya three times and would return a fourth time two weeks after our visit. I didn't know she planned to return so soon. I didn't know the only reason we were able to find her at home was because we had come during Orthodox New Year. She had decided to stay with her husband and teenage daughter for the holiday. She had received our telegrams but had not replied because she had nothing to say. She spoke now only because we were there. There was no polite way to send us away. In small Russian villages hospitality is a requirement of existence.

A kitten played in her lap as she spoke. A small icon of Jesus was pinned to the wall behind her. In pictures her son Denis came across as a slim teen with boyish wavy blond hair and dressed in an ill-fitting army uniform. He had been serving his two years of mandatory military service when he was captured in 2000. Yelena learned about his capture not from the military but from another young man who had just returned from serving in Chechnya. If the military had said anything, it would have said he was a deserter. It was easier that way. There was no institutional responsibility, no need to mount a rescue. The conscripts were mere teens, too young to have wives, too ill-trained and too ill-equipped to be a serious danger. To many of their commanders they were cannon fodder, worth even less than the uniforms they wore. Only their mothers missed them.

There were no winners in Chechnya, just survivors. The first war in 1994 was supposed to be a short operation, as they always are, to bring Chechnya back under Russian control. Less than a year later twenty-five thousand people had been killed, and Russia withdrew in disgrace. The Russians returned in 1999 following a series of Moscow bombings blamed on Chechens. The fighting destroyed the Chechen economy, leaving the selling of captives as one of the few ways to make a living. Middlemen sprang up to meet the demand. Some were legitimate; others were con artists. The mothers relied on these men. They trusted them more than the Russian military commanders who were known to bomb the villages the mothers visited. They believed if the mothers were there, then captives were there and thus rebels were there. That the mothers, captives, and civilians might also be killed in the bombings did not seem to bother them.

The mothers took to wearing head scarves to blend in. They carried photos of their teenage sons to cafés, asking anyone who would listen if they had seen them. Natalya was one of the first to travel to Chechnya. She went in the beginning and had since helped hundreds of other mothers through the organization she had set up. Some came back alive, as her son

Sergey had; others came back in body bags. Then there were those who remained missing, like Denis. Yelena had been told that if she could arrange the transfer of an imprisoned Chechen, her son would be returned to her. It was just the latest in a long list of negotiations she had tried to take part in. The negotiators and terms changed, but she remained convinced at the end of all of them that she would be reunited with her son. Natalya was less sure. "As a rule, if you don't get him at the very beginning, according to our bitter experience you won't get him at all," said Natalya. "Or if you do, it will only be his body."

That can be a relief in itself. A woman who didn't want to give her full name for fear the government would punish her spoke about the awful happiness she felt when she found her son's body. She had spent months tracking clues to his whereabouts in Chechnya, always one step behind his captors. She stumbled on the bombed building where he was last held only after it had been destroyed and all the captives killed. She found his body in a morgue, identifiable only by his dental records.

Dima and I almost always worked together now. I had quit the *Kyiv Post* and was writing solely for Western publications. When they accepted my stories, I recommended Dima as a photographer. Somehow he found time to continue working for the *Kyiv Post* and also to shoot my stories. He liked the work I got him better; it paid well and was more prestigious. It was also one of the few times we had together. We made a good team. We even made up little business cards calling ourselves "Eastern European Features Agency" or EEFA for short. I still have a few. They are nicely done, white with red type and a little map of the world with an arrow pointing to Eastern Europe. I took care of all of the business—rounding up work, showing Dima how to invoice, making sure he got the right visas to travel. All Dima had to do was shoot. I didn't mind; I liked working with him, and in Kyiv he did other things for me. We worked well together; it was easy.

The whole marriage thing was another matter. I kept changing my mind. He was too charming sometimes, especially with other women. There was one woman in particular we used to fight over. I caught him holding her hand once. He was always complimenting her feminine ways, encouraging me to be more like her. When I complained, he insisted I misunderstood, that she had a boyfriend and that the two of them were just friends, colleagues. I wanted to believe him, but I doubted him. Later, in the States, there would be another woman he spent too much time with. But by then there were probably men I spent too much time with as well. The woman in Kyiv was just the first to find an opening. Maybe it was my fault for not knowing how to close it.

There was too much going on for us to waste much time arguing about our relationship. We would have our fights and then get back to work. Most of the work I did then provided enough drama to spare. The only stories I could sell to U.S. publications immediately after 9/11 had to do with terror or the Ukrainian protest movement. The topics fed on public fear. I found the reality more depressing than sinister.

The former Soviet scientists who the United States feared might sell their secrets to rogue nations were a desperate lot. The lights in their apartments were broken, duct tape covered their doors, and paint was chipping from their walls. One leading thinker drank weak coffee from a mug that he had bought during a trip to the United States three years before. They all clung to their memories. Life had once been better for them—not great, but better. There had been a time when their offices were heated and the typewriters they used were not obsolete. Heavy smokers who survived on salaries of one hundred dollars a month or less, they were a sad group I pitied more than feared. Their danger lay not in ideology but in desperation.

Politics were a far more explosive topic. The month before Ukraine's parliamentary elections a group of parliamentary deputies called for President Kuchma's impeachment. The tapes that implicated Kuchma in Gongadze's disappearance had finally been authenticated. Ukraine had never been known for its transparency, but in the aftermath of Gongadze's disappearance and the resulting protests, the parliamentary elections were particularly fraught with allegations of corruption. The Western world wanted details. I had never reported directly on Ukrainian politics, but I somehow convinced the *Wall Street Journal* and the *Baltimore Sun* I was the best person to do so. I was in over my head, and the subtle warnings from some of those I interviewed proved how ill-suited I was for the job. It was one thing to write about such matters for the *Kyiv Post*, another to write about them for the *Wall Street Journal*. No direct threats were made. None needed to be. All they needed to tell me was what they did: they knew who I was.

Until then I had never had to face the details of how the political machine worked in Ukraine. It was both complicated and incredibly simple. The government made sure companies had the right conditions in which to operate their businesses, and the companies in turn made sure their employees voted for the pro-government candidate. Threats of pay cuts were enough to ensure employees did what they were told, and state funds further helped government-supported candidates run successful campaigns, while independent candidates were blocked from accessing the media. Most of the work was done in the open with little attempt at cover-up. The assailants who destroyed the entire weekly run of one opposition paper in the run-up to the elections were dressed as police.

Surveys showed the majority of Ukrainians had no faith in the democratic process. I tended to agree with them. The thing was, no one seemed to care much. Two things had happened since the spark had ignited: 9/11 and increased government suppression. The terror attacks had refocused world and even domestic attention. Possible outside enemies became a higher priority for both the government and protesters. Government suppression had squashed independent voices so effectively after the widespread protests of the year before that there seemed little energy or strength left to fight. Inertia had set in. The elections were carried off just as predicted. Kuchma and his cronies remained in power. It would be another two years and another round before the revolution succeeded.

35 Shot in the Butt

The attack came in the middle of the night. I managed to half crawl, half slither to the bathroom, where I spent the next six hours hunched over the toilet. Throwing up is never enjoyable, but throwing up into a toilet that belongs to two bachelors is particularly distasteful. I would think about this briefly, focusing on one particular stain or another, in between my heaves. Occasionally I would contemplate what I would do if one of the apartment's other two occupants needed to use the bathroom. Morning came without interruption, and I called weakly for my host. When he found me by the toilet, he was surprised but not overly concerned. That wouldn't happen until later, when he found himself stuck with me indefinitely.

"Were you here all night?" he asked.

I nodded my head.

"Was it something you ate?"

I nodded again.

"The food yesterday was too rich, wasn't it?"

I nodded.

"What should I do?"

I finally spoke. "Call a doctor."

He moved me to his absent roommate's room for the examination. The doctor was a little guy who spoke some English, some Russian, and a lot of Bulgarian. My host, Michael, helped translate. I learned what I already knew. I was having a pancreatitis attack.

"He wants to give you a shot to help," Michael said.

"What kind of shot?"

Before Michael could answer the little doctor interrupted.

"A shot in the butt," he said.

"No, not where," I said. "What kind?"

"In the *butt*," the doctor repeated loudly in his bastardized English.

Michael and I looked at each other. The little doctor got a syringe ready. He made a show of demonstrating the clean packaging, emphasizing that he used fresh needles, not like in Africa. Then he shot me in the butt.

"That it then?" Michael asked.

"No, now she must come to the hospital for fluids."

"But I thought the whole reason of the house call was so she wouldn't have to leave the house," Michael said.

"Yes, but now she needs to go."

I was too weak to argue and almost too weak to walk to the clinic. It was only a block away, but it took us a good twenty minutes to get there. I leaned heavily on Michael the whole way. The doctor hooked me up to an IV that delivered fluids and pain killers. I told Michael to come back in a few hours when it was done and drifted off to sleep. When I woke up, he was still there, sitting in a chair across from me, reading a newspaper.

"In the *butt*," Michael said.

"In the *butt*," I echoed.

I didn't even know his last name.

I had realized that a few days before, when I had once again found myself in a foreign airport without the slightest clue how to find my way around. Michael had promised to meet me at the Sofia airport in Bulgaria. I hadn't thought about what I would do if he wasn't there. I scanned the waiting crowd, looking for a tall American. I kept looking as all the waiting people claimed the other passengers until I was the only one left. I spent the next half hour studying several lingering men, most likely taxi drivers. After forty minutes I approached one of the men and asked if he was Michael. He wasn't, but he offered to let me use his cell phone to call Michael. That is when I realized I didn't have Michael's number.

"Maybe he decide meet you at home," the man said. "Tell me address." I didn't know that either. "Silly girl," he said. "No one can help you." He laughed as he walked away.

Michael and I had met online. He was looking for information about Trans-Dniester, and I had told him what I knew. By way of thanks he invited me to report on a retirement home for dancing bears in Bulgaria. It sounded like a fun story; the plane ride was short and the ticket relatively cheap. I didn't put much more thought into it than that, which is how I found myself stranded at the Sofia airport. I didn't have enough cash to buy an early return ticket and hadn't brought my bank card. Credit cards were not used at that time in that part of the world. I talked myself into the idea that Michael would still come because I had no other option. And he did come, an hour and a half late. Traffic had been horrendous, and he was terribly sorry. All the apologies after that would be mine. Michael was American, like me, and working as a freelancer. He had already made arrangements for a translator/fixer to accompany us to the village where the bear retirement sanctuary was located. We left the following day.

The sanctuary was former movie star Brigitte Bardot's idea. She wanted to buy dancing bears from their gypsy owners and offer them a chance to live out their remaining years in peace without having to perform. The bears were housed in a vast grassy enclosure in an impoverished rural village. We walked alongside the fencing and saw the roly-poly black bears lounging in the sun. Inside the sanctuary office, a cabin-like enclosure, we were shown videos about how the gypsies got the bears to dance. They pierced the creatures' snouts with a large metal ring and kept the bears chained up when they weren't forced to stand on their hind legs and do a sort of jig. The bears in the videos were small, no bigger than most men, with shabby coats and dull eyes.

The Western press loved it. A beautiful reclusive woman had set out to save abused animals. The locals had a slightly different take on things, which we heard when we left the sanctuary and walked through the quiet village.

"You know they feed those bears watermelon," a young villager told us. "I don't eat watermelon."

"Those bears eat better than we do," another said.

In winter cold air seeped in through the broken windows at the village school. Fresh fruit and vegetables were treats the village children seldom saw, but the bears were fed them daily. It might have been funny if it hadn't been tragic. I liked the bears. I liked the villagers. I even almost liked the public relations people who had organized the whole celebration for the sanctuary. They had somehow managed to convince one of the bears' former owners to attend. When I asked what he had done with the money he had received for his bear, he told me he had used it to buy a performing monkey.

It was toward the end of the day that I started feeling nauseous. I had eaten several cookies and went outside the room where the presentations were being given for fresh air. I sat on a step and threw up. Another guest found me there a few minutes later and got Michael to take me home. It was a long, bumpy road back to Sofia, but I managed to survive it without throwing up again. I might have been okay if I hadn't ordered a creamy noodle dish at the restaurant Michael took me to that evening.

I spent the next several days on Michael's couch watching the Hallmark Channel, one of only two English-language channels available. The movies were pure mush, and I cried at the end of every single one. I called Dima one evening and my mother on another. There wasn't really anything anyone could do. Once an attack started, I had to rest my pancreas, which meant no eating and little drinking. Without food I lacked energy and could handle nothing more than watching Hallmark classics.

Michael bought me clear juices, and on the third day I tried dry toast. On the fourth I got off the couch long enough to pack and take a taxi to the airport with Michael. The driver was erratic, swerving in and out of traffic and stopping and starting suddenly, all customary for that part of the world but brutal when you are nauseous.

"Michael, I'm not feeling so good," I said.

"Just hang in there; we're almost there."

He was right; in a few more turns we were at the airport, and he was helping me up the steps. He settled me on a bench before going off to find out where I needed to check in. "Wait here, I'll be right back," he said. "Just don't throw up."

I was still sitting there five minutes later when he returned. A janitor was mopping up the floor to my right.

"I'm sorry," I said. "I tried."

"It's okay. Come on let's get you on your plane."

An official looking man approached.

"What's wrong?" he asked Michael. "Is she pregnant?"

"No, just a little car sick," said Michael.

I stood up and tried hard to look healthy as Michael and I walked away. The official called after us.

"She cannot fly like that," he said.

"Like what?" said Michael. "She's just a little sick; she'll be fine."

"Then you can return with a doctor's note tomorrow, and we will let her fly."

"But the next flight to Kyiv isn't for four more days," I said.

The official wouldn't budge. We kept arguing. Another official was found. The same argument was made. Two hours later the flight to Kyiv left without me. I returned to the couch and Hallmark. Somehow I managed not to throw up on the taxi ride back, a guilty success if there ever was one. I tried to be as good a house guest as I could. When Michael's Bulgarian girlfriend came over, I pulled the covers up to my neck, hoping she wouldn't notice the sick American chick huddled on her boyfriend's couch.

In order to get me back to Kyiv it was necessary for a doctor to write a note saying it was safe for me to fly. Neither Michael nor I wanted to revisit the little doctor who made house calls, so we agreed to meet with a friend of a friend of Michael's who knew a doctor. The meeting spot was several blocks away. We had to walk because I could not be trusted on transportation. Michael wrapped one arm around me and offered the other for me to lean on. I watched pedestrians hurry past us, talking as they went. There was so much activity outside, so much movement. My world had stood still the last few days, and now everything was whirring past. I stopped every few feet to catch my breath. I thought about how I used to run a half mile in a little over two minutes. I wondered where that body was; it seemed impossible it had ever belonged to me and that I would ever inhabit it again.

At the doctor's office we revealed as little as possible. We decided that telling him I had pancreatitis would not help our cause. The doctor did a quick examination and decided it was too risky. I couldn't blame him. My blood pressure, heart rate, and temperature were all almost too low for the living. Without food and liquid my body slowed down dramatically. If he signed a note saying I was healthy and then my heart stopped working, he would be in trouble. Still, I wanted to get home.

For the second doctor we tried a different tactic. We told him even less but paid him even more. He agreed to write the note if I returned in a few days looking better. A few days later I didn't look any better but I was still alive, so he wrote the note and we returned to the airport. I didn't throw up this time. I also didn't have a ticket. When they had kicked me off my original flight, they had canceled my ticket and had not rebooked me. I was out the money for the original ticket and had no money with which to buy a new one. Michael ended up buying the ticket. I sent him a check a month later from California. He never cashed it. I wish I could remember his last name.

I didn't go to California right away. First I returned to Kyiv and Dima's care. In truth it was his mother who cared for me, making me a special broth with dumplings every few days. Even with her soup and ministrations I continued to deteriorate. Only this time it wasn't just my pancreas. I started suffering vertigo and had trouble hearing out of my right ear. The first time it happened I was cooking on the stove when the floor came up in front of me and I fell to meet it. When I straightened myself out, I noticed I had burned my arm on the stove's flame. I looked outside to see if the children in the yard had noticed the earthquake. They were playing the same as they had been a minute before. The earthquake had been in my head.

Dima and his mother took me to another hospital, where I waited for hours while they gave me IVs that took just as long as the old ones had. They put me in a booth, tested my hearing, and told me I had 50 percent hearing loss in my right ear. I went for treatments daily for a week, but I was still dizzy and suffering from ringing in my ears. I fell down a flight of stairs in my apartment building. I worried about walking alone. Sveta took me to a doctor who used magnets and wires to cure people. Another doctor did a CAT scan and suggested brain surgery. My mother begged me to come home.

I stayed because of Dima. Sveta told me he was the reason I should go. She worried he would get tired of taking care of me; I wondered if that meant she had. I don't believe Sveta could relax while I was in Ukraine.

She worried about me too much. I never really worried about her. I thought she would always be there when I needed her. Later I lost touch with her. When I tried to find her again, she seemed reluctant to reconnect. I had contacted her because I needed help with something. Only after I had completed that task and still hadn't heard from her did I realize I missed her and wanted to hear her voice. We hadn't had a lot in common, and if we had met at a different time in a different place, we might not have been friends. But we met in Kyiv in the run-up to the Orange Revolution, and for three years we were inseparable.

I spent several weeks in California recuperating. I gained back some of the weight I had lost and the ringing in my ears subsided. I still had hearing loss, but the vertigo didn't flare up while I was in California, and I felt well enough to return to Ukraine. I was the only one who thought it a good idea. But I wasn't ready to give up on my life there yet. I wasn't ready to leave Dima or the freelance work that was starting to take off.

The vertigo and ringing in my ears returned almost immediately after I landed in Kyiv. I had more pancreatitis attacks and lost more weight. Then my landlady decided to raise my rent. Dima's mother took me to look at apartments. She conducted the interviews with prospective landlords in Russian, advising me to stay silent. I listened as she introduced me as her son's friend. Then she told them I worked for the *Wall Street Journal*. Nothing she said was exactly a lie, but it wasn't the truth either. When I protested, she silenced me, explaining that she knew what was best in these situations. I wasn't sure she did. I didn't see the advantage in telling them the things she said, only the worry of having to maintain a false existence.

She spoke conspiratorially, elaborating far too easily on my fictional background. I didn't recognize the young woman she was describing. I didn't recognize the woman she had become. The duplicity came so easily to her, developed no doubt out of necessity; it was maintained now more out of habit. When I complained to Dima later, he took her side.

"You do work for the *Wall Street Journal*, and you are my friend," he said.

"I did one story for the *Journal* as a freelancer," I corrected. "She said I had worked for it for years, had been in its offices in the States, and all sorts of other details."

"What does it matter? Those babushkas will never know the difference."

"But I do. I don't want her calling you 'my friend.'"

"Why do you make problems where there aren't any? She was trying to help you."

"I didn't ask her to lie. I can't move to any of those places now, I can't pretend to be the things she said I was."

"You don't understand how things work here; not everything is so easy as in America."

That was his favorite refrain: I didn't understand. The thing was, he never bothered to explain. I could see he was growing frustrated with my problems. I was just as aggravated. It was hard to concentrate while my ears were ringing and hard to hear when the pressure filled them. I was scared of losing my balance and falling and avoided balconies and street crossings. When we went out, I seldom ate, fearful the rich food in the restaurants would make me sick again. There wasn't much I did anymore. I couldn't bike because of the vertigo, I had trouble hanging out with friends because of the distracting ringing in my ears, and work was almost impossible because I spent so much time in hospitals.

I didn't want to, but I decided the only thing left to do was to leave Ukraine. I asked Dima to come with me. I knew he couldn't come to America unless he came as my fiancé or husband. I viewed marriage more as a necessary annoyance than a lifetime commitment, something that needed to be done in order for us to stay together. It was what normal lovers did, and I wanted desperately to be normal, to be healthy and live like other twenty-somethings did. I didn't think much about what it meant beyond that. I didn't think about what it would look like in ten or twenty years. It was hard to plan beyond the present. Whenever I did, it seemed a hospital stay would end up altering my plans.

One of the last stories I wrote before I left was about military tourism. The cash-strapped Ukrainian military was offering rich tourists a chance to fly its fighter jets and drive its military vehicles. But that's not the last story I remember. That one belongs to Dima. We had been on a boat the *Kyiv Post* had rented for its employees that day. The boat took us to an island where we ate spiked watermelons and bathed in the sun. On the way back we learned about a plane accident in Lviv. Dima had orders to leave that night to photograph it. I didn't listen to details. I only knew work was taking him away once again. There was always some tragedy in Ukraine.

He didn't return for several days. By then I knew more than I wanted to. A Ukrainian plane had crashed into spectators at an air show, killing seventy-seven people, nineteen of them children. Hundreds more were injured. Dima talked about the number of coffins for days afterward, bringing up again and again the small size of those in which the children had been enclosed. He didn't usually talk about his difficult assignments, and he didn't talk much about this one except to mention the coffins. It was the worst air show accident in history.

I moved back to the States soon after. I was too exhausted and sick to be sad—or to pack. Trevor came to help. Dima took him places he had never taken me.

We agreed Dima would follow me on a fiancé visa. It bought us both a little more time. We would marry in America and live there until I was healthy again. Both the marriage and my being healthy again seemed distant dreams, but they were something to cling to, and in my mind they were almost linked. On my last night in Kyiv I tried to get Dima to answer the questions on the visa form. He wouldn't pay attention and promised to send it later. We spoke weekly once I was in America, and each time we talked, I bugged him about the form. Finally he sent it. It was only half filled out, and it took another several conversations before I could complete it. He had always been a procrastinator, but looking back, I wonder if he had ever wanted to come. I know what his family wanted, I know what I thought I wanted, but I don't believe I really knew what Dima wanted. I don't think he did either.

PART 4 Kentucky

Hi Katya,

Here is the blurb of what I am working on:

I am a US-based visual artist, currently working on a project related to Maidan which is about the recent events in Ukraine that started as a pro-democracy movement and escalated into a standoff with Russia.

The goal of this project is to encourage people to have a dialogue and think for themselves instead of consuming the readily-available propaganda . . .

Best,

Dima

36 A Revolution

Nine months later he arrived. A month later we married. Another two and we were sleeping in separate beds. Within the year we were divorced.

The wedding was in Kentucky, where I had finally found a job as a features reporter at the *Louisville Courier-Journal.* Dima was so nervous that he fumbled his vows. I started doubting what I was doing on the short walk down the aisle.

We stayed at a local bed and breakfast on our wedding night. Dima spent most of the time filming the interior with a video camera. I spent it alone in a bath. The next morning we returned to our apartment. My mother and stepfather were staying there for the wedding, and when Dima threw open the door he shouted, "Parents!" his arms wide for a hug. I cringed. He had married my family, not me. He was especially attached to my stepfather, Trevor. He admired the way Trevor had made money in business early in life and now lived his life more or less how he pleased. As the marriage faltered, I would rely on Trevor more and more to help me out, sending Dima to him so they could go skiing together. Trevor had come late to fatherhood and was eager to make up for his earlier interactions with me, which had been tainted by his foul temper. Trevor even helped me locate a good place to honeymoon in the Caribbean several months later.

That's when the separate beds started. I slept on the large bed, and Dima slept on the couch, insisting I kicked in my sleep and it disturbed him. Back in our apartment in Louisville he again said he couldn't sleep in the same bed with me, and I ended up on the couch while he got the bed. No one before or since has voiced such a concern. On New Year's Eve I went to bed early, and he celebrated with a family of Russian immigrants he barely knew. He told me daily how much he hated America, how backward Kentucky was. He talked about joining the army one week and living in a fraternity the next. I didn't have a husband; I had a child.

In truth I wasn't much of a wife. I spent all my energy on my work, on building up my professional reputation in America. It had been hard to land a job at a large U.S. newspaper, and I felt the need to prove myself. I came home tired and not in the mood to listen to Dima's struggles with his new country. The cruel truth is that I no longer needed him. He didn't really need me either; he needed my family. He had been disappointed to learn we wouldn't be living with them in California. I explained Kentucky was where I had found work. He saw it as a step down in society. He had lived in the capital of his country, known important people, gone to prestigious schools. He had given up a career, status, and everything he owned. He felt he deserved better than to have to fight for a job in middle America. I helped him get freelance work at the paper, but he got turned down when a full-time position became available.

In Ukraine there had always been distractions, dire things that couldn't wait: my sickness, the revolution. We were good in disasters. It was everyday life that we found difficult. Cultural differences that had been easy to ignore in Ukraine became barriers between us now that we were tied together. I would catch him in a little lie, and he wouldn't understand why I was upset. They were small things. But the lying was a big thing. That he could do it so easily made it hard for me to trust him.

When I introduced him to my friends and colleagues, he was incredibly charming, always complimenting them. Out of earshot his tone would change. He would mock the people he had just praised. I had never seen anyone so good at subterfuge. I started to doubt his words, wondering when he was being sincere and when he was just saying what he thought I wanted to hear. The one thing he couldn't give me was the only thing I wanted: the truth. I don't know that he even knew it. I am not sure how I missed all this before, except that maybe age and the revolution and everything else had changed him, had changed me. It also could be that we never lived together in Ukraine, so we were both able to hide the traits we didn't want seen. It was probably a little of both, and so much more.

He seldom wore his wedding ring, and one day I stopped minding. We slept not just in separate beds but in separate rooms. I started to spend more and more time away from home. I found myself avoiding him, resenting his presence. We ate separately. We stopped talking. We stopped listening.

Dima spent more and more time with a new female friend I had never met. I thought about staying married for his visa, but it would require living a lie for another two years. So he moved out. Trevor came to help with the transition. First Dima stayed with friends, then with strangers in Salt Lake City. It was Trevor who took him to the bus station. He liked Dima, but he remained loyal to me and made sure Dima was safe so I wouldn't have to take care of Dima anymore.

Dima came back once while he was still staying with friends in Louisville. He needed to collect a few things. He had to hurry because his friends were waiting outside in the car. Before he left he gave me a hug. "Katiusha, don't make me go back there," Dima pleaded.

I held on to him in silence. His puffy red jacket stank of cigarette smoke. Neither of us were smokers, and we both hated the smell of cigarette smoke.

"They smoke all the time. All my clothes stink. You would hate it there."

"I'm sorry," I said.

And I was. But I didn't feel anything else.

"I'll do whatever you want. It will be different, I promise," he said.

"I can't, Dima."

It was true. I couldn't go back. And I knew he couldn't give me what I wanted. We had drifted too far apart. I served him with divorce papers not long after and mailed back the rings.

37 Repeat Performance

The Ukrainian government didn't last much longer than our relationship. Kuchma did not run for a third term in the 2004 elections. Instead he put his weight behind Viktor Yanukovych, who was also backed by Russian president Vladimir Putin. Yanukovych promised to bring those responsible for Gongadze's murder to justice. His rival candidate, Viktor Yushchenko, had trouble concentrating on his campaign after eating with the chairman of the Ukrainian secret service and becoming gravely ill. It was later confirmed Yushchenko had been poisoned with the same chemical that had been used on Gongadze's body: dioxin.

The protest movement was reignited. The protesters wore orange, Yushchenko's campaign color. They called the movement the Orange Revolution. Yushchenko was elected president, and heroine Yulia Tymoshenko, of the Princess Leia locks, became prime minister. The euphoria proved short lived.

Before the end of 2005 Yushchenko got rid of Tymoshenko and the rest of his ministers. His pro-Russian rival, Yanukovych, became prime minister, putting the government in a tug of war between those wanting closer ties with Russia and those wanting closer ties with the West.

In 2007 Tymoshenko replaced Yanukovych and continued to serve until 2010, when she ran for president, losing to none other than Yanukovych. Under Yanukovych, Ukraine officially abandoned its goal of joining NATO. In 2011 Tymoshenko was sentenced to seven years in prison for abuse of power. She went on a hunger strike the next year. Despite the revolution, little had changed.

In the Gongadze case, there was also a lack of resolution. In 2004 the former interior minister died of two gunshot wounds to the head on the day he was scheduled to give testimony in the case. In 2008 three former police officers were sentenced to twelve and thirteen years for assisting in Gongadze's abduction and murder. In 2013 the former police general who partially confessed to carrying out the murder was sentenced to life in prison. No one has been tried for ordering Gongadze's murder.

In the winter of 2013–14 it all started again. The president this time was Kuchma's crony Viktor Yanukovych. The dead journalist was first Vyacheslav Veremyi—and then Vasily Sergiyenko. Neither of their killings spurred the unrest; they happened later. The spark that set the blaze was Yanukovych's decision to sign a treaty with Russia instead of establishing closer ties with the European Union. That was the official reason at least, but unrest had been building for years. People were tired of the corruption, the currency devaluations, and the increasingly heavy-handed control of the press. They were tired of things being the way they always had been in Ukraine: the elites living grandly, the masses missing out.

In February 2014 Yanukovych fled Ukraine, and a new interim government was put in place that Russia refused to recognize. The West supported it. It was more complicated than that. Both sides tried to simplify things by defining it as a fight between the west of the country, which favored Western values and integration into Europe, and the eastern pro-Russia segment. The western contingent was accused of being right-wing nationalists and the eastern of being thugs. Both accusations held some truth.

Ukraine's ships and military bases in Crimea were taken by Russian soldiers in unmarked green uniforms, leading to the euphemism "little green men." Putin insisted they were "self-defense groups," not invaders. It was an old Kremlin tactic of *dezinformatsiya*, a mix of fact and fiction designed to confuse people. Pro-Russian groups started to take territory in the east of the country with Russian help. In almost five years of fighting around thirteen thousand people died. U.S. support of the Ukrainian government has impacted the U.S. relationship with Russia. So have revelations that Russian-backed groups bought advertisements on social media, establishing fake Facebook personae to incite dissension among American voters in 2016. In spring 2018 U.S. president Donald Trump referred to the U.S.

relationship with Russia as being worse than it has ever been. Ukraine once again was in the middle of the fighting, literally. Eastern Ukraine is a battleground where Russian-backed forces fight Ukrainian forces that are minimally supported by the West.

By fall 2018 the level of deception had gotten downright crazy. A Ukrainian hero and patriot, fighting against Russian-supported separatists, was arrested for plotting with those same separatists. A Russian journalist in exile in Ukraine was killed by Russian forces. Only he wasn't dead; it was a hoax perpetrated by the Ukrainian government to thwart a Russian attack. It is impossible to know what to believe and whom to trust.

Maybe that is the point. We lose track of reality. It happens every day in little ways. Several years ago I had to wake in the middle of the night while on assignment in a remote area. The photographer I was with, who had been raised in Moscow after the fall of the Soviet Union, insisted on taking time to put on makeup despite the time and our remote surroundings. When I asked her why she was bothering with makeup, she said she was scared of what people would think of her without it. She was young and relatively pretty, so I was surprised by her answer. She had become so accustomed to hiding behind mascara, eyeliner, and foundation that she was no longer sure how people would react when they saw her naked face. It was a small deception, but it stuck with me.

The Soviet leaders lied to their people. The people in turn have come to expect, and in some ways accept, deception. American politicians and the American people in general are not immune to falsifying the facts. But I think it is less expected or accepted. Americans tend to take things at face value. We take pride in being straightforward and straight-talking. Some accuse Americans of being naïve. We may be. That may be why the social media hoaxes Russia sends out about vaccines causing autism scare us. We still believe in truth.

Or maybe we just believe in our own truth. We always have. In 1932 *New York Times* Moscow correspondent Walter Duranty won a Pulitzer Prize for a series of articles on the success of collectivization, the main cause of the Ukrainian famine that killed millions. The old woman whose parents were sent by Moscow to keep order in Ukraine during the famine told me people weren't starving back then—they just liked to eat birds. That is what she saw because that is what she wanted to see, what she was capable of seeing. It is the same way I continue to see Ukraine.

I have never been back, maybe in part because I still want to see the Kyiv I remember: the hope, the beauty, the excitement, the youth—my youth. Was it ever really that way? For me, yes, it was. And as long as I don't see anything different, it still is; it still can be. Maybe that is my own deception, learned from my years living in the former Soviet Union. Or maybe it is just human nature.

If I were to return to Ukraine today, I am not sure I would recognize it. I remember an ease of relations between Russians and Ukrainians. But the separation I never saw must have been there all along. Now that it has surfaced, it will take time, maybe generations, to smooth it over. The same might be said of my own country. Trump's presidency has highlighted a separation the intensity of which I hadn't realized existed, and I know I am not the only one. The naïve hope at the start of the century has been replaced with a more sober view of a battleground that only seems to be growing by the day.

Afterword

The old *Baltic Times* office in Riga is now a hostel. Latvia became a member of the EU in 2004. The EU stopped mattering to many Western Europeans half a decade or so later. The *Kyiv Post* is now owned not by an American playboy but by a Syrian businessman. Daniel works as a journalist in Spain. After more than a decade working at the weekly news magazine *Korrespondent*, Vitaly resigned as editor-in-chief before Yanukovych was ousted. The government had been putting increasing pressure on the press and limiting the topics journalists could cover.

Nastya and Steve live in Brooklyn with their two daughters. Yulia also lives in the United States with her husband and children, as does Diana. Last I heard from Greg, he was wandering around Asia with possibly a wife and child in tow. Dima is a father, U.S. citizen, and divorced once again. My pancreatitis has been in remission for years. The vertigo returned in 2017. Like the pancreatitis, the reason remains a mystery.

Maybe it was that one extra trip to Chernobyl.

Acknowledgments

There is no way to properly thank everyone who has played a role in this story. I am going to do my best to note those who played a particular role in this book.

Peter Nichols was one of the first to understand what I was trying to do with this narrative. Tom Swanson is one of those wonderful editors who trusts and supports his writers. Rosemary Sekora does an amazing job in marketing. The rest of the Nebraska team also deserves special thanks, including Abby, Mark, Sara, and Tish. Language experts Bojana and Olga did a great job. As always my mother and stepfather proved valuable readers, supporters, and critics, and my brother Tom, a great fan. John Jackson has been handling my website for years and is long overdue an official thanks, as are best buds Alisa and Jax. Andrea, Lisa, Eileen, Karen, Larry, Courtney, Mike, David, and the Trotts also need a mention. In memory of Karin Foster, Anne Karst, and my one-man European staff, Brian Pitts.

This book would not be possible without the courageous people of Latvia and Ukraine who shared their stories and lives with me. I owe a special thanks to all of those who took care of me when I was sick, especially Michael in Bulgaria and Ludmilla, Dima, and Sveta in Kyiv.

Bibliography

Memories are imperfect. I have done my best to be as accurate as possible by relying on old articles, journal entries, and photos. Conversations are recreations. The number killed in fighting in Ukraine comes from the United Nations Human Rights Monitoring Mission in Ukraine.

Byrne, Peter. "Has Gongadze Been Found?" *Kyiv Post*, November 23, 2000.

Cengel, Katya. "Behind Enemy Lines: Mothers Risking All to Find Their Lost Sons." *Marie Claire Australia*, April 2002.

———. "Believing in a Button." *Baltic Times*, March 4, 1999.

———. "Big Bad Disasters." *Baltic Times*, July 23, 1998.

———. "Bones Exhumed from Mass Grave Near Kyiv." *Kyiv Post*, November 1, 2001.

———. "Cossacks Bury Head of Old Chief." *Kyiv Post*, August 23, 2000.

———. "Delayed Trial Halted in Mass Confusion." *Kyiv Post*, November 29, 2001.

———. "Dying Mines, Dying Towns." *Kyiv Post*, November 16, 2000.

———. "Famine Survivors Laud Reforms." *Kyiv Post*, September 7, 2000.

———. "Ghosts in Latvia's Fastest Graveyard." *Baltic Times*, January 4, 1999.

———. "Hasids Flock to Uman Answering Call of Legendary Rabbi." *Kyiv Post*, September 20, 2001.

———. "Hearing the Voices That Never Spoke." *Baltic Times*, August 27, 1998.

———. "International and Individual Truth." *Baltic Times*, July 16, 1998.

———. "Latvian Legion Revisited." *Baltic Times*, November 5, 1998.

———. "Life in the Shadow of Chernobyl." *Kyiv Post*, July 13, 2000.

———. "Living Dangerously: Ukraine Journalists Risk Their Lives to Tell the Truth." *San Francisco Chronicle*, June 11, 2001.

———. "Matchmakers Tout Ex-Soviet Women to U.S." *San Francisco Examiner*, March 22, 1999.

———. "Miner Determined to Revive Dying Coal Mines." *Kyiv Post*, November 23, 2000.

———. "Police Raid Does Away with Tent City." *Kyiv Post*, March 7, 2001.

———. "Pope to Take on Ukraine: Religious Factions Divided over Pontiff's Visit." *San Francisco Chronicle*, June 22, 2001.

———. "Post-Protest Police Roundup Leaves Suspects Battered." *Kyiv Post*, March 15, 2001.

———. "Ready or Not—Chernobyl Closing Dec. 15." *Kyiv Post*, December 14, 2000.

———. "Reunited Families: When the Boys Came Home." *Baltic Times*, January 14, 1999.

———. "The Rise and Fall of a Radical Movement." *Kyiv Post*, November 8, 2001.

———. "The Road to Latvia." *Baltic Times*, October 29, 1998.

———. "The Russian Women and Children Left Behind in Estonia: Tiina's Widows Start a New Life." *Baltic Times*, August 20, 1998.

———. "Separatists Seek Help from Mother Ukraine." *Kyiv Post*, November 22, 2001.

———. "Sevastopol Still Reels from *Kursk* Sub Tragedy." *Kyiv Post*, January 18, 2001.

———. "Shopkeepers Find Profits, Loans Elusive." *Kyiv Post*, February 1, 2001.

———. "Show Bears Bask in Retirement: Dancing Bruins Live Better Than Most in Bulgaria." *San Francisco Chronicle*, July 8, 2002.

———. "Skydiving in Kyiv: From Total Fear to Peaceful Floating." *Kyiv Post*, October 19, 2000.

———. "Tension Rises in Break-Away Trans-Dniester." *Kyiv Post*, November 15, 2001.

———. "Terror and Temptation: Since Sept. 11, Worry Abounds about Fate of Ex-Soviet Researchers." *San Francisco Chronicle*, March 19, 2002.

———. "Trials and Tribulations of Life in Tent City." *Kyiv Post*, March 1, 2001.

———. "Ukraine's Elections Are Rife with Charges of Political Abuse." *Wall Street Journal Europe*, March 28, 2002.

———. "Water-Skiing in the Dnipro: Why Not?" *Kyiv Post*, August 3, 2000.

———. "When We Returned We Were Treated as Guilty." *Kyiv Post*, November 2, 2000.

———. "Zvarde: The Town That Time Forgot." *Baltic Times*, July 22, 1999.

Heleniak, Timothy. "Latvia Looks West, but Legacy of Soviets Remains." Migration Policy Institute, February 1, 2006. https://www.migrationpolicy.org/article/latvia-looks-west-legacy-soviets-remains.

International Students Center Commonwealth. "The Ukrainian Capital Kiev." 2010. http://commonwealth.in.ua/engli/ukraine_city/kiev.htm (site discontinued).

Misiunas, Romuald, and Rein Taagepera. *The Baltic States: Years of Dependence 1940–1990*. Berkeley: University of California Press, 1993.

Noble, John, Nicola Williams, and Robin Gauldie. *Estonia, Latvia and Lithuania*. Hawthorn, Victoria, Australia: Lonely Planet, 1997.

Rupar, Terri. "Remember When a Ukrainian Presidential Candidate Fell Seriously Ill?" *Washington Post*, March 12, 2014.

"Ukraine Gongadze Case: Court Convicts Journalist's Killer." BBC, January 29, 2013. https://www.bbc.com/news/world-europe-21245784.

Wakefield, Jane. "TED 2018: Ukrainian Journalist Fights Fake News." BBC, April 11, 2018. https://www.bbc.com/news/technology-43568238.

"Whipped." *The Economist*, January 23, 2003.

Williams, Matthias. "Murdered Journalist Buried in Ukraine 16 Years after Beheading." Reuters, March 22, 2016. https://www.reuters.com/article/us-ukraine-gongadze-idUSKCN0WO2LH.